WINDOWS

WINDOWS

Compiled by Emmett K. Vande Vere

**Selected
Readings in
Seventh-day
Adventist
Church History
1844-1922**

Southern Publishing Association
Nashville, Tennessee

**Southern Publishing Association
appreciates Dr. Vande Vere's work
in verifying the accuracy of the material
in this volume.**

*The compiler has kept editorial comment to a
minimum because of space limitations and a desire to
make the volume adaptable to any denominational
history text. At the close of each chapter appear
suggestions for further study. Some are starred (*) to
indicate special recommendation.*

*Basic also are "The Advent Review and Sabbath
Herald," "The Youth's Instructor," "Battle Creek
Daily Journal" (Battle Creek Willard Library),
"Seventh-day Adventist Yearbook," "The General
Conference Daily Bulletin." The "Comprehensive
Index to the Writings of Ellen G. White" (three
volumes) is useful for systematic references, and the
"Seventh-day Adventist Encyclopedia" for articles on
selected subjects.*

Copyright © 1975 by
Southern Publishing Association
Library of Congress Catalog Card No. 75-27641
SBN 8127-0104-6

This book was
Edited by Gerald Wheeler
Designed by Dean Tucker

Type: Century Schoolbook

Printed in U.S.A

To Rhonda, Robert, Jolinda, and David

Contents

Millerite Disappointment

Seventh-day Adventists contend that the Millerite religious movement in America, lasting from approximately 1831 to 1844, provides the historical background of their origin. Perhaps up to two hundred ministers and two thousand lay lecturers participated in it, and possibly several hundred thousand people more or less responded to the teaching of Christ's second coming.

It has been said that when God desires to move mankind, He first moves a man. William Miller of Low Hampton, New York, felt himself to be such a man—a man with a message from the Bible. He became an effective evangelist.

D. Millard of Portsmouth, New Hampshire, described Miller's impact on his town:

> On the 23rd of January brother William Miller came into town, and he commenced, in our chapel, his course of lectures on the second coming of Christ. During the nine days he remained, crowds flocked to hear him. Before he concluded his lectures, a large number of anxious souls came forward for prayers. Our meetings continued every day and evening for a length of time after he left. Such an intense state of feeling as now pervaded our congregation, we never witnessed before in any place. Not infrequently from sixty to eighty would come forward for prayers on an evening. Such an awful spirit of solemnity seemed to settle down on the place, that hard must be that

sinner's heart that could withstand it. . . . All was order and solemnity. Generally, as soon as souls found deliverance, they were ready to proclaim it, and exhort their friends, in the most moving language, to come to the fountain of life. Our meetings thus continued on evenings for six weeks. . . .

For weeks together the ringing of bells for daily meetings rendered our town like a continual sabbath. Indeed such a season of revival was never before witnessed in Portsmouth, by the oldest inhabitant. It would be difficult at present to ascertain the number of conversions in town. It is variously estimated at from 500 to 700. [D. Millard extract in the *Christian Herald,* as quoted in *Signs of the Times* (J. V. Himes, ed.), April 15, 1840, p. 13.]

Elder Fleming, of Portland, Maine, recorded the success of Miller's revival in that city in the spring of 1840:

At some of our meetings, since Br. M[iller] left, as many as 250, it has been estimated, have expressed a desire for religion, by coming forward for prayers; and probably between *one* and *two hundred* have professed conversion at our meetings; and now the fire is being kindled through the whole city, and all the adjacent country. A number of Rum-sellers have turned their shops into meeting rooms, and those places that were once devoted to intemperance and revelry, are now devoted to prayer and praise. . . . *Infidels, Deists, Universalists,* and the most abandoned *profligates,* have been converted. . . . Prayer meetings have been established in every part of the city by the different denominations, or by individuals, and at almost every hour. . . . I was conducted into a room over one of the Banks, where I found from 30 to 40 men of different denominations, engaged with one accord in prayer, at 11 o'clock in the daytime! [L. D. Fleming extract in

10

Millerite Disappointment

Signs of the Times (J. V. Himes, ed.), April 15, 1840, p. 14.]

Joseph Bates recounted Miller's meeting with a group of ministers at New Bedford, Massachusetts, in the spring of 1841:

> I was not a minister then, but I had a strong desire to attend this meeting, to learn how the ministers received the Second-advent doctrine. . . . When the meeting commenced in the morning, I counted twenty-two ministers present, belonging to the place and within a circle of a few miles around the city, and about forty lay members. After the meeting was organized, Bro. Miller proposed they begin with the prophecy of Daniel, and requested the reader of the Scriptures to commence with the second chapter. Occasionally Bro. Miller would request the reader to pause, and then ask the ministers how they understood what had just been read. At first they looked upon each other in silence, seemingly unwilling to expose their ignorance in this matter, or to see who would reply. After some time, one of the learned ministers replied, "We believe it as you do, sir." "Well," said Bro. M[iller], "if you are all agreed on this point, we will proceed." No other one replied. The reader proceeded until another question. All was silent again until the same learned minister answered, "We believe as you do, sir." And thus they professed to believe with him to the end of the chapter. It was truly cheering to see how all these ministers of the various denominations were admitting and believing the doctrine of the second advent. [Joseph Bates, *The Autobiography of Elder Joseph Bates* (1868), pp. 255, 256.]

During 1843 the Millerites emphasized the limited

11

period of time remaining to the earth (spring of 1843 to spring of 1844), the destruction of the earth by fire, and the cleansing of the church. By 1844 (spring to autumn of 1844) their teaching centered more on Christ's coming out of the heavenly sanctuary to gather His faithful, waiting saints. A number of factors prompted the shift.

1. The weight of typology: that just as Christ "fulfilled" all the Jewish spring-festival types during His first advent, so He would complete the autumn festivals at His second advent.

2. The recognition that the 2300 days-years began in the autumn of 457 BC and ended AD 1844.

3. An awareness that the Jewish Karaite calendar placed the 7th (or atonement-judgment) month in the civil month of October.

4. The parable of the ten virgins in which they interpreted the night of tarrying into six months of actual time (May to October) with the "Midnight Cry" breaking forth at its halfway mark.

(William Miller and Samuel S. Snow early promoted factors No. 1 and No. 2; Sylvester Bliss pointed to No. 2 and No. 3; George Storrs emphasized No. 4.)

But after Christ failed to return in the spring of 1844, the Millerites struggled with a great spiritual depression. Then Snow spearheaded the concept that Christ would come in the fall of 1844 in various articles as early as February, 1844. He presented his conclusions at the large Boston Tabernacle on July 21, and at a camp meeting at Exeter, New Hampshire, from August 12-17, where he lectured three times.

From among the accounts of the important camp meeting at Exeter we have selected three—the first by James White, who was present; the second by John Orr Corliss, who was not there; and the third by Joseph Bates, who spoke at the meetings. Corliss, although he wrote long afterward, pro-

vides some additional insights. There is also an observation from J. V. Himes.

James White's recollection in 1868:

It was in the month of August, 1844, that the memorable Second-Advent camp-meeting was held at Exeter, N. H. This meeting was large. . . . Believers were in a state of suspense and uncertainty, . . . and there were other things besides the passing of time [in the spring of 1844], that cast a degree of general gloom over the Second-Advent cause at that time.

Storrs' Six Sermons on the immortality question were being widely circulated among Adventists, and the doctrine of man's unconsciousness in death and the destruction of the wicked, was being adopted by some and regarded with favor by many. . . . [However], lecturers, such as Litch, Hale, Bliss, Himes, and Miller, who did not agree with Mr. Storrs, not only failed to see that good could result from the agitation of the subject, but were grieved that the once united and happy flock, who were looking for the immediate return of the great Shepherd, should have their minds divided by this question. . . .

And not a few men and women in the Advent ranks who professed to be wonderfully led by the Holy Spirit . . . and so directly taught by the Holy Spirit in relation to their entire duty, how could they err? The idea of mistakes on their part, in doctrine or in duty, was banished from them. . . .

And with their false notions of entire consecration [sanctification?], they were in readiness for the torch of fanaticism. . . .

But none among the preachers and speakers generally had shown up to this time that they had the burden of the meeting upon them. . . . Several spoke from the stand, but they failed to move the people. . . . Just then, as one was speaking with but little force

13

and interest, and the people were becoming weary of
being told, in a dull, prosy style, what they already
knew, a middle-aged, modest-appearing lady [Mrs.
Couch] arose in the centre of the audience, and in a
calm manner, and with a clear, strong, yet pleasant
voice, addressed the speaker as follows:

"It is too late, Bro. [Bates]. It is too late to spend
our time upon these truths, with which we are
familiar, and which have been blessed to us in the
past, and have served their purpose and their time."

The brother sat down, and the lady continued,
while all eyes were fastened upon her.

"It is too late, brethren, to spend precious time as
we have since this camp-meeting commenced. Time is
short. The Lord has servants here who have meat in
due season for his household. Let them speak, and let
the people hear them. 'Behold the Bridegroom cometh,
go ye out to meet him.'"

This testimony seemed electrifying, and was
responded to by choked utterances of "Amen," from
every part of the vast encampment. Many were in
tears. . . . [The power of the fanatics] was broken.

By the request of many brethren, the next
morning, the arguments were given from the stand
[by S. S. Snow], which formed the basis of the tenth
day of the seventh-month [October 22, 1844]
movement. . . .

The deepest solemnity pervaded the entire
encampment. But one view was taken of the subject
presented, by nearly all present, namely, that in all
probability the speaker was correct, and that in a few
short weeks human probation would close forever.

The next day, by unanimous request of the people,
the same speaker repeated with still greater clearness
and force, the same proofs. . . . This was followed with
solemn and stirring discourses in harmony with the
time, from Elders Heath, Couch, and Eastman. . . .

14

Millerite Disappointment

[They dwelt at length on the parable of the ten virgins.]

On returning from the Exeter camp-meeting, I visited the Advent congregation at Poland, M[ain]e, and attended camp-meetings at Litchfield and Or[r]ington. At these two camp-meetings ministers and people became imbued with the spirit of the seventh-month message. The evidences upon which it was based seemed conclusive, and a power almost irresistable attended it; and the fruits of this message everywhere were alike excellent. Whatever of differences of opinion, division in feelings and plans of action, or schisms of any kind that had sprung up during the time of suspense represented by the tarrying . . . were now being swept away and lost sight of in the onward course of this mighty movement. The hearts of the believers were being unified as never before. [James White, *Life Incidents* (1868), pp. 153-168.]

J. O. Corliss's composition of 1904:

Many theories were advanced to explain the [spring] disappointment, both by Mr. Miller and by others, but none of these seemed satisfactory. Before the end of the year, however, a conference was called at Exeter, N. H., in which the matter was intelligently adjusted, and the message received new life and vigor. At the conference mentioned, several were making commonplace remarks, when a sister arose and said: "It is too late to be dealing in these platitudes; a brother in the audience has light for the people." Immediately upon the sister's taking her seat, John Couch [her husband] arose and reviewed the data of the prophetic utterance upon which their message had been based. He showed that the 2,300 years reaching to the cleansing of the sanctuary must

15

include both the first and the last day of the full time given; that inasmuch as the 2,300 years, if beginning with the first day of the year 457 BC, could not be called completed before the last day of 1843, since it required 457 full years BC and 1843 full years AD to make 2,300 years. He then showed that the commandment on which their time message depended for its data did not take effect until *autumn* of 457 BC, and so the term of 2,300 years would extend to the *autumn* of 1844. This would designate the autumn of 1844 as the time for the coming of the Lord.

This explanation was so simple and satisfactory that the whole audience was electrified. They went forth from that conference with the cry on every lip: "Behold the Bridegroom cometh." Men sold their homes, and gave their means to the proclamation of the Lord's return, believing that now they would surely see the fruition of their fondest hope. But again disappointment overtook them. [J. O. Corliss, *Review and Herald,* August 11, 1904, p. 8.]

Bates describes how the "Midnight Cry" inspired him and others:

At Midnight, in the dead of the night of this tarrying of the Bridegroom, "the cry was raised," which caused great agitation and excitement, looking with unparalleled interest at definite time, 10th of the seventh month.

A camp meeting was held in Concord, N. H., somewhere about the first of August. Here, as we afterwards learned, the cry resounded throughout the camp. On the 12th of August, another was held at Exeter, N. H. On my way there, something like the following seemed to be continually upon my mind. You are going to have new light here, something that will give an impetus to this work. How many thousand living witnesses there still are scattered

16

Millerite Disappointment

over the land that experienced the manifestation of
the spirit's power in applying to their hearts the many
scriptures, and especially the clear exposition of the
parable of the ten virgins, at that meeting. There was
light given and received there, sure enough; and when
that meeting closed, the granite hills of New
Hampshire rang with the mighty cry, *Behold the
Bridegroom cometh, go ye out to meet him!* As the
stages and railroad cars rolled away through the
different States, cities and villages of New England,
the rumbling of the cry was still distinctly heard.
Behold the Bridegroom cometh! Christ is coming on
the tenth day of the seventh month! Time is short, get
ready! get ready! [Joseph Bates, *The Advent Review,*
November, 1850.]

J. V. Himes observed:

From July these movements were in different
parts of New England and were distinct from each
other. . . . At the Exeter Campmeeting all these
influences met, mingled into one great movement,
and rapidly spread through all the advent bands in
the land. [Joshua V. Himes, *Signs of the Times,*
October 30, 1844, p. 99.]

**Many of those urging the October 22 date may have leaped
for joy when they learned that on October 6, William Miller
had reluctantly accepted it.**

I see a glory in the seventh month which I never
saw before. Although the Lord had shown me the
typical bearing of the seventh month, one year and a
half ago, yet I did not realize the force of the [Jewish
festival] types. Now, blessed be the name of the Lord,
I see a beauty, a harmony, and an agreement in the
Scriptures, for which I have long prayed, but did not
see until today. Thank the Lord. . . . I am almost

17

home. Glory! Glory!! Glory!!! [William Miller letter to
J. V. Himes, October 6, 1844, as quoted in Francis D.
Nichol, *The Midnight Cry,* p. 229.]

**The passing of October 22, 1844, disappointed and shocked
the entire religious movement. Many had disposed of their
property and paid off their debts. Some farmers left their
crops unharvested. Washington Morse recalled:**

> As the time shortened there was all anxious
> waiting and watching for the hour that should
> witness the coming of our dear Saviour. Our Ministers
> hastened their movements in order to reach their
> homes and be with their families before the decisive
> hour arrived. We began to count the days that
> remained—only a few of them—and arranged to close
> up all our work so as to be in that waiting condition
> prophesied of: Lo, this is our God; we have waited for
> him, and he will save us. Isa. 25:9. We felt [ready] to
> lay down our burden for souls and to leave all with
> the Lord. Many who wer without homes assembled in
> companies at the home of some believer, there to wait
> for the few remaining hours to pass.
>
> It was our privilege to arrive at Bro. Cushmans in
> Tunbridge[,] Ver the evening of the last day. Here we
> met from fifty to seventy-five brethren and sisters and
> several of the leading Ministers. Brother Cushmans
> large Brick House was all lighted up during the night.
> Great solemnity prevailed. Each one turned his eyes
> within and inquired "Am I ready to meete the dear
> Saviour?" Deep anxiety was depicted upon every
> countenance, but no word of doubt was uttered.
>
> The morning came on, we were gathered in a
> group in the front yard standing in silence. Presently
> someone asked "Watchman, what of the night?" We
> waited breathlessly for a few moments until a
> prominent Minister spoke and said "If we are right in
> our interpretations of the parable of the ten virgins,

we must stay here until a part of our brethren go down and act the part of the foolish virgins."

This statement fell with crushing weight upon our hearts. It seemed more than we could bear to think of remaining longer in this world especially for such a development as was suggested. Our hearts wer greatly saddened at the mere thought that part of our dear brethren and sisters wer to go down and act the part of the foolish virgins. We had become dead to the world and had lost all relish for the things of the world in its present condition. Our confidence remained firm that we had ben lead by the Lord in making the proclamation of the close of time. . . . The thought of again turning our attention to the things of this world and engaging in the various avocations was exceedingly distasteful to us not to say distressing. The injunction to remember Lots Wife came to us with special forse. We could not but realize that we should meete with many sneers and expressions of ridicule from our fellow men: but this was a consideration of minor importance, as compaired with the disappointment in not seeing our Saviour. With extreeme reluctance we relinquished the hope of Christs coming at that time, and with much bitterness sought our several occupations. [Washington Morse, MS memoir. Paragraphing supplied. Held by the compiler.]

Later on, SDA editor-author Uriah Smith likewise composed a memoir that recalled his experiences on October 21 and 22, 1844:

In 1843 Elder J. V. Himes started in New York City a paper called The Midnight Cry. His opponents changed its prospectus, and called it The Midnight Yell, and Junk Bottle of Destruction. Cartoonists were not idle with their slurs. One represented the

19

saved ascending to meet the Lord in the air, and
devils trying to drag them back. One picture showed
the devil holding by the coat-tails, Elder J. V. Himes,
then known as the leading Millerite, and saying,
"Rev. Joshua V., you must go with me." These are the
characters described in Jude, verses 13-15. Such
scoffing will follow Adventists all their journey
through.

Oct. 21, 1844, the writer, in company with his
mother and an older brother, attended an Adventist
meeting in the dooryard of a Brother Tolman, in
Fitchburg, Mass. In the evening, a rabble came up
from the village, and began to pelt the tent where the
meeting was held, with apples from the orchard.
Waxing bolder, as the meeting became more earnest,
they gathered around the door, and began to direct
their missiles against the lanterns hanging on the
center-poles in the house-shaped tent. These were
soon hit and demolished, and the glass scattered over
the floor of the tent, and all were left in total
darkness. The rabble grew bolder, and seizing hold of
the framework of the tent, and cutting the guy-ropes,
soon leveled it to the ground. Meanwhile the crowd
had seized a large hog, brought him to the tent, lifted
up the curtain, and pushed him in, and there we
were—women, children, and the hog—in darkness
under the cover of the tent—not a very pleasant
companion, and not a very agreeable situation.

Brother Tolman immediately opened his house to
those gathered there; and the women and children
were piloted out of the darkness, into the house. But
the liquor began to work on the baser sort, and they
then attacked the house. Pretty soon something
harder than apples were used, and sticks and chunks
of wood demolished the lights and the sash of the
windows, and we had to seek some other quarters.
The writer and his brother took shelter in the barn.
Soon the mob, as I will now call them, came through

the barn, apparently searching for some one who had tried to restrain them in the yard, and threatening to do him violence.

The next day was Oct. 22, 1844, the famous "tenth day of the seventh month," on which we were expecting the Lord to appear. The mob finally left us to ourselves. Quite a number went forward in baptism. . . .

The brethren scattered out from the meeting at Fitchburg, and were soon all at home, bewildered by their great disappointment. And the false reports followed them. For instance, it was said that the writer took cold by exposure at the meeting, and lost a leg in consequence. We received no harm from that meeting. No report could be more false than that. We have no charge of that kind to make against Adventism. [Uriah Smith, *Review and Herald,* January 13, 1903, pp. 3, 4.]

Some have asked why the Millerites set a time for Christ's second advent contrary to Matthew 24:36. Besides citing 1 Thessalonians 5:4 in justification, they argued, as Miller did during a sermon "at the tabernacle" in Boston, probably in early February, 1844, as follows:

In the afternoon and evening he [Miller] took for his text, Eccl. viii, 5, 6, "Whoso keepeth the commandment shall feel no evil thing: and a *wise* man's heart discerneth both *time and judgment. Because to every purpose there is time and judgment."* He showed from the Scriptures that those only are wise, who keep the commandments of the Lord and believe his word, and which is accounted to them for righteousness, producing a corresponding life. Such will discern both *time* and *judgment,* because to every purpose there is both time and judgment. It was there shown that every *judgment* brought upon the world, as predicted in the Scriptures, was in connection with

21

Windows

a specific time, which was discerned by the wise. The flood, the destruction of the cities of the plain, the sojourning of the children of Israel in Egypt, and in the wilderness, the Babylonish captivity, and its end, and the dispersion of the ten tribes, with many other judgments, all occurred at the predicted time, which was discerned by those who feared the Lord; as was the time of our Saviour's First Advent. It was therefore argued that the time of the Second Advent, at the end of all the prophetic periods, in the fullness of times, will also be discerned by those who are wise in the sight of God. [*Advent Herald and Signs of the Times Reporter,* February 14, 1844, p. 8.]

Naturally, the Millerites produced numerous defenses of their movement. Joshua V. Himes, Sylvester Bliss, and Apollos Hale editorialized in their "Advent Herald" after the Disappointment:

At first the definite time was generally opposed [by us]; but there seemed to be an irresistable power attending its proclamation, which prostrated all before it. It swept over the land with the velocity of a tornado, and it reached hearts in different and distant places almost simultaneously, and in a manner which can be accounted for only on the supposition that God was in it. [J. V. Himes, et al, *Advent Herald,* October 30, 1844.]

J. B. Cook, a minister, wrote:

The Midnight Cry was the largest and tallest of the whole. It bore us quite out of the world; we supposed it would have been the last [message]. [J. B. Cook, *The Advent Review,* September, 1850, p. 32.]

Joseph Bates graphically depicted the bewildered Millerites as—

22

Millerite Disappointment

. . . his [Christ's] "scattered," "torn," and "peeled people," since the closing up of our work for the world in October, 1844. [Joseph Bates, "Remarks," *A Word to the Little Flock,* May, 1847, p. 21.]

William Miller, however, was as conscientious and nearly as optimistic after 1844 as before:

But I believe in the main . . . we were honestly preaching what we supposed to be the word of God; and I have no reflections to cast, only trust in God and He will shortly reconcile these seeming difficulties. That God has been in this cause, I have not a shadow of doubt; and that *time* has been the main spring, is equally as clear; and that if we leave out *time,* no mortal could prove that Christ is near, even at the door.

That parable [of the virgins] was never given to show the exact order or time of marriage and shutting of the door; but as an illustration of the kingdom of heaven when these things should transpire, i.e., in its character "likened unto." [William Miller's letter to Bro. Marsh, March 15, 1845, as quoted in *The Advent Review,* August, 1850, p. 11; and Miller as quoted by Sylvester Bliss, *A Brief History of William Miller the Great Pioneer in Adventual Faith* (1910), p. 268.]

And according to Ellen G. White the experience had its benefit:

The weak and the wicked united in declaring that there could be no more fears or expectations now. The time had passed, the Lord had not come, and the world would remain the same for thousands of years. This second great test revealed a mass of worthless drift that had been drawn into the strong current of the Advent faith, and been borne along for a time with the true believers and earnest workers. . . .

23

Windows

We were firm in the belief that the preaching of definite time was of God. It was this that led men to search the Bible diligently, discovering truths they had not before perceived. . . .

They had obtained valuable knowledge in the searching of the word. The plan of salvation was plainer to their understanding. Every day they discovered new beauties in the sacred pages, and a wonderful harmony running through all, one scripture explaining another, and no word used in vain. [Ellen G. White, *Testimonies,* Vol. 1, pp. 56, 57.]

for further reading:

* Bliss, Sylvester, *A Brief History of William Miller the Great Pioneer in Adventual Faith* (1910), 387 pages.

Dick, Everett N., "The Adventist Crisis of 1843-1844" (PhD dissertation, University of Wisconsin, 1930).

_____, *Founders of the Message* (1938, chaps. 1, 2).

* Froom, Leroy Edwin, *The Prophetic Faith of Our Fathers* (1954), Vol. IV, Part III.

* Nichol, Francis David, *The Midnight Cry* (1944), 560 pages.

Spalding, Arthur W., *Origin and History of Seventh-day Adventists* (1961), Vol. 1, chap. 5.

Wellcome, Isaac C., *History of the Second Advent Message and Mission, Doctrine and People* (1874), 707 pages.

Reorientation

It could be startling to learn that a few Adventists after October 22/23, 1844, began to reorient their Biblical exegesis almost overnight—unless we note that Hiram Edson, the principal exponent of the new sanctuary view, had read the important scriptures "a hundred times." Under such circumstances the correct interpretation could come as a flash of insight as it did to Martin Luther in the "little room" [cloaca] in the tower. The Millerites had believed that on October 22 Christ would return to earth. Now, suddenly on October 23, the idea dawned that He would move *into* the most holy place of the heavenly sanctuary rather than out of it.

Edson's own account of what happened, though written some time afterward, is fundamental to understanding what took place:

> Our expectations were raised high, and thus we looked for our coming Lord until the clock tolled 12 at midnight. The day had then passed, and our disappointment became a certainty. Our fondest hopes and expectations were blasted, and such a spirit of weeping came over us as I never experienced before. It seemed that the loss of all earthly friends could have been no comparison. We wept, and wept, till the day dawn. I mused in my own heart, saying, My advent experience has been the richest and brightest of all my christian experience. If this had proved a failure,

what was the rest of my christian experience worth?
. . . Is all this but a cunningly devised fable? Is there
no reality to our fondest hope and expectation of these
things? And thus we had something to grieve and
weep over, if all our fond hopes were lost. And as I
said, we wept till the day dawn. A second glance over
our past experience, and the lessons learned, and how
when brought into strait places where light and help
was needed by seeking the Lord, he had answered by
a voice and other ways, I began to feel there might be
light and help for us in our present distress. I said to
some of my brethren, Let us go to the barn. We
entered the granary, shut the doors about us and
bowed before the Lord. We prayed earnestly; for we
felt our necessity. We continued in earnest prayer
until the witness of the Spirit was given that our
prayer was accepted, and that light should be given,
our disappointment be explained, and made clear and
satisfactory. After breakfast I said to one of my
brethren, "Let us go and see, and encourage some of
our br[ethre]n." We started, and while passing
through a large field I was stopped about midway of
the field. Heaven seemed open to my view, and I saw
distinctly, and clearly, that instead of our High Priest
coming out of the Most Holy of the heavenly
sanctuary to come to this earth on the tenth day of the
seventh month, at the end of the 2300 days, that he
for the first time entered on that day, the second
apartment of that sanctuary; and that he had a work
to perform in the Most Holy before coming to this
earth. That he came to the marriage at that time; in
other words, to the Ancient of days to receive a
kingdom, dominion, and glory; and we must wait for
his return *from the wedding;* and my mind was
directed to the tenth ch[apter] of Rev[elation] where I
could see the vision had spoken and did not lie; the
seventh angel had begun to sound; we had eaten the
little book; it had been sweet in our mout[h], and it

Reorientation

had now become bitter in our belly, embittering our whole being. That we had to prophesy again &c., and that when the seventh angel began to sound, the temple of God was opened in heaven, and there was seen in his temple the ark of his testament, &c. While I was thus standing in the midst of the field, my comrade passed on almost beyond speaking distance before missing me. He inquired "Why I was stop[p]ing so long?" I replied, "The Lord was answering our morning prayer, giving light with regard to our disappointment." I talked these things to my brethren. In those days I was closely associated with O. R. L. Crosier and Dr. F. B. Hahn, Crosier making his home with me a portion of the time. He examined the Bible on the subject of the sanctuary. F. B. Hahn, and myself, was connected with Crosier in the publication of the paper called, "The Day Dawn." Br. Hahn and myself, held a consultation with regard to the propriety of sending out the light on the subject of the sanctuary. We decided it was just what the scattered remnant needed; for it would explain our disappointment, and set the brethren on the right track. We agreed to share the expense between us, and said to Crosier, "Write out the subject of the sanctuary. Get out another number of the Day Dawn, and we will try to meet the expense." He did so, and the Day Dawn was sent out bearing the light of the sanctuary subject. It fell into the hands of Elders James White and Joseph Bates, who readily endorsed the view; and it was shown in vision [to Ellen G. White] to be light for the remnant. This number of the Day Dawn opened a communication between us and these Eastern [states] brethren. We appointed a conference of the scattered brethren to be held at my house, and invited these our Eastern brethren to meet with us. Br W[hite] made the effort to come; but his way was hedged up. Father Bates came on. His light was the seventh-day Sabbath. From my

27

understanding of the opening of the tabernacle of the *testimony* in heaven, and the seeing of the ark of his testimony, and a few lines I had seen from the pen of T. M. Preble, I had been looking at the subject of the seventh-day Sabbath and talking it to my Br[ethre]n. I had said to them, "If we abide by . . . [end of fragment]. [Hiram Edson, MS "Life and Experience." Xerox copy, Heritage Room, Andrews University.]

A 1904 interview with former schoolteacher Owen R. L. Crosier by J. W. Hofstra produced the following recollection penned by William A. Spicer:

Our periodicals and books dealing with the 1844 movement have frequently mentioned the name of O. R. L. Crosier. He was a friend of Hiram Edson, of western New York. Hiram Edson was the first[?] to catch a glimpse of the Bible doctrine of the heavenly sanctuary. Young Crosier, schoolteacher and preacher, was the man walking over the fields with Edson on that morning of October 23, 1844, the day after the disappointment when Elder Edson stopped alone for a few moments of prayer by a shock of corn. Then it was that the truth was flashed into Brother Edson's mind, "The sanctuary to be cleansed is in heaven." This earth was not the sanctuary to which Christ was to come in 1844! Hiram Edson told his experience to Crosier and others, and they began immediately to study the Bible doctrine of the sanctuary. Crosier was the student penman who wrote out the exposition. Hiram Edson led out in securing funds and arranging for its publication. . . .

"I [J. W. Hofstra] then asked him [Owen R. L. Crosier], 'Were you interested in the early advent movement, and did you pass through the experience and disappointment of 1844?' To this Brother Crosier replied, 'Yes, I did; I passed through it all. I shared its grief and its distress, and I was present in that all-night prayer meeting and Scripture study held after the disappointment. When the light came concerning the temple in heaven, showing that this had been the object of the prophecies which we thought referred to the return of Jesus and the cleansing of the earth by fire, what a joy this light was to us! Very early in the morning I was on horseback going from place to place to tell the good news and to cheer those whom I could reach.' " [W. A. Spicer, *Review and Herald,* March 29, 1945, p. 5.]

Loughborough's story of Hiram Edson's experience in the field agrees essentially with Edson's manuscript except in minor details. Apparently Loughborough did not know about Edson's manuscript when he wrote his "Review and Herald" article:

> I will relate it as he related it to me in the winter of 1852, while we were holding meetings together for two months. The man was Hiram Edson, of Port Gibson, N.Y. He gave me an account of his 1844 experience, and especially of his seventh month experience. His residence was one mile from Port Gibson, on the Erie Canal. The meeting on the 22nd of October was in a schoolhouse one mile up the canal. He went to the place of meeting by way of the town, inviting people to meet with them, for they expected the Lord to come that day. The people refused to go, and he bade them good-by.
>
> The Adventists had a glorious meeting all day at the schoolhouse, expecting any moment to hear the blast of the Archangel's trumpet. But the sun set, the day was ended, and the Lord had not come. Brother Edson said they stayed all night, talking and praying over their disappointment, which they could not explain.
>
> In the morning he said to O. R. L. Crosier, who was staying with him, "I cannot go home by the town.

Windows

I do not know what to say to the people. Let us go
home cross-lots through the shocks of corn." So they
started, walking slowly and talking of the situation.
Kneeling by a shock of corn, they prayed for light.
When they had thus knelt the third time and while
Brother Edson was praying, he had this experience:

"A mighty wave of the power of God came upon
me, with an impression almost as distinct as though
spoken in an audible voice, 'The sanctuary is in
heaven, and Jesus has gone in to cleanse the
sanctuary.' "

As they arose, he repeated this to his companion,
and said, "What does that mean?" They hastened
home, determined to seek light on this matter from
the Scriptures. There they prayed the Lord to guide
them to the portions that would give light on the
subject. Brother Edson said he let his Bible drop on
the table, to see where it would open. It opened
between the eighth and ninth chapters of Hebrews. As
they began to read, Brother Edson said, *"I suppose I
have read that a hundred times, but it never appeared
to me as it does now.* The sanctuary is in heaven, and
Christ has gone in to cleanse it."

They then made a careful study of the sanctuary,
Crosier writing out the points as they studied, and
thus they began to get hold of that part of the third
angel's message; also on their finding that the
original law of God was in the ark, in the second
apartment of the sanctuary, the little company at Port
Gibson, and Crosier with them, began the observance
of the seventh-day Sabbath. [J. N. Loughborough,
Review and Herald, September 15, 1921, p. 5. Italics
supplied.]

The Edson group became the first band of Sabbathkeeping
Adventists, also accepting the restoration of the heavenly
sanctuary and the gift of prophecy. Though small at the

30

outset, their spiritual descendants would number millions. They developed a fierce determination to avoid making erroneous assumptions as they had in 1844. Therefore they developed a system of belief only after careful Bible study and through prophetic guidance:

Many of our people do not realize how firmly the foundation of our faith has been laid. My husband [James White], Elder Joseph Bates, Father [Stephen] Pierce, Elder [Hiram] Edson, and others who were keen, noble, and true, were among those who, after the passing of the time in 1844, searched for the truth as for hidden treasure. I met with them, and we studied and prayed earnestly. Often we remained together until late at night, and sometimes through the entire night, praying for light and studying the Word. Again and again these brethren came together to study the Bible, in order that they might know its meaning, and be prepared to teach it with power. When they came to the point in their study where they said, "We can do nothing more," the Spirit of the Lord would come upon me, I would be taken off in vision, and a clear explanation of the passages we had been studying would be given me, with instruction as to how we were to labor and teach effectively. Thus light was given that helped us to understand the scriptures in regard to Christ, His mission, and His priesthood. A line of truth extending from that time to the time when we shall enter the city of God, was made plain to me, and I gave to others the instruction that the Lord had given me.

During this whole time I could not understand the reasoning of the brethren. My mind was locked, as it were, and I could not comprehend the meaning of the scriptures we were studying. This was one of the greatest sorrows of my life. I was in this condition of mind until all the principal points of our faith were made clear to our minds, in harmony with the Word of

31

Windows

> God. The brethren knew that when not in vision, I
> could not understand these matters, and they
> accepted as light direct from heaven the revelations
> given. For two or three years my mind continued to be
> locked to an understanding of the Scriptures. [Ellen
> G. White, *Selected Messages,* Book One, pp. 206, 207.]

**Though the struggle to unify a core of Sabbath-observing
Adventists was enormous, the task to attract more ex-
Millerites proved gargantuan. Six "Sabbath conferences" in
1848 brought only about fifty participants. Ellen White's description of the conference at Volney, New York, hints of the
difficult times they had:**

> Our first general meeting in western New York,
> beginning August 18, was held at Volney, in Brother
> David Arnold's barn. About thirty-five were
> present,—all the friends that could be collected in
> that part of the State. But of this number there were
> hardly two agreed. Some were holding serious errors,
> and each strenuously urged his own views, declaring
> that they were according to the Scriptures.
>
> One brother held that the one thousand years of
> the twentieth chapter of Revelation were in the past,
> and that the one hundred and forty-four thousand
> mentioned in the seventh and fourteenth chapters of
> Revelation, were those raised at Christ's resurrection.
>
> As we had before us the emblems of our dying
> Lord, and were about to commemorate His sufferings,
> this brother arose and said that he had no faith in
> what we were about to do; that the Lord's supper was
> a continuation of the Passover, and should be
> partaken of but once a year.
>
> These strange differences of opinion rolled a heavy
> weight upon me. I saw that many errors were being
> presented as truth. It seemed to me that God was
> dishonored. Great grief pressed upon my spirits, and I

Reorientation

fainted under the burden. Some feared that I was
dying. Brethren Bates, Chamberlain, Gurney, Edson,
and my husband prayed for me. The Lord heard the
prayers of His servants, and I revived.

The light of heaven then rested upon me, and I
was soon lost to earthly things. My accompanying
angel presented before me some of the errors of those
present, and also the truth in contrast with their
errors. These discordant views, which they claimed
were in harmony with the Scriptures, were only
according to their opinion of Bible teaching; and I was
bidden to tell them that they should yield their errors,
and unite upon the truths of the third angel's
message.

Our meeting closed triumphantly. Truth gained
the victory. Our brethren renounced their errors and
united upon the third angel's message, and God
greatly blessed them and added many to their
numbers. [Ellen G. White, *Life Sketches* (1910), pp.
110, 111.]

**In another place Mrs. White outlined what she considered to
be the church's fundamental doctrinal points:**

The passing of time in 1844 was a period of great
events, opening to our astonished eyes the cleansing
of the sanctuary transpiring in heaven, and having
decided relationship to God's people upon the earth,
[also] the first and second angels' messages, and the
third, unfurling the banner on which was inscribed,
"The Commandments of God and the Faith of Jesus."
One of the landmarks under this message was the
temple of God, seen by His truth-loving people in
heaven, and the ark containing the law of God. The
light of the fourth commandment flashed its strong
rays in the pathway of the transgressors of God's law.
The nonimmortality of the wicked is an old landmark.
I can call to mind nothing more that can come under

33

the head of the old landmarks. [Ellen G. White, *Counsels to Writers and Editors* (1946), pp. 30, 31.]

for further reading:

* Froom, Leroy Edwin, *The Prophetic Faith of Our Fathers,* Vol. IV, Part III.

Haskell, Stephen N., *The Cross and Its Shadow.*

Heppenstall, Edward, *Our High Priest* (1972).

Jemison, T. Housel, *A Prophet Among You* (1955), 505 pages.

Loughborough, John N., *Rise and Progress of the Seventh-day Adventists* (1892), chaps. 1–8.

Reiner, Edwin, *The Atonement* (1971).

Spalding, Arthur W., *Origin and History of Seventh-day Adventists,* Vol. 1, chaps. 6–13.

_____, *Footprints of the Pioneers* (1947), 224 pages.

White, Ellen G., *Life Sketches of Ellen G. White* (1915), 480 pages.

Joseph Bates

Three persons particularly shaped the emerging Seventh-day Adventist Church: Joseph Bates, James White, and Ellen Gould White. The next three sections will examine them.

Bates, having retired from the sea and his captaincy at the age of thirty-six, evidently intended to devote his life and fortune (ten thousand dollars) to the reform causes agitating his countrymen, many of whom felt that not to have been a reformer was not to have lived.

In his autobiography Bates explains how he first learned of the Millerite movement:

> In the fall of 1839, while engaged in my orchard, one Eld. R., an acquaintance of mine, and a preacher in the Christian connection, called upon me and inquired if I would like to go to New Bedford, about two miles distant, that evening, and hear him preach on the second coming of Christ. I asked Eld. R. if he thought he could show or prove anything about the Saviour's coming. He answered that he thought he could. He stated that the North Christian meeting-house in [New] Bedford was offered him to give a course of five lectures on that subject. I promised to go with him, but I was very much surprised to learn that any one could show anything about the *time* of the Saviour's second coming. . . .
>
> When I heard Eld. R. present the Scripture

testimony on the subject in his first lecture, I was deeply interested, as was also my companion. After meeting, we had ridden some distance toward home, absorbed in this important subject, when I broke the silence by saying, *"That is the truth!"* My companion replied, "Oh, you are so sanguine always!" I argued that Eld. R. had made it very clear to my mind, but we would hear further. The meeting continued with crowded congregations and increasing interest to the close, and I felt that my mind was much enlightened on this important subject.

I now obtained Wm. Miller's book of nineteen lectures, which I read with deep interest, especially his argument on the prophetic periods of Daniel's vision, which heretofore, when I read the Bible in course, appeared to me so intricate, and led me to wonder what importance there could be attached to those days connected with his pictor[i]al prophecy of chapters vii and viii. But I now began to learn that those days were so many years, and those years were now to close in about 1843, at which period of time, according to Mr. Miller's view of the prophecies, Christ would personally appear the second time. [Joseph Bates, *The Autobiography of Elder Joseph Bates* (1868), pp. 243, 244.]

In 1913 John Orr Corliss described Bates' use of conversational prayer:

I had the privilege of laboring with Father Bates. This I shall never forget. He taught me how to pray. I had prayed a good deal before that, but I had never learned how to talk with the Lord as I did after I had been with Father Bates. That good old soul would bow down in my presence and talk with the Lord just as if he was a friend of his and had hold of his hand. Brethren, I love to think of those days and my association with such men as Joseph Bates and J. N.

Joseph Bates

Andrews. [J. O. Corliss, *Review and Herald,* May 22, 1913, p. 5.]

In 1923 Corliss recounted another experience with Bates:

I first met him [Bates] in 1869, under peculiar circumstances. I had been for some time publicly connected with our work, while a member of the Battle Creek church. The leader of that church conceived the idea that the church ought to be purified. His method for doing this was for all but twelve of the members whom he would name, to withdraw from the church, and then singly to apply for membership under rigid examination. Feeling rather displeased with this arrangement, I departed for the north [of Michigan], and located in the neighborhood of my wife's relatives. Not long afterward, Brother Bates came that way, and after preaching to the church, said without further preliminary, "Brother Corliss is not a member of any church among us. You that are in favor of his joining this church, raise your hands."

This novel method of doing business drew a unanimous vote in favor of the proposition. His next suggestion was for me to accompany him in travel, which I did, to the blessing of my soul; for I found in him one who had a tender heart, and knew how to set wrongs right without "fuss or feathers." I had never before known the real efficacy of prayer, but when I knelt with him to address the heavenly throne, I was touched with his quiet earnestness and familiar confidence expressed in the power of God to help and save. I probably felt much the same as the Lord's disciples when they asked to be taught to pray as John taught his followers. I have often thought since, Why should not older ministers now kneel with younger ones, and teach them the efficacy of prayer, without seeming to show them how?

37

His method of teaching the message was peculiar to him. He did not wait for an audience in some public building, though he had the power to interest large gatherings. But upon finding a friendly home in some community, as soon as he settled, he would invite the family to a study from the Bible. Then hanging up his prophetic chart, he would cover the world's history in prophetic outline so tersely and earnestly as to convince his hearers of the truth in a single study. He knew nothing about many side issues by which to draw the mind toward the truth, yet his work was often far-reaching in effect. . . .

After I had been associated with "Father" Bates as a joyous and eager learner for a brief period, one day a man came from an adjoining county, begging him to go to his neighborhood and deliver a series of Bible studies. The old gentleman cut short the interview by saying, "I am too old to go." Then pointing to me, without further debate he added, "Here is a young man who will go." To make good his word, he at once laid his hand on my head and said, "Now, young man, prime yourself and get ready." Of course at this word I was forced to leave my dear exemplar to "try the woods alone."

But the time spent with my fatherly teacher was not unappreciated. From him I learned most that I then knew about the rise of the message; for in our talks together the various phases of its development were recalled, and so firmly implanted in my mind as never to be forgotten.

I now recall a meeting held in the old Battle Creek church in the spring of 1871, the year before the death of Brother Bates. The question of health reform was up for consideration. In response to a call for his testimony, the old gentleman, then in his seventy-ninth year, arose to tell what it had done for him. He recalled the experience of his entire past, and the result of dropping one bad habit after another

38

until he reached the point of total abstinence from all things hurtful, and closed with the declaration that he was then entirely free from aches and pains, with the gladdening, cheering prospect that if he continued in the way he had chosen, he would stand without fault before the throne of God.

Nor did his looks belie his words; for at that very moment he stood as straight as a marble shaft, and tripped about as lightly as a boy. The audience was so electrified by the aged man's eloquence that for a moment only deep "amens" were to be heard. Elder J. N. Andrews was then called for, but upon rising said, "What shall the man do who comes after the King?" This occasion went far toward elevating the cause of health reform to its rightful place as a part of the message. [J. O. Corliss, *Review and Herald,* August 16, 1923, p. 8.]

for further reading:

* Anderson, Godfrey T., *Outrider of the Apocalypse: Life and Times of Joseph Bates* (1972), 141 pages.
* Bates, Joseph, *The Autobiography of Elder Joseph Bates* . . . (1868), 248 pages.

Dick, Everett N., *Founders of the Message* (1938), chap. 3.

Spalding, Arthur W., *Footprints of the Pioneers* (1947), 224 pages.

_____, *Origin and History of Seventh-day Adventists,* Vol. 1, chap. 2.

* White, James (ed.), *The Early Life and Later Experiences and Labors of Elder Joseph Bates* (1878), 320 pages.

James White

If any one man can be said to have designed and shaped the denominational structure, it was James White. His dedication, drive, and activity laid the foundation of today's church. He established many church institutions—including the first publishing house, college, and sanitarium—and served the church as theologian and administrator.

The section below shows James White's theological reasoning as he defended the teaching of the "shut door," a transitional doctrine of the late 1840's:

> Mark this: The great Redeemer then [in 1844] approached the mercy-seat in behalf of sinners. Was the door of mercy closed? This is an unscriptural expression, but, if I may be allowed to use it, may I not say that in the fullest sense of the expression the door of mercy was opened on the tenth day of the seventh month, 1844?
>
> Beside the ark of God containing the ten precepts of his holy law, over which was the mercy-seat, did the trusting ones now behold their merciful High Priest. They had stood in harmony with the whole Advent host at the passing of the time, then represented as "the church in Philadelphia," meaning brotherly love. And with what inexpressible sweetness did the following words addressed to that church come home to their stricken hearts: "These things saith he that is holy, he that is true, he that hath the key of David, he that openeth, and no man

shutteth; and shutteth, and no man openeth. I know thy works. Behold, I have set before thee an open door, and no man can shut it." Rev. iii, 7, 8.

Adventists were agreed that the seven churches of Rev. ii and iii, symbolized seven states of the Christian church, covering the entire period of the first advent of Christ to his second appearing, and that the sixth state addressed represented those who with one united voice proclaimed the coming of Jesus, in the autumn of 1844. This church was about to enter upon a period of great trial. And they were to find relief from it, so far as ascertaining their true position is concerned, by light from the heavenly sanctuary. After the light should come, then would also come the battle upon the shut and open door. Here was seen the connecting link between the work of God in the past Advent movement, present duty to keep the commandments of God, and the future glory and reward. And as these views were taught in vindication of the Advent movement, in connection with the claims of the Sabbath of the fourth commandment, these men, especially those who had given up their Advent experience, felt called upon to oppose. And their opposition, as a general thing, was most violent, bitter, and wicked.

The shut and open door of the heavenly sanctuary constituted the strong point upon which the matter turned. If we were right on the subject of the cleansing of the sanctuary, then the door or ministration of the holy place was shut, and the door or ministration of the most holy place was opened, the 2300 days had ended, the preaching of time was correct, and the entire movement was right. But let our opponents show that we were in error upon the sanctuary question, that Christ had not entered the most holy place to cleanse the sanctuary, then the 2300 days had not ended, the preaching of the time was an error, and the entire movement was wrong.

Windows

And, again, if the door or ministration of the most
holy place was opened, and the faith of the waiting
ones was to view Jesus standing before the mercy-seat
and the ark of the ten commandments in Heaven, how
forcible the arguments for the perpetuity and claims
of the entire law of God, the fourth precept not
excepted. The hand of the Lord was with those who
took a firm position that the great Advent movement
had been in his direct providence, and that the time
had come for the Sabbath reform, and many embraced
these views. Then it was that our opponents arose in
the spirit of persecution, manifesting the wrath of the
dragon against those who kept the commandments of
God, and labored to open the door that had been shut,
and to shut that door which had been opened, and
thus put an end to the matter. Hence the strong
expressions quoted above—"He that openeth and no
man shutteth, and shutteth and no *man* openeth."
"Behold I have set before thee an open door, and no
man can shut it." Nothing can be plainer than that
man, or a set of men, near the close of the history of
the church, would war against the truth of God in
reference to the shut and open door.

And to this day those who retain the spirit of war
upon those who keep the commandments of God,
make the belief in the shut and open door odious, and
charge it all upon Seventh-day Adventists. Many of
them, however, are not aware of the injustice of this.
Some of this people did believe in the shut door, in
common with the Adventists generally, soon after the
passing of the time. Some of us held fast this position
longer than those did who gave up their Advent
experience, and drew back in the direction of
perdition. And God be thanked that we did hold fast
to that position till the matter was explained by light
from the heavenly sanctuary.

And it may be worthy of notice that although the
belief in, and abandonment of, the shut-door position

42

had been general, there have been two distinct and opposite ways of getting out of it. One class did this by casting away their confidence in the Advent movement, by confessions to those who had opposed and had scoffed at them, and by ascribing the powerful work of the Holy Spirit to human or satanic influences. These got out of the position on the side of perdition.

Another class heeded the many exhortations of Christ and his apostles, applicable to their position, with its trials, dangers, and duties—Watch—Be ye therefore patient—Cast not away therefore your confidence—For ye have need of patience—Hold fast. They waited, watched, and prayed, till light came, and they by faith in the word saw the open door of the heavenly sanctuary, and Jesus there pleading his precious blood before the ark of the most holy place.

But what was that ark? It was the ark of God's testimony, the ten commandments. Reader, please follow these trusting, waiting ones, as they by faith enter the heavenly sanctuary. . . . Yes, dear reader, there, safe from the wrath of man and the rage of demons, beside his own holiness, are the ten precepts of God's holy law.

The waiting, watching, praying ones, embraced the fourth precept of that law, and with fresh courage took their onward course to the golden gates of the city of God, cheered by the closing benediction of the Son of God: "Blessed are they that do his commandments, that they may have right to the tree of life, and may enter in through the gates into the city." Thus they came out of the position of the shut door on the side of loyalty to God of high Heaven, the tree of life, and the eternal city of the redeemed. The reader will not fail to see the difference between their course and getting out of the shut door on the side of perdition. God pity the apostate. [James White, *Life Incidents in Connection With the Great Advent*

Windows

Movement as Illuminated by the Three Angels of Revelation XIV (1868), pp. 205-209.]

White pioneered Battle Creek College, the first Seventh-day Adventist institution of higher learning. In 1880 he wrote about it:

In the spring of 1874, when the College was established, two departments of instruction were opened; one in the Arts and Sciences, the other in Theology. In the fall of 1876, a department was opened for the preparation of teachers. In the fall of 1877, a department of Hygiene was established for those who desire to become familiar with the facts and principles upon which health and temperance reforms are based. In the fall of 1879, a Commercial department was instituted, and a primary school was opened.

The range of study in Battle Creek College through its different departments, includes those usually pursued in the very lowest grades and upward through all the branches of a full collegiate course. There are two courses of study, the Classical and the English, which, when completed, will entitle the graduate to a degree. . . .

Besides these there is a course of three years for students in Theology. . . .

The College receives its students from almost every State and Territory in the Union. From the fall of 1873, to June 15, 1880, 1375 persons have been enrolled as students of this institution. . . .

The important considerations which parents usually take into account in sending their children to school, are the character of the instruction, the influence under which their children will be placed, and the expense incurred while pursuing their studies.

It has become a kind of mania among young people

44

in our public and preparatory schools throughout the country to attach very great importance to the higher branches, while the common branches are looked upon as something to be passed over in a superficial manner. The teachers of Battle Creek College are endeavoring to correct this false view among its students. Great importance is attached to the common branches, which are regarded as constituting a foundation for a liberal education. Indeed, the thoroughness with which the youth are taught to perform their tasks, will in a great measure determine their success in after-life. . . .

The good influences which surround the students at Battle Creek College, and the vigilance exercised by those in charge, warrant parents in intrusting their sons and daughters to the watch-care of the institution. Teachers and officers feel that the hearts and lives of those they seek to educate are in a peculiar sense consigned to their care. They recognize the responsibility thus devolving upon them. Students are not left to themselves without care or sympathy. A personal interest is taken in each one, and a strong moral and religious influence is thrown around each member of the school. . . .

The necessary expenses of students attending Battle Creek College are probably less than any similar institution in the land. The whole expense of board, room-rent, tuition, books, and incidentals, need not exceed one hundred and twenty dollars a year. The annual expense incurred by the majority is less than one hundred dollars for each. Club boarding is very popular among the students of this institution. This system enables them to economize, in this the greatest of college expenditures. As these students fully adopt the two-meal system, they assemble at the eating-house only twice each day, where order and sobriety are observed, becoming Christian gentlemen and ladies.

45

Windows

But the victories gained in adopting the restricted diet are of far more importance to young men and women who are preparing by study to bless others with their influence, than simply the sum of money saved. However important this may be to the poor student, dollars and cents can hardly compare with the moral value of practical lessons of self-control, and physical and mental culture. All scientific physicians in the land, who have not lost proper regard for truth and honesty, agree in testifying that a nutritious hygienic diet is the safest and best for the young student. Most of our students are conforming to hygienic rules of living, and, as a consequence, sickness is almost unknown among them, and they are able to make greater progress in their studies.

The true friends of the health reformation will be gratified to know that the experiment of the Hygienic Boarding Club system of our good school is proving a perfect success. Some may be ready to cry "starvation" when we state that restricted diet is adopted by these students. But the writer with pleasure looks back thirty-nine years, when, thirsting for education and grappling with poverty, he and his room-mate, now Judge Smith, lived three months on corn-meal pudding and raw apples. By way of variety we had flour-cakes for each Sunday morning. But these young gentlemen and ladies . . . feast twice each day on the best grains, fruits, and vegetables, at a cost of about one dollar a week. With them the keen relish of healthful appetite, secured by their restricted diet, far exceeds the gustatory enjoyment of the sweetened, spiced, salted, and buttered dishes of fashionable living. Thank God for health reform. It is a mighty lever to lift up the student to physical, mental, and moral improvement. . . .

One of the principal objects of the College is the preparation of ministers and missionary workers. The results from the efforts already put forth are very

James White

encouraging. There are one hundred young men and almost as many young women laboring in the missionary field who received the impetus and preparation for their work at Battle Creek College. And of the many that have been students at our College, who made no profession of religion, not less than three-fourths have gone away hopefully converted. Hundreds of youth who have received their education in this institution, have been preserved from the ruin into which they would have been led, had they attended school under the circumstances less favorable to morality. These results are noticed particularly because they are largely peculiar to our school. . . .

The rapid increase of students in attendance during the past five years will doubtless continue. This will create a demand for more buildings and enlarged plans.

The means necessary to remove the debt now on the College, and to meet the demand for more room, should be raised as cheerfully and promptly by the many of our people who have taken no stock, as the sum of $54,000 has been raised by the few who have already taken stock.

There should be equality in our sacrifices and efforts to build up the College. [James White, *Life Sketches* (1880), pp. 370-375.]

Actively involved in various aspects of church administration, White had definite ideas of what kind of leadership the church needed:

In the providence of God, we [I] have been permitted to bear a part in the work of the last message from its commencement. And it has fallen to our [my] lot to lead out in the publishing work, church organization, systematic benevolence, and to take an active part in bringing our institutions into existence,

47

and also in their management. The success which has
attended the several branches of the great work, has
come from the direct providence of God. This has
given our people confidence in our plans and our
general management. Some, taking extreme positions
upon the subject of leadership, have been ready to
acknowledge us [me] as the leader of this people. This
position, however, we [I] have never for a moment
accepted. . . .

Those who drew the plan of our [SDA] church,
Conference, and General Conference organization,
labored to guard the precious flock of God against the
influence of those who might, in a greater or less
degree, assume leadership. They were not ignorant of
the evils and abuses which had existed in many of the
churches of the past, where men had assumed the
position which belongs to Jesus Christ, or had
accepted it at the hands of their short-sighted
brethren.

It was designed that the General Conference
Committee should be men of experience, deep piety,
and tender care for the flock, especially for younger
ministers, a board of fathers in Christ, who should
prayerfully and in the fear of God counsel with one
another and their brethren in the ministry in
reference to the best good of the cause of God, and
those who are laboring for its advancement. . . .

We call to mind scenes that frequently transpired
at the close of our little Conferences thirty years
since, when such meetings were held in private
houses in the warm season of the year. At the
suggestion of our venerable brother, Elder Joseph
Bates, we would usually enjoy a parting season of
prayer out of doors, bowed upon the green turf. These
were seasons of weeping. Our minds and hearts were
imbued with the Spirit of our Great Leader as we
wept for joy. . . . God grant that the day may never
come when our dear ministers shall go from our

48

James White

general assemblies with a spirit of unsanctified emulation, willing to build themselves up at the expense of the reputation and influence of their brethren in the ministry. [James White, *Life Sketches* (1880), pp. 396, 397, 408-410.]

About fifteen years before his death James White suffered several strokes. They left him sometimes pessimistic and abrupt. Eight entries selected from the diary of George W. Amadon, a Review and Herald press foreman, portray how difficult it became to get along with White after his strokes:

January 12, 1870. Wed. Another meeting at the office. Dr. Russel was spoken to plainly. I was spoken of *very sharply*. Aldrich was reproved severely, & U. S[mith's] course was spoken of some. Not much going on at the office. Several girls dismissed. It has rained for 24 hours. Bro. Gale came & went off. Bro. Leighton's folks are at Bro. Whites. I am in some trial, but I pray that I may stand free.

January 14, 1870. Fri. . . . Bro. W. still feels led to bear down on me. Praise God, that I am worthy of reproof, for that is good for the soul. Made up some of the paper 2 da. Got some shavings for cow bedding. Byron drew some for office. John is hauling wood from Depot. I am feeling down in mind[;] I think I don't overcome fast enough.

February 7, 1870. Mon. About 8 got down to the office. Pitched into work. . . . God seemed to sustain. Haven't been reproved by Bro White but twice. God knows whether I try to do my work faithfully or not. Worked till eight this evening. Laura here to-day. Worked extra about Russell with Review. . . .

February 8, 1870. Tu. Worked 7th form of Sol[emn] Appeal. Bro. White seemed to be much tired with me today. Accused me of "yelping," when I spoke to Bro. Miller. I hope the Lord will help me to humbly do right. Bro. White went to Chicago today. We

49

ordered 300 lbs. small pica. A good meeting to our
house to night. I have had a terribly congested brain,
caused by trials, sweetcake & beans. . . .

March 20, 1870. Sun. Worked all day at the office.
Didn't attend any of the meetings. Made up most of
the Review. Have been addressed very sharply by Bro.
W. several times. Surely, no chastening for the
present is joyous; but reproof *is* good for the soul.
Better are the reproofs of the righteous than the
kisses of a friend. Didnt stay long at the meeting
to-night. Bro. Canright preached.

March 25, 1871. Sat. A good day. Bro. White spoke
in the forenoon—Sr. W. in the afternoon. How faithful
these servants of God are. Oh may we improve on our
many privileges.

May 27, 1871. Sat. Sister W. preached in the
morning. Bro. W. in the afternoon. Very plain—very
sharp. A session at the close of the Sabbath sharper &
sharper. They come right to the point.

August 7, 1875. Sat. Bro. White preached
vigorously in the forenoon. In afternoon a good social
meeting. Time mostly occupied by delegates. In
evening, Bro. White elaborated the "present
situation" till near midnight. God helped him
wonderfully. He was clear & sharp as a sword.
[George W. Amadon, MS Diary. Heritage Room,
Andrews University.]

**Joseph Harvey Waggoner, a fellow minister, however, wrote
kindly of the intensity of White's disposition:**

It was often remarked by those who were
associated with him [James White] more than a
quarter of a century, that we never knew a man
whose being and personality were so entirely
identified with his work. . . .

No man ever occupied a position where the
careless would more readily misunderstand his

50

James White

motives. It was to his credit that they who stood with him the longest, and were the most intimately acquainted with him, clung to him the closest and trusted him most fully.

About fifteen years ago he was stricken down with paralysis, which brought him very near to the grave; and as slighter shocks followed the first one, he never fully recovered from their effects. They who knew him only since that time cannot realize with what strength and energy he labored in this cause previous to that time. [Joseph H. Waggoner, ed., *Signs of the Times,* August 11, 1881, p. 354.]

And George I. Butler, General Conference president in 1881 and a White protégé, eulogized White at his funeral:

For about thirty years I have known Elder White, and for ten years I have been acquainted with him intimately. He was a man of a remarkable mind. In some respects I never saw his equal. For force of character, for the grasp of the details necessary to the success of his plans, for foresight, and looking quickly and deeply into difficult and perplexing matters, and for preparing for emergencies when his plans were threatened, I think his mind was most remarkable. As an organizer, and in laying the foundation of an enterprise, his mind was far-reaching, and he could see the bearing and connection of things with surprising clearness.

With integrity of purpose, he labored most earnestly for what he thought would advance the cause—that cause which with all his soul he believed to be the cause of God. . . . With such force of character, such aggressive instincts and tenacity of purpose as he possessed, it was inevitable that he should come into conflict with the men he found in his way in the carrying out of his plans. This is always so with men of earnest purpose who attempt the work of

51

a reformer. Yet he made hosts of ardent friends, who will cling to his memory with fondest affection. When free from care, suffering, and perplexity, he was a most pleasant companion, cheerful, hopeful, and full of life.

His influence has reached thousands, to benefit and lift them in the scale of virtue and religion. He was eminently a man of faith and prayer, going to God in all times of perplexity for comfort and guidance. How many times we have seen him do this, pouring out his soul to the Lord of Heaven. With all his force and firmness and tenacity, when he clearly saw he was wrong, he would confess it as freely as any one I ever saw. . . .

I never knew a man who could more generously forgive a wrong when he thought it was truly repented of than he. Yet with many he never received credit for this trait.

His labors in this cause have been truly wonderful, and were often performed in suffering and weakness. [George I. Butler, *Review and Herald,* August 16, 1881, pp. 120, 121.]

Twenty-four years later Butler still retained the same memory of him:

He was one of those lordly men[,] . . . for I believe he was a man whom God used to do great good, and that in some respects he was a greater man than any other in the Denomination, but he had his failings like other mortals. [George I. Butler letter to Dr. J. H. Kellogg, June 11, 1905. John Harvey Kellogg Papers. The Museum, Michigan State University.]

for further reading:

Ashbaugh, Kraid I., "An Analysis of the Sermons of James White" (MA thesis, SDA Theological Seminary, 1951), 84 pages.

* Dick, Everett N., *Founders of the Message* (1938), chap. 4.

Spalding, Arthur W., *Footprints of the Pioneers,* chap. 5.

_____, *Origin and History of Seventh-day Adventists,* Vol. 1, chaps. 3, 9.

White, Ellen G., *Testimonies for the Church,* Vol. 1, pp. 105-112.

White, James, *Bible Adventism* (1877; reissued 1972), 198 pages.

_____, *Sermons on the Coming and Kingdom of Our Lord Jesus Christ* (1870), 182 pages.

53

Ellen White

Ellen Gould White was unique. Though the church leadership rejected all other nineteenth century claims to the prophetic role, they accepted her gift as genuine. Though she spoke with authority, what she said did not always mark out a clear line of action because her colleagues seldom had the understanding, manpower, and money enough to expedite the matter. Though she often could have said "I told you so" after some failure she had warned about, she remained humble. And though a woman, she became the most notable platform attraction in her church.

J. N. Loughborough, minister and pioneer denominational historian, portrayed Ellen and her visions:

> I will state some facts relative to the visions. The first time I saw Mrs. E. G. White (formerly Miss Harmon) was on the first Sabbath in October, 1852. On that day I saw her in a vision that lasted over one hour. Since that time I have had the privilege of seeing her in vision about fifty times. . . .
>
> In passing into vision she gives three enrapturing shouts of "Glory!" The second, and especially the third, fainter, but more thrilling than the first, the voice resembling that of one quite a distance from you, and just out of hearing. For about four or five seconds she seems to drop down like a person in a swoon or one having lost his strength; she then seems to be instantly filled with superhuman strength,

54

sometimes rising at once to her feet and walking about the room. There are frequent movements of the hands and arms, pointing to the right or left as her head turns. All these movements are made in a most graceful manner. In whatever position the hand or arm may be placed, it is impossible for any one to move it. Her eyes are always open, but she does not wink; her head is raised, and she is looking upward, not with a vacant stare, but with a pleasant expression, only differing from the normal in that she appears to be looking intently at some distant object. She does not breathe, yet her pulse beats regularly. Her countenance is pleasant, and the color of her face as florid as in her natural state.

Her condition as to breathing, loss of strength, and being made strong as the angel of God touches her, all agree perfectly with the description given by the prophet Daniel of his own experience in vision. [J. N. Loughborough, *Rise and Progress of Seventh-day Adventists,* pp. 93, 94.]

Though many church members regarded Ellen as a prophet, she little relished the title. But not until 1906 did she explain why she preferred the phrase "the Lord's messenger" instead:

Some have stumbled over the fact that I said I did not claim to be a prophet; and they have asked, Why is this?

I have had no claims to make, only that *I am instructed that I am the Lord's messenger;* that he called me in my youth to be his messenger, to receive his word, and to give a clear and decided message in the name of the Lord Jesus. . . .

Why have I not claimed to be a prophet?—Because in these days many who boldly claim that they are prophets are a reproach to the cause of Christ; and because my work includes much more than the word "prophet" signifies. . . .

To claim to be a prophetess is something that I have never done. If others call me by that name, I have no controversy with them. But my work has covered so many lines that I can not call myself other than a messenger, sent to bear a message from the Lord to his people, and to take up work in any line that he points out. [Ellen G. White, *Review and Herald,* July 26, 1906, p. 8.]

Mrs. White saw the world as a constant conflict between good and evil. She viewed the spiritual warfare not as an abstract thing, but as something intensely personal:

Those who are exalting education above everything else, may become much more intelligent in regard to the work that is going forward in this high contest of the two opposing forces between the principalities and powers. They need not imagine a battle going on in some distant field with celestial pomp, in all the terribleness of superhuman strength, but bring the imagination down to the reality of the war and conflict in the domain of the human heart, and give this battle the character of a moral conflict, a struggle between principalities supported by opposite parties which appear as combatants. They must consider they are either to become champions of falsehood or of truth. But this view of things is not poetical enough for the fancy of very many who are fighting with Satan the game of life for their souls. [Ellen G. White, *Review and Herald,* July 19, 1887, pp. 449, 450]

Some readers supposed her ideas fell into categories—that her writings contained "I-was-shown" material which was inspired, and "personal-opinion" material which was unin-

spired. Concerning such distinctions she wrote:

> Some have taken the position that the warnings,
> cautions, and reproofs given by the Lord through his
> servant, unless they come through special vision for
> each individual case, should have no more weight
> than counsels and warnings from other sources. In
> some cases it has been represented that in giving a
> testimony for churches or individuals, I have been
> influenced to write as I did by letters received from
> members of the church. There have been those who
> claimed that testimonies purporting to be given by
> the Spirit of God were merely the expression of my
> own judgment, based upon information gathered from
> human sources. This statement is utterly false. . . .
>
> The Lord does not give a vision to meet each
> emergency which may arise in the different attitudes
> of his people in the development of his work. . . .
>
> For the last forty-five years the Lord has been
> revealing to me the needs of his cause, and the cases
> of individuals in every phase of experience, showing
> where and how they have failed to perfect Christian
> character. The history of hundreds of cases has been
> presented to me, and that which God approves, and
> that which he condemns, has been plainly set before
> me. God has shown me that a certain course, if
> followed, or certain traits of character, if indulged,
> would produce certain results. He has thus been
> training and disciplining me in order that I might see
> the dangers which threaten souls, and instruct and
> warn his people, line upon line, precept upon precept,
> that they might not be ignorant of Satan's devices,
> and might escape his snares. . . .
>
> With the light communicated through the study of
> his word, with the special knowledge given of
> individual cases among his people under all
> circumstances and in every phase of experience, can I
> now be in the same ignorance, the same mental

uncertainty and spiritual blindness, as at the
beginning of this experience? Will my brethren say
that Sister White has been so dull a scholar that her
judgment in this direction is no better than before she
entered Christ's school? . . .

If you, my brethren, who have been acquainted
with me and my work for many years, take the
position that my counsel is of no more value than the
counsel of those who have not been especially
educated for this work, then do not ask me to unite
with you in labor; for while you occupy this position,
you will inevitably counteract the influence of my
work. . . .

And now, brethren, I entreat you not to interpose
between me and the people, and turn away the light
which God would have come to them. Do not by your
criticisms take out all the force, all the point and
power, from the Testimonies. Do not feel that you can
dissect them to suit your own ideas, claiming that God
has given you ability to discern what is light from
heaven, and what is the expression of mere human
wisdom. If the Testimonies speak not according to the
word of God, reject them. [Ellen G. White,
Testimonies, Vol. 5, pp. 683, 685, 686, 688, 691.]

**Church members sometimes assumed that she had all the
answers, that she "saw" all things in detail. Some Notes
From the General Conference of 1901 bear upon the matter:**

Mrs. E. G. White: I did not know how we should
get along at this meeting [of the General Conference].
. . . [But] I was never more astonished in my life than
at the turn things have taken at this meeting. This is
not our work. God has brought it about. Instruction
regarding this was presented to me, but until the sum
was worked out at this meeting, I could not
comprehend this instruction. God's angels have been
walking up and down in this congregation. I want

Ellen White

every one of you to remember this, and I want you to remember also that God has said that He will heal the wounds of His people. [Ellen G. White, *Review and Herald,* May 7, 1901, p. 296.]

Often when some problem threatened denominational ranks, the church sought the Whites' help. President Sands H. Lane, of the Indiana Conference, relates their skillful dealing with one such emergency in his report of the 1879 camp meeting.

Wrote Lane in the Supplement of the "Review and Herald" that year:

The meetings from the first day were good. Thursday we were all cheered by the arrival of Bro. and Sr. White and W. C. White and wife. . . . Monday morning Sr. White bore a straight testimony to the ministers and members of the Conference, presenting important facts to the satisfaction of all on many points which had been matters of sore perplexity, clearing up and dispelling difficulties which would ere long have proved a source of distraction and ruin to the cause and Conference. Hearty confessions were afterward made, publicly and privately. The Lord blessed. Light came at last, union and harmony revived, and a good state of feeling now exists. As the result, all business sessions of the Conference . . . passed off pleasantly and harmoniously.

It is well known by the readers of the *Review* that some two years ago Eld. A. W. Bartlett took extreme views on the subject of sanctification, and that he and several others ran into fanaticism on the subject. This caused the Conference much perplexity, as some sympathized with him and were gradually losing sight of the message, and drawing off from the body. Sr. White bore a very plain testimony to Eld. Bartlett

59

and his sympathizers, and to the Conference in general, in regard to the subject of sanctification as held by Eld. B., showing that it was the work of Satan to distract and draw away precious souls from the truth, and lead them into darkness where they would be blinded to their own danger.

Elder Bartlett was deeply affected by the straight testimony, and publicly confessed it all to be true, stating that he had often deplored the fruits of the move. He expressed a willingness to surrender his positions on the subject of sanctification, and to labor to build up that which his course had torn down.

The Lord gave victory, and Brother Bartlett's heart seems to be again united with the cause of God.

Bro. and Sr. White left us Monday noon; and as they rode off the ground we felt like saying, The Lord's hand is in this work. [Sands H. Lane, *Review and Herald,* October 23, 1879, Supplement, p. 2.]

Having a prophet in the midst of the church may have led many to place on her responsibilities that they should have assumed. Mrs. Sarepta M. I. Henry, a recent convert and a person influential in the Women's Christian Temperance Union, attended the 1899 General Conference. From the conference floor, in South Lancaster, Massachusetts, Mrs. Henry commented:

Now I have one other thing to say, which has been resting upon me very heavily for a day or two, and that is concerning a danger which I recognize among this people—a danger of spiritual paralysis; a resting upon the fact that the Lord sends special messages to meet special needs, through his servant to this people; and in knowing this fact, and resting upon it, each man for himself, which is the privilege of this people. When a question comes up which ought to be settled quickly, under the influence of the Spirit of God, upon principle, instead of practicing the self-denial, instead

Ellen White

of bringing yourself up to the point of consecration and that earnest self-surrender to God which would bring you to the place into which you could yourself see, in the light of the Spirit, just what to do with that case, you think, "Well, we will get help through Sister White;" and then you just leave it. You lay the burden off on her, instead of carrying it yourself.

I do not think this is fair. I want to make an appeal to my brethren right here. I want to exhort you earnestly to bring yourselves to the point from which you can settle every personal question yourself; and when every personal question is settled, you will come together in conference, and be able to settle conference questions. I know that this is the privilege of every one of us. God is no respecter of persons, and he is perfectly willing to give that measure of the Holy Spirit to every one of his servants that will enable them to see clearly, so that we shall not be obliged to wait, as I said the other evening, six weeks to get an answer [by correspondence with Ellen White] from the Lord. [Mrs. S. M. I. Henry, *The General Conference Daily Bulletin* (1899), p. 171.]

What sort of person was Ellen White? The following selections will give some hints. Pastor John Matteson writes following a brief acquaintance. Doctor Sanford P. S. Edwards writes after lifelong experience. Matteson wrote:

This is the first opportunity [1866] I have had of seeing her, and I considered and weighed well all her actions and words. I have been at one period of my life a skeptic, and I now let skepticism bring in her objections, and let the Bible, the Spirit, and reason answer. As the result of this examination I will here present one argument to prove that Sr. White is led by the Spirit of God.

We have the best evidence that gold is genuine, by the excellent quality of its own matter. . . .

61

Windows

I happened accidently to overhear her family prayers twice, unknown to her, as she was alone with her husband and children. What was she doing? Planning cunningly how she might lead her admirers to bring their sacrifices before her? Or how she might be revenged upon her enemies and bring shame upon them? No! Childlike and earnest pleadings were heard, not only by me, but by Jesus and angels. She communed with God. She was moved by the same Spirit that moved upon me when I heard the first comforting word from my Saviour.

If she does not have the things presented before her mind, which she purports in her testimonies, then she is a deceiver, and one of the worst kind too. But her prayers were not such as deceivers bring forth. . . . In her home she did not betray the least sign of one who is exalted. She engaged in household duties, and appeared just as humble and social as one who had never spoken in public.

When she spoke to the people, she manifested no human learning or art. No studied eloquence, nor gestures, nor display of education. But there was an earnestness, power and yet simplicity, which told that she had been with Jesus and learned of him. Appeals came from the heart and went to the heart. . . . When she spoke, she appeared to me like one crying in the wilderness. Those appeals ought to stir every soul to renewed action and consecration. But they seem to be partly lost amid all the worldliness, and pride, and surfeiting, of the latter days. [John Matteson, *Review and Herald,* May 29, 1866, p. 206.]

Edwards' letter:

Of Sister White's appearance and characteristics I fear to start; the paper is to[o] short. Structurally she was short, about 5 ft. 4 in., I judge, rather stockily built but not overly obese. Her features were round and full; her hair dark and always parted and combed back simply to a braided knot at the back of her neck. She always looked you straight in the face unless she was reading. She was not handsome nor was she homely; she always looked *good*. I mean it did you good just to look at her face. You never thought of how she looked—it was always what are you seeing. She had the sweetest smile that broke out frequently and made her face beautiful. Her eyes were large and became larger if she was in earnest or excited and grew smaller when she smiled. Her voice was a contralto tone but very soft and pleasing to listen to. When in conversation she spoke . . . with a deep, almost bass voice. It had tremendous carrying power. . . . When she was much in earnest, as when giving instruction to an individual or group, her eyes were wide open, her voice indescribable—you heard the words rather than the voice. I know for I have been there more than once.

I knew her love, her pity, her sympathy and her reproof. It all brought joy. The sound was lost in the joy of the presence and the message. Even the reproof was sweet. . . . She talked to me as a long lost friend, as tho she never had a care in the world, when I knew that she was holding back a message she knew would hurt, but she could not say it until she was sure I was ready to take it like a man.

When I was recovering from a severe stroke in 1910 and had just been prayed for by Elder Daniel[l]s and others of the ministers available, she sent for me to come to her home. I went and found her sitting in her easy chair by the door of her study. I was welcomed with a warm handshake and asked to be seated, and then for half an hour[,] her face smiling all the time, she talked to me about the times we had met and visited. . . . Suddenly her face straightened and she looked so kindly at me and said, "Willy tells me that the brethren prayed for you yesterday. You were blessed?" I answered "Yes," and then she continued "It was right that you should be prayed for, but I am instructed to tell you that you will not be completely healed. You are a willing Horse and will do any thing that the brethren ask of you and the brethren are willing to ask a lot of you. God cannot trust you with your old strength and vigor. You have done more than your share already, and He wants others to carry the load. He has work for you yet but it is your job to sit still and wait His time. There will be things come up which you can do better than anyone else, or that no one else is willing to do. He will then give you strength for the task and lay you aside when it is finished. Let us kneel in prayer."

And we knelt and the prayer is unquotable. She talked with God and told Him all about me and my suffering and my need and my failings and my efforts in the cause and then she turned to me and laid her hands on my head and said, "And now Father as I lay my hands on his head and his shoulders and his arms and his back, let the healing power, as Thou seest best come in." And she prayed on for my wife and for wisdom for me to use wisely the health that He trusted to me. If she had told me I was to die the next day, I would have been happy about it, for that was the nearest to God's presence I had ever known and I was satisfied whatever came. That was forty-seven years ago this summer. . . .

I could tell much more about her. We all called her Mother. She was much more than a mother to all who knew her. She was not eloquent in the sense we com[m]only use it. She never used a big word in talking. The largest word I ever heard her speak was "righteousness." [Sanford P. S. Edwards letter to the compiler, October 29, 1957. Paragraphing supplied. Held by the compiler.]

Ellen White

for further reading:

Delafield, D. Arthur, *Ellen G. White and the Seventh-day Adventist Church* (1963), 90 pages.

Dick, Everett N., *Founders of the Message* (1938), chap. 5.

* Jemison, T. Housel, *A Prophet Among You* (1935), 505 pages.

Nichol, Francis D., *Why I Believe in Mrs. E. G. White* (1964), 128 pages.

* Noorbergen, Rene, *Prophet of Destiny* (1972), 241 pages.

Rebok, Denton E., *Believe His Prophets* (1956), 320 pages.

Spalding, Arthur W., *Origin and History of Seventh-day Adventists,* Vol. 1, chap. 4.

* Spicer, William A., *The Spirit of Prophecy in the Advent Movement* (1937), 128 pages.

* Teesdale, W. Homer, "Ellen G. White, Pioneer, Prophet" (PhD dissertation, University of California at Berkeley, [ND]), 300 pages.

* White, Arthur L., *Ellen G. White—Messenger to the Remnant* (1969), 129 pages.

White, Ellen G., *Christian Experience and Teaching of Ellen G. White* (1940), 268 pages.

——————, *Life Sketches of Ellen G. White* (1915), 480 pages.

——————, *Testimonies for the Church,* Vol. 1, pp. 1-105.

Wilcox, Francis M., *The Testimony of Jesus* (1944), 160 pages.

Witness of the Pioneers Concerning the Spirit of Prophecy (1961), 92 pages.

Sabbath Reform

Settlers brought to America four worship or rest-day ideas. (1) The most ancient consisted of the seventh-day Sabbath, represented by the Seventh Day Baptists. (2) The next oldest tradition involved Sunday, or "Continental Sabbath," allegedly authorized at the Council of Laodicea (AD 336). (3) Several heavy sermons on Sunday and Old Testament Sabbath-style behavior characterized the Sunday "Puritan Sabbath." (4) A fourth, stressed by the Quakers, placed goodness, uprightness, and human freedom above the mere formal details of Sunday-keeping. Wars and materialism gradually nudged Sunday-keeping Americans toward the continental practices.

Eugene W. Farnsworth described how seventh-day Sabbath observance came to the Adventists:

> Mrs. Rachel D. [Oakes] Preston . . . is the one whose name has gone down in history as being among the very first, if not the first, Seventh-day Adventist.
>
> She came from the State of New York in the early advent times, probably in the latter part of the year 1843, to visit her daughter, who was teaching school in Washington, N.H. She was a Seventh-day Baptist. She had no sooner arrived here than the believers in the advent message, true to the message, gave her the light, which she readily accepted, saying to them, "I believe you are right."
>
> Then she said, "I want to ask you one question,

66

Sabbath Reform

Why do you keep Sunday for the Sabbath?" They in turn asked, "Why, isn't Sunday the Sabbath?" To which she replied, *"No, indeed!"* Then she gave them the Bible testimony on the true Sabbath. It is said that William Farnsworth, who had given her the message and had listened to this testimony, took his hat and went home without saying a word. But he kept the next Sabbath. Others of that company of Adventists followed. Elder Frederick Wheeler, who died a few years ago at the age of one hundred years, was a member of that company and began the observance of the Sabbath in March, 1844.

[Information] obtained from Edgar W. Farnsworth, of South Lancaster, Mass., who is a grandson of Mrs. Preston, with whom he spent the early years of his life. [E. W. Farnsworth, *Review and Herald,* February 21, 1918, p. 16.]

T. M. Preble, a minister near Washington, New Hampshire, wrote an article and a pamphlet on the Sabbath in 1845. John N. Andrews and Joseph Bates soon accepted the doctrine. Bates influenced Hiram Edson, of New York, James and Ellen White, of Maine, Albert Belden and E. L. H. Chamberlain of Connecticut, and Otis Nichols, of Massachusetts. Also, Bates prepared and published a forty-page tract, *The Seventh-day a Perpetual Sign,* in 1846.

What doubt lingered in the minds of the Adventists regarding the true Sabbath vanished after an 1846 vision by Ellen White:

But the Lord gave me a view of the heavenly sanctuary. The temple of God was open in heaven, and I was shown the ark of God covered with the mercy seat. Two angels stood one at either end of the ark, with their wings spread over the mercy seat, and their faces turned toward it. This, my accompanying

67

angel informed me, represented all the heavenly host looking with reverential awe toward the law of God, which had been written by the finger of God.

Jesus raised the cover of the ark, and I beheld the tables of stone on which the ten commandments were written. I was amazed as I saw the fourth commandment in the very center of the ten precepts, with a soft halo of light encircling it. Said the angel, "It is the only one of the ten which defines the living God who created the heavens and all things that are therein." [Ellen G. White, *Life Sketches*, pp. 95, 96.]

Thus began a vast literature on the perpetuity, obligation, restfulness, and significance of the seventh-day Sabbath. For example, the *Index to the Writings of Ellen G. White* contains over twenty-five pages of Sabbath references.

A problem eventually arose among Adventists, however. Did one determine its beginning and end by mechanical contrivances or by natural indicators? In 1855 James White asked J. N. Andrews to study the matter. The conclusions of Andrews and his committee appeared in the general church paper:

A most important consideration is this: if the Sabbath commences at six o'clock, no one can tell when that hour arrives unless they have a clock or watch. Now these were not invented until about 1658. See *Putnam's Hand Book of Useful Arts.* So that for nearly the whole space of 6000 years the people of God have been without the means of telling when the Sabbath commenced. But such a conclusion would be a manifest absurdity. And we have already seen that there is not a single testimony of Holy Scripture that can be adduced for the six o'clock time. We conclude

Sabbath Reform

this article by summing up the argument as follows:

1. There is no Scriptural argument in support of six o'clock, as the hour with which evening commences.

2. If that is the hour, the people of God for about 5,600 years were unable to tell when the Sabbath commenced.

3. The Bible, by several plain statements, establishes the fact that evening is at sunset. [J. N. Andrews, *Review and Herald,* December 4, 1855, p. 78.]

Nearly all accepted their conclusions except Bates and Ellen White. However, a few days later a vision corrected her understanding:

> I saw it is even so, "From even to even shall ye celebrate your Sabbaths." Said the angel, "Take the word of God, read it, understand, and ye cannot err. Read carefully, and ye shall there find *what* even is, and *when* it is." I asked the angel if the frown of God had been upon His people for commencing the Sabbath as they had. I was directed back to the first rise of the Sabbath, and followed the people of God up to this time, but did not see that God was displeased, or frowned upon them. I inquired why it had been thus, that at this late day we must change the time of commencing the Sabbath. Said the angel, "Ye shall understand, but not yet, not yet." Said the angel, "If light come, and that light is set aside or rejected, then comes condemnation and the frown of God; but before the light comes, there is no sin, for there is no light for them to reject." [Ellen G. White, *Testimonies,* Vol. 1, p. 116.]

Why had it taken a decade to decide on the point? Andrews admitted that in part it was because of their ignorance of Seventh Day Baptist exegesis which "always held to this doctrine."

It occurred, however, to the Adventists that inasmuch as they had accepted the seventh-day Sabbath, the Seventh Day Baptists might join them. The Seventh-day Adventists kept up a friendly relationship with the Baptist group for the next several decades.

Seventh Day Baptist history hints how the two groups interacted:

1843: SDB General Conference at Plainfield (N. J.): recommends to all the brethren "that the first day of November next be observed by our churches as a day of fasting and prayer that Almighty God would arise and plead for his holy Sabbath."

1844: SDB General Conference at Verona (N. J.): "To recommend, in view of the Divine blessing since last Conference, that the first day of January next be observed as a day of fasting and thanksgiving, and of prayer that God would continue to plead for His Sabbath and prepare us for the labor thus devolved upon us. . . ."

1869: SDB General Conference at Shiloh (N. J.): "Conference adopted a fraternal reply to a communication from the Seventh-day Adventists, and appointed Jonathan Allen a delegate to the next meeting of that body."

1870: SDB General Conference at Little Genesee (N. Y.): Resolved upon "Co-operation with the Seventh-day Adventists, but without compromising distinctive principles. . . ."

70

Sabbath Reform

1871: SDB General Conference at Adams Center (N. Y.): "A Mr. Prescott was received as representing the Central Association of Baptists, and J. N. Andrews from the Adventists."

1872: SDB General Conference at Southampton (Ill.): "Uriah Smith was welcomed as delegate from the Adventists."

1873: SDB General Conference at Westerly (R. I.): "J. N. Andrews was cordially received as delegate from the Seventh-day Adventists; . . . Stephen Burdick, delegate to the Conference of the Adventists, reported concerning the work and organization of that people."

1874: SDB General Conference at De Ruyter (N. Y.): "L. C. Rogers, delegate to the Adventist Conference, told of the enlarged missionary, publishing and educational work of that body."

1875: SDB General Conference at Alfred (N. Y.): "Delegates . . . [including] Elder Canright, accompanied by Elder Smith, from the Adventists."

1876: SDB General Conference at Walworth (Wis.): "Elder James White appeared as delegate from the Adventists, and, later, gave an address on the relations of the two denominations. W. C. Whitford, delegate to that body, reported their activity and advancement, vigor and religious fervor." [Approved]: "The interchange of delegates with the Adventists, but not the consolidation of the two bodies holding such opposite views concerning important doctrines. . . ."

71

Windows

1878: SDB General Conference at Plainfield (N. J.): "Elder J. H. Waggoner was welcomed as delegate from the Adventists." "Essays were read by A. H. Lewis, on evolution; and by Varnum Hull on the differences between our denomination and the Adventists."

1879: SDB General Conference at Brookfield (N. Y.): "Nathan Wardner, delegate to the Seventh-day Adventist General Conference, expressed the opinion that that people are modifying in their sentiments; and that each change brought them nearer to us in belief." "Elder James White, of the Adventists, was introduced and welcomed to a seat in our Conference; and his report of their prosperity was met by a resolution expressing fraternal joy."

1885: SDB General Conference at Alfred Centre (N. Y.): "A resolution stating a definite and literal doctrine of the certain and personal coming of Christ was laid on the table."

1886: SDB General Conference at Milton (Wis.): "Resolutions were adopted indorsing the doctrine of the certain and personal coming again of our Lord, and of the resurrection of the dead. . . ."

1889: SDB General Conference at Ashaway (R. I.): ". . . extended thanks to the Seventh-day Adventist New England Conference, owner of the auditorium tent [used by us]. . . ." SDB author, Alexander McLearn [former president of Battle Creek College, 1881-1882] issued *Seventh-day Adventism; Some of Its Errors and Delusions.* [*Seventh Day Baptists in Europe and America,* 2 vols. (Plainfield, New Jersey; 1910), Vol. 1, pp. 149-233; Vol. 2, p. 1346.]

72

Many Seventh Day Baptists did join the Seventh-day Adventists—but the two groups drifted apart. The Seventh-day Adventist Church mushroomed far ahead of the Seventh Day Baptists in growth.

for further reading:

* Andreasen, M. L., *The Sabbath, Which Day and Why?* (1942), 255 pages.

Bronner, Frederick L., "The Observance of the Sabbath in the United States, 1800-1865" (PhD dissertation, Harvard University, 1937).

Knappen, M. M., *Tudor Puritanism* (1939), pp. 442-450.

Lewis, Richard, *The Protestant Dilemma* (abridged, 1961), 96 pages.

Morse, Alice Earle, *The Sabbath in Puritan New England* (1891), 335 pages.

Seventh Day Baptists in Europe and America, Vol. 2 (1910).

Shuler, J. L., *God's Everlasting Sign.*

Spalding, Arthur W., *Origin and History of Seventh-day Adventists,* Vol. 1, chap. 7.

* Thomsen, Russel J., *Seventh Day Baptists—Their Legacy to Adventists* (1971), 95 pages.

Weaver, Horace B., "A Historical Study of the Sabbath in the American Colonies From 1664 to 1800" (MA thesis, SDA Theological Seminary, 1946), 62 pages.

* Wood, Kenneth H., "God's Holy Day," *Review and Herald,* November 27; December 4, 11, 18, 1969.

73

Adopting a Name and Organizational Structure

Much as the English Sabbath observers around 1754 received the name Seventh Day Baptists because of similarity to the Baptists, so now around 1853 the Seventh Day Baptists styled the American Sabbath-observing Adventists as the "Seventh-day Advent" people—and the idea and essential phraseology stuck.

Concerning the development of a denominational name, William A. Spicer, himself of Seventh Day Baptist origin, wrote in 1946:

> The name Seventh-day Adventist was adopted in 1860. Before that we find the workers speaking of this people as "the brethren," "the little flock," "the believers." When a general meeting was called in a State or district, the notice spoke of a "general gathering of the Advent brethren." Opposition papers of the scattered parties into which the old 1844 main body of Adventists was dividing sometimes called our people Sabbatarian Adventists.
>
> In 1853 the secretary of a Seventh Day Baptist organization, J. C. Rogers, of De Ruyter, New York, wrote to James White, at the Rochester headquarters, saying he was instructed to "correspond with the Seventh-day Advent people and learn their faith." That was suggesting a phrase pretty close to the name finally adopted. [W. A. Spicer, *Review and Herald*, February 7, 1946, p. 5.]

Adopting a Name

In 1856 Joseph H. Waggoner, Merritt E. Cornell, and Joseph Bates established a church of sixty-six members at Hillsdale, Michigan, and from October 17 to 20 convened a "conference." A contemporary, John N. Loughborough, points out how nearly two hundred people located the meeting place there:

> As there has been feeling with some in regard to the name proposed [and adopted] at Battle Creek Conference [in 1860] by which we as a people should be known, I would say I think the name, "Seventh-day Adventists," is the most natural and appropriate name we could take. In Hillsdale I came across a handbill that was used there some four years ago when our brethren were going to have a conference there. It reads, "There will be a conference of the *Seventh-day Advent* people held in Waldon's Hall," &c. This name I suppose was used in the handbill because everybody would know at once who it meant. [J. N. Loughborough, *Review and Herald,* November 13, 1860, p. 205.]

However, as late as summer, 1860, the influential Joseph Clarke of Ohio still placed arguments for "Advent Sabbatarians" before the readers of the "Review":

> It is to me a matter of no little surprise, that the name "Advent" is considered by some of those who look for the soon coming of Christ, a term of reproach, so much so that they even would deny its application, and reject the name.
>
> A little investigation and sober reflection will soon set this matter right; for there is a peculiar propriety in the name; and its application is so fitting, that for one I rejoice in it. A purer word, and one more significant and applicable, is not to be found. . . .
>
> There is a necessity that every individual, and body of individuals, have some name to distinguish

Windows

them; and there is no wrong in this. We may see an illustration of the innocence of this proceeding, in the act of bringing the animals to Adam, for the purpose of seeing what he would call them. See Gen. ii, 19.

The disciples were first called Christians at Antioch, and the name has clung to them ever since; and who is ashamed of the name Christian? . . .

Names are of some consequence; and a fitting and appropriate name is a good thing. Sabbatarian is a name which has for a long time distinguished those who kept holy the true Sabbath. "Sabbatti" was the name applied to the Waldenses, who kept and venerated the precepts of the decalogue; and of course the name has been applied to those who have embraced the third [angel's] message; and this, too, is a fitting and appropriate name; it is a pure name, from the word Sabbath which name was applied by God himself to the seventh or rest (Sabbath) day: and who could wish for a more honorable name?

Taking into consideration these names, their origin, and meaning, and appropriateness, their peculiar bearing upon our own eventful times, it must be conceded, that as to the name Advent Sabbatarians, we are the most fortunate of all people, in having a name beautiful, significant, appropriate, natural and becoming. O that none of us bring disgrace upon so pure a title.

But says one, the world despise the name. Very well; they despised Emanuel and his chosen followers. It is the fashion of this world to despise all that pertains to purity and holiness; all that reproves the world, and that leads to God and his holy law is held in disrepute by the world, and always has been, since the fall of Adam; and doubtless the Antediluvians despised Noah's title, whatever it was, as much as the world now hate the term "Advent." [Joseph Clarke, *Review and Herald,* June 12, 1860, p. 29.]

Adopting a Name

Few Seventh-day Adventists wrote of the denominational organization so personally and perceptively as James and Ellen White, inasmuch as they participated actively in it.

Early in 1881 James reviewed what had taken place:

> Organization was designed to secure unity of action, and as a protection from imposture. It was never intended as a scourge to compel obedience, but, rather, for the protection of the people of God. . . .
>
> Christ never designed that human minds should be molded for Heaven by the influence merely of other human minds. . . . However important organization may be for the protection of the church, and to secure harmony of action, it must not come in to take the disciple from the hands of the Master.
>
> Those who drafted the form of organization adopted by S. D. Adventists, labored to incorporate into it, as far as possible, the simplicity of expression and form found in the New Testament. The more of the spirit of the gospel manifested, and the more simple, the more efficient the system.
>
> The General Conference takes the general supervision of the work in all its branches, including the State Conferences. The State Conference takes the supervision of all branches of the work in the State, including the churches in that State. And the church is a body of Christians associated together with the simple covenant to keep the commandments of God and the faith of Jesus.
>
> The officers of a local church are servants of that church, and not lords to rule it with church force. . . . These officers should set examples of patience, watchfulness, prayer, kindness, and liberality, to the members of the church, and should manifest a good degree of that love to those they serve exhibited in the

life and teachings of our Lord. [James White, *Review and Herald,* January 4, 1881, p. 8.]

Ellen appraised what had occurred from a later perspective:

I was one of the number who had an experience in establishing it [gospel order] from the first. I know the difficulties that had to be met, the evils which it was designed to correct, and I have watched its influence in connection with the growth of the cause. At an early stage in the work, God gave us special light upon this point; and this light, together with the lessons that experience has taught us, should be carefully considered.

From the first our work was aggressive. Our numbers were few, and mostly from the poorer class. Our views were almost unknown to the world. We had no houses of worship, but few publications, and very limited facilities for carrying forward our work. . . .

Our numbers gradually increased. The seed that was sown was watered of God, and he gave the increase. At first we assembled for worship, and presented the truth to those who would come to hear, in private houses, in large kitchens, in barns, in groves, and in school houses; but it was not long before we were able to build humble houses of worship.

As our numbers increased, it was evident that without some form of organization, there would be great confusion, and the work would not be carried forward successfully. To provide for the support of the ministry, for carrying the work in new fields, for protecting both the churches and the ministry from unworthy members, for holding church property, for the publication of the truth through the press, and for many other objects, organization was indispensable.

Yet there was strong feeling against it among our people. The First-day Adventists were opposed to

Adopting a Name

organization, and most of the Seventh-day Adventists entertained the same ideas. We sought the Lord with earnest prayer that we might understand his will, and light was given by his Spirit, that there must be order and thorough discipline in the church, that organization was essential. . . .

We had a hard struggle in establishing organization. Notwithstanding that the Lord gave testimony after testimony upon this point, the opposition was strong, and it had to be met again and again. . . . We engaged in the work of organization, and marked prosperity attending this advance movement. As the development of the work called us to engage in new enterprises, we were prepared to enter upon them. The Lord directed our minds to the importance of educational work. . . . Our work was not sustained by large gifts and legacies; for we have few wealthy men among us. What is the secret of our prosperity? We have moved under the order of the Captain of our salvation. God has blessed our united efforts. The truth has spread and flourished. Institutions have multiplied. The mustard seed has grown to a great tree. . . .

The business of our Conference session has sometimes been burdened down with propositions and resolutions that were not at all essential, and that would never have been presented if the sons and daughters of God had been walking carefully and prayerfully before him. The fewer rules and regulations that we can have, the better will be the effect in the end. When they are made, let them be carefully considered, and, if wise, let it be seen that they mean something, and are not to become a dead letter. Do not, however, encumber any branch of the work with unnecessary, burdensome restrictions and inventions of men. In this period of the world's history with the vast work before us, we need to observe the greatest simplicity, and the word will be stronger for its simplicity.

Let none entertain the thought, however, that we can dispense with organization. It has cost us much study and many prayers for wisdom that we know God has answered, to erect this structure. It has been built up by his direction, through much sacrifice and conflict. Let none of our brethren be so deceived as to attempt to tear it down, for you will thus bring in a condition of things that you do not dream of. . . . Then let every one be exceedingly careful not to unsettle minds in regard to those things that God has ordained for our prosperity and success in advancing his cause. . . .

In reviewing our past history, having travelled over every step of advance to our present standing, I can say, Praise God! As I see what God has wrought, I am filled with astonishment and with confidence in Christ as Leader. We have nothing to fear for the future, except as we shall forget the way the Lord has led us, and his teaching in our past history. We are now a strong people, if we will put our trust in the Lord; for we are handling the mighty truths of the word of God. . . .

We have an army of youth to-day who can do much if they are properly directed and encouraged. We want our children to believe the truth. . . . We want them to act a part in well-organized plans for helping other youth. [Ellen G. White, *The General Conference Daily Bulletin* (1893), January 29, 30, pp. 22-24.]

for further reading:

* Crisler, Clarence C., *Organization: Its Character, Purpose, Place, and Development in the Seventh-day Adventist Church* (1938), 265 pages.

Loughborough, John N., *The Church, Its Organization, Order, and Discipline* (1907), 184 pages.

Olsen, M. E., *A History of the Origin and Progress of Seventh-day Adventists* (1926), chap. 10.

Spalding, Arthur W., *Origin and History of Seventh-day Adventists*, Vol. 1, chap. 12.

Conditional Immortality and the Resurrection

Adventists early confronted the puzzle of death. Even in the Millerite period George Storrs, one of their ministers, introduced the "nature of man" into their discussions.

Washington Morse later reflected on the situation:

> I was troubled to know what kind of a Resurrection was taught in the Bible and I was answered that it would be a Spiritual Body[,] nothing tangible[.] But as one Elder said, a body of spirit. I was taught to believe that all men had an Immortal Soul that went at death either to Heaven or Hell and was either Happy or in eternal torments throughout the endless ages of eternity[.]
>
> And In the summer of 1843 While attending Camp Meeting in Chelsea[,] Vt[.,] I chanced to go into the tent oc[c]upied by Elder George Storrs of Philadelphia and seeing his large trunk that was filled with Books I took up one entitled The Sleep of the Dead and Annihilation of the Wicked. A good sister whome I was united with in church fellowship said, "Bro. Morse do not touch that Book[,] its teachings are rank poison." Such was our Ignorance then upon such a great subject. [Washington Morse, MS Memoir, c 1888. Held by the compiler.]

Seventh-day Adventists shortly reasoned, as did Storrs, that at death man ceases breathing and goes to sleep "for a

Conditional Immortality

little moment" (Isaiah 26:20), awaiting the resurrection event when the righteous mortal receives the gift of eternal life. To them the Biblical doctrine (as in 1 Corinthians 15) seemed humane, meaningful, and comforting, especially in an age that stressed hellfire. Within a score of years some Adventists refined the "unconscious state of the dead" and the "morning of the resurrection" ideas to the utmost.

Paragraphs written by James White about 1880 indicate his approach to the doctrine—and his dealing with a problem that had arisen:

> At the General Conference held at Battle Creek, April, 1861, we spoke upon the resurrection, as set forth in the fifteenth chapter . . . [of 1 Corinthians]. The strong tendency with many members of the popular churches, to surrender the time-honored doctrine of the literal resurrection of the dead, led us to speak upon the subject before such representative men as Elders Andrews, Waggoner, Loughborough, and Smith. We had adopted the view that it was not necessary to a resurrection that the same particles of matter which constitute the mortal man should enter into the immortal being; and that the identity between the present mortal and the immortal is not in matter, but in organization.
>
> We were happy to know that the position taken relieved the subject of the resurrection from the difficulties of the identical-particles-of-matter theory, urged by skeptics, which difficulties were leading thousands, like the Sadducees of old, to deny the resurrection of the dead. It seemed evident to us that Paul refers to these when he says, "But some men will say, How are the dead raised up? and with what body do they come?" 1 Cor. 15:35. He then shows by the figure of the grain, that the matter which constitutes

83

the mortal body does not enter into the immortal being.

The ministers before mentioned did not accept our view of the subject, and conforming to the rule we had adopted, that new views should not be urged until there should be harmony among the leading men of the denomination, we let the matter rest during a period of sixteen years. . . .

When we returned from California a few weeks later, we found Doctor Kellogg presenting to his physiology class the identity question from a scientific view. But the subject was still under the heavy pressure of the prejudice which would naturally exist in the minds of the brethren at Battle Creek, because of the position and influence of leading ministers. Many of the students accepted the Doctor's position, while but few of them dared to express their real convictions, lest they should be doomed to the regions of infidelity, where the Doctor had been consigned by those under the influence of narrow prejudice. We take pleasure in stating that the church at Battle Creek, and our people generally, are relieved upon this subject by the able and patient labors of Doctor Kellogg. The views of Mrs. W[hite] on this subject, in manuscript three years since, are clear and definite. And when she can be spared from arduous labors in the field, into which she is urged, she will be able to give them in connection with other important matter in the fourth volume of the "Spirit of Prophecy." [James White, *Life Sketches* (1880), pp. 399-401.]

As White suspected, Dr. J. H. Kellogg did not refrain from urging his concept of the doctrine. In 1878 the doctor spoke at camp meeting on "The Harmonies of Science and Religion" in an effort to brighten the prospect of the tomb.

Conditional Immortality

In 1879 Kellogg lectured a General Conference session on "Human Identity" and put forth a book on "The Nature of the Soul," from which we extract the following paragraphs:

In this record [in Heaven's books] is embodied a detailed plan of each person's organization, whether he be good or bad. The record forms a perfect photograph of the individual, being, indeed, a representation of the abstract organization which was once represented in matter. In the case of the righteous, after the resurrection the soul or organization becomes immortal, as forming a part of an immortal organism. . . .

Another advantage in the new view is this: To most people who have believed in a conscious, independent soul, after death, the doctrine of a material soul lying in the grave and undergoing natural dissolution, or scattered to the ends of the earth, has seemed anything but satisfactory. Indeed, to the minds of the majority of the people, such a soul is equivalent to no soul at all. But in this view, which regards the soul as safely lodged in Heaven, while the worthless body is being scattered by the ruthless elements of organic change, there is something more secure, more satisfying to the mind, more in accordance with the general idea of the soul held in common by the human race. . . .

The resurrection must concern especially the same elements of man's nature that were involved in creation. The thing that was created, goes into the grave; a human body dies, is disorganized. At the resurrection we have a restoration of the same person by re-organization of matter in the same order, manner, or arrangement. The matter of which Adam's body was composed was not created at his creation. The only new thing made in the creation of man was an organization. God formed man from the dust of the ground; that is, he gave to inorganic matter an

85

arrangement which invested it with life. The organization was created, not the matter. Through the creation of an organization and its representation in matter, Adam was created. In death, the material representation of the organization is destroyed. The *person* is dead. In the resurrection, the same organization is again represented in matter, the re-organization being effected by the same omnipotent power which created the first organization. Thus the resurrection concerns chiefly the very same thing which was created; viz., the organization. It appears, then, that a resurrection which excludes or ignores the original atoms of the body is not in any proper sense a new creation, since the same individual is reproduced. The creation of man was making a living being out of dead matter without reference to any previously existing man. The resurrection is making a living man out of dead matter, with direct reference to a previously existing man, who is reproduced by the preservation and reproduction of the identical organization. There is no new creation involved, but a resurrection in every sense of the word. [John H. Kellogg, *Harmony of Science and the Bible on the Nature of the Soul and the Doctrine of the Resurrection* (1879), pp. 104-106, 217-219.]

James White suggested that Ellen was hoping soon to explore the nature of human identity, too, but not until 1900 did she get around to it. The vital portion of her essay follows:

Our personal identity is preserved in the resurrection, though not the same particles of matter or material substance as went into the grave. The wondrous works of God are a mystery to man. The spirit, the character of man, is returned to God, there to be preserved. In the resurrection every man will have his own character. God in His own time will call

86

Conditional Immortality

forth the dead, giving again the breath of life, and bidding the dry bones live. The same form will come forth, but it will be free from disease and every defect. It lives again bearing the same individuality of features, so that friend will recognize friend. There is no law of God in nature which shows that God gives back the same identical particles of matter which composed the body before death. God shall give the righteous dead a body that will please Him.

Paul illustrates this subject by the kernel of grain sown in the field. The planted kernel decays, but there comes forth a new kernel. The natural substance in the grain that decays is never raised as before, but God giveth it a body as it hath pleased Him. A much finer material will compose the human body, for it is a new creation, a new birth. It is sown a natural body, it is raised a spiritual body. [Ellen G. White, *Seventh-day Adventist Bible Commentary,* Vol. 6, pp. 1092, 1093.]

And as a sort of exclamation point Ellen added:

Christ became one flesh with us, in order that we might become one spirit with Him. It is by virtue of this union that we are to come forth from the grave,—not merely as a manifestation of the power of Christ, but because, through faith, His life has become ours. Those who see Christ in His true character, and receive Him into the heart, have everlasting life. It is through the Spirit that Christ dwells in us; and the Spirit of God, received into the heart by faith, is the beginning of the life eternal. [Ellen G. White, *The Desire of Ages,* p. 388.]

87

for further reading:

* Andreasen, M. L., *The Faith of Jesus and the Commandments of God* (1939), chap. 16.

Froom, Leroy E., *The Conditionalist Faith of Our Fathers*, Vol. II (1939), chap. 16.

* Kellogg, John H., *Harmony of Science and the Bible on the Nature of the Soul and the Doctrine of the Resurrection* (1879), 224 pages.

Seventh-day Adventists Answer Questions on Doctrine (1957), chap. 9.

Spalding, Arthur W., *Origin and History of Seventh-day Adventists,* Vol. 1, chap. 13.

* Vandeman, George E., *Destination Life* (1966), 92 pages.

Preachers
of the Faith

The developing denomination desperately needed preachers. They valued each one. Even as late as 1892 historian Loughborough remembered to count and name most of those who in each of the early critical years began to preach.

1849: Three or four ministers decided to help Bates and the Whites speed "the message."

1850: Eight more ministers entered the ranks. They included Samuel W. Rhodes, Hiram Edson, Frederick Wheeler, E. P. Butler, and John Nevins Andrews.

1851: An additional eight assumed responsibilities, some of whom were Roswell F. Cottrell, Charles W. Sperry, William S. Ingraham, and Joseph Baker.

1852-53: Fifteen more volunteers joined, including Joseph Harvey Waggoner, A. S. Hutchins, Merritt G. Kellogg, J. B. Frisbie, Merritt E. Cornell, T. M. Steward, Uriah Smith, and John N. Loughborough.

1854-55: Five more ministers came into the ranks. Two of them were brothers, Augustin C. and Daniel T. Bourdeau.

The handful of Adventist preachers tried to find as many former Millerites as possible. Their letters reveal their evangelistic zeal:

Windows

Jackson, Mich. Aug. 18, 1849

Dear Brother White—

I would say for your encouragement, that the little band here have received the truth on the Sabbath, without exception [Dan Palmer, Cyrenius Smith, and others]. And we thank the Lord for ever inclining Bro. Bates' mind to come to Jackson. O, sound the alarm, and let the message fly! I think it is the last one to the remnant. We herein send you ten dollars for the spread of the truth. . . .

Give our love to Sister White, and Bro. Bates. Tell him we are all strong in the Lord, rejoicing in the truth. How thankful I am that this blessed truth has not divided us. O, praise the Lord!

Yours, in Hope, J. C. Bowles.

Oswego, N.Y. Nov. 26, 1849

Beloved Brethren, scattered abroad— ˙

God is reviving his people, and building up his cause in Western New York. . . . Divisions are being thoroughly healed, and strong union, and fervent Christian love increase among us. . . . The little flock here in this region are established on the Sabbath, and our past advent experience. Our number is constantly increasing. . . .

Our general meeting . . . in Centreport, Nov. 17 and 18, was one of the best I ever attended. Here we met some of our beloved brethren from the east—Brethren Ralph and Belden from Connecticut, and Brother and Sister White from Maine. . . . It was a melting, confessing, refreshing season. . . .

About ten days before the Centreport Conference, I was deeply impressed with a sense of duty to make

90

one more effort to rescue our beloved Bro. Rhodes. . . .

Bro. Rhodes was one of the most faithful, and self-sacrificing lecturers on the Second Advent, that ever labored to this region, and that most of those who now stand on present truth, received their first light on the advent through him. He spent a handsome property in the [Millerite] cause . . . until his means were entirely exhausted. . . .

With tenderest feelings for the torn flock [after 1844], he left them, and retired to the wilderness; for he feared that some of them might lean on him, and be lost. Most of the time for three years he has been in the wilderness, about thirty miles from any settlement. He has sustained himself principally by fishing and hunting. . . . Twice within the past year, in company with other brethren, I have been about 180 miles to see him, and we tried to persuade him to come among the brethren; but without success.

At the close of the Centreport Conference, I introduced Bro. Rhodes' case to Bro. Ralph. . . . We both felt deeply Bro. Rhodes' case. . . . Bro. Ralph asked the Lord, in secret, [for guidance]. . . . The Spirit was poured out, and it settled upon us, so that the place was awful, and glorious. . . .

Monday Nov. 19, we started on our journey. . . . We did not have to go into the wilderness; for Bro. Rhodes had come out a few days previous, and we found him at work in a field, on a rise of ground on the east side of Black River.

We told him that we had come in the name of the Lord to get him to go with us and see the brethren, and go with us into the Kingdom. . . .

Bro. Rhodes finally consented to come with us, and went about arranging his business in order to leave. [Next day, however], he turned from us and said, "It is too much, I cannot stand it" and started for the woods. I feared that he was going away from us not to return again, so I started and ran after him, and found him on his face, asking the Lord what all this meant, why his children should feel so much for him.

Friday, Nov. 23, we returned as far as Bro. Arnold's, of Volney, and our dear Bro. Rhodes with us. Sabbath morning we came to this place, in company with Brother and Sister Arnold, where many of the brethren of this region were assembled. They were all rejoiced to see Bro. Rhodes. Tears of joy and tenderness flowed freely as they greeted each other. We had a sweet, heavenly sitting together during the meeting, and Bro. Rhodes' faith and hope are fast increasing. He stands firm in all the present truth; and we heartily bid him God speed, as he goes to search out and feed the precious, scattered flock of Jesus.

Hiram Edson.

March, 1850

[White's notice of a] conference.

There will be a conference of the brethren at Oswego, N.Y. to hold Sabbath and first-day, March 16 and 17. Brethren Rhodes and Holt expect to [be] with us. . . . Brethren Holt and Rhodes returned to this city last week, in good health, and strong in the faith. Their labors for a few weeks past, have been effectual. . . . About forty have embraced the Sabbath within a few weeks where they have labored. They feel that they cannot rest; but must go on as fast as possible, and hunt up the scattered "sheep" who are perishing for want of spiritual food. Brethren, let them have your prayers; also, be careful to see that their temporal wants are supplied.

Preachers of the Faith

Michigan, Aug. 22 [1850]

[Dear Brother White—]

I started Tuesday after the meeting at Jackson, and after traveling two days over loose rails, rough log-ways and through the mud, I found the North Plains about seventy-five miles north of Jackson. I found dear Bro. Case at work in his shop. . . . We went to the meeting. . . . Bro. Case's eyes were opened wide by the Bible class.

Friday afternoon I had the time to talk, and spoke on the 2,300 days. Bro. Case saw . . . [the truth]. I attended the meeting, Sabbath[;] E. Miller preached on the sleep of the dead (it seems that many know but little else). . . . We went Monday to see B. B. Brigham, the principal one among those who profess to believe in the Advent[.] I think there is but little doubt but that he will, with his wife and son, come into the truth.

Tuesday morning, by Bro. Case's request, I went with him down into the woods—we knelt by the side of a beautiful stream of water, where we prayed for the Spirit to come upon us. The Lord heard and answered. Bro. Case was there buried with Christ in baptism. I think he will yet go into the field, when the way shall open.

S. W. Rhodes.

Jackson, Ind., Sept. 2 [1850]

[Dear Brother White—]

I will here say that we had one of the best meetings with the Saints in Jackson, Mich. Five were baptized. . . . Glory to God! for salvation that can be felt in the flesh. Bro. Bowles and myself left Jackson, Mich., last Monday. Stopped at Battle Creek, found one brother nearly lost in the darkness of the Laodiceans. We think there is strong hopes of his embracing the truth.

We next went to Climax Prairie; found a few poor souls drowning in the "age to come" doctrine—the return of the Jews—a sacrificial age, &c., &c. Some hopes of their coming into the present truth. We have held meetings here (Jackson) three days, and the Lord has blessed our testimony. Two have embraced the present truth, and I think more will come to the light. I shall start, "if the Lord will," for LaPort[e] [Indiana] to-morrow. I am stronger in the truth now, than I was when I left New York. O how clear it all looks to me. The Lord is giving me clearer light on his word every day. I feel now much as Elisha did when he said— "Yea, I KNOW IT, hold your peace."

Kingsbury, Ind., Sept. 9; I am satisfied that the Lord is about to work by the present truth, and he will send laborers into the vineyard. Some three or four confessed the truth yesterday, and others are deeply convicted. Bro. Joseph Catlin has come into the present truth like a giant. He has been a leader here. I expect to start to-morrow for Wisconsin.

S. W. Rhodes.

North Plains, Mich., Sept. 15, 1850

Dear Bro. White—

For the first time I sit down to write you a few words. . . . O, how shall I be thankful enough to the Lord that he put it into the heart of Bro. Rhodes to come to this dark part of the world. . . . This truth ravishes my soul. . . . Glory to God! the path is plain and glorious. . . .

If Bro. Rhodes had not come to see me, I think that I should have fallen into the "ditch." . . .

94

Preachers of the Faith

I feel the truth in my soul, like fire shut up in my bones. I want to proclaim the third angel's message [especially to those in New York whom I buried in baptism]; but I have not the means. . . .

The excitement that the truth has produced here is not small. . . . If the way opens I want to go into the field once more, to get some precious "jewels" for the "second casket."

Yours in hope.
H. S. Case.

Jackson, Mich., Sept. 17, 1850

Dear Bro. White—

I left Bro. Rhodes the 9th inst., 160 miles west of here, (at LaPort[e], Indiana.) . . . Bro. Rhodes has been the means in the hands of God of raising up three in the West that will be able to give the message, . . . Brn. Case, Kemp, and Catlin. Several were brought in on our way. I left Bro. Rhodes at Bro. Catlin's, with a good prospect that others would embrace the truth. From there he goes to Illinois and Wisconsin. I think he will be back here in about two or three weeks.

J. C. Bowles.

Greece, N. Y., Oct. 14, 1850

Dear Bro. White—

Oh! What floods of light continue to shine upon my ravished vision. . . .

I . . . will begin the history of my journey, and labors in Wisconsin. I found Bro. Holcomb and his wife . . . they both confessed the truth. [Also a daughter and a neighbor woman at Lake Pleasant.]

Windows

[Before that, however], I had a more severe battle to pass through, than at North Plains, *Mich*. . . . The blessed Lord palsied the influence of six or seven preachers, and stood by poor unworthy me, in power, and took a few from the mouth of the lion. . . . I baptized three the morning that I left. . . . Arrived in Jackson, Mich., by Railroad, stopped with the Brethren over the Sabbath, broke bread, washed the Saint's feet, got abundantly blessed. Left the band in Jackson in as good a place as any band I have seen in all my travels. . . . I felt that I must see Bro. Case again before I left for the East. I went to North Plains, found him in the present truth, and more than a match for all his enemies. . . . Bro. Case left with me for Bro. Guilford's, found them in an awfully dark place. The eldest one confessed all the truth, several others came into the Sabbath. . . . Bro. Case came with me to Detroit, and then returned with horse and wagon to Jackson. Spent last Sabbath, probably there. I think he will go in search of the scattered sheep, for the Lord is showing him his light and truth very fast. I pray God to make him mighty in the truth. I want to see you very much, God bless you, Amen.

S. W. Rhodes.

Oswego, [NY] Oct. 21 [1850]

[Dear Brother White—]

I feel strong in the strength of the living word of God. We have had a meeting similar to the one you wrote of at Topsham, Me. The brethren at Oswego and Sterling were free.

You have my heart and prayers in publishing a paper. I know that a paper is needed very much. I start this P.M. for Volney, Schroeple, Bro. Miller's, Fayetteville, Brookfield and Camden.

Preachers of the Faith

Pray for unworthy me. I ask it with tears. O, how I love you. Love and fellowship in the Holy Ghost to all in Christ.

S. W. Rhodes.

Oswego, N. Y., Oct. 21, 1850

Dear Bro. White—

Since I returned from Canada[,] . . . seven were baptized. [Then I visited the brethren in Copenhagen and Lorain.]

I then went to Oswego, . . . fourteen were baptized. . . . One week yesterday I met with Dear Bro. Rhodes four miles from Rochester. . . .

We met in conference the 18th, at Bro. Storrs'. . . . Thirty-three were baptized. I rejoice to see the people of God rising in Western New York. I feel like going night and day to bear the glorious message. It grows better and better. Glory to God. My love to yourself, wife and all the saints.

Geo. W. Holt.

[November, 1850?]

Conferences—

The blessing of the Lord attends such meetings in a wonderful manner. The Vermont conference, held at Sutton, Sept. 26, 27, 28 and 29, was well attended, and we are sure resulted in much good. The number of believers present was about seventy. Eight of our dear brethren from Canada East were among the number. . . .

Bro. George, the son of our beloved brother and sister Morse of Sutton, and two others, were also

97

buried with Christ in baptism. . . .

We met in conference with the brethren at Fairhaven, Mass. Oct. 19 and 20. It was a very interesting meeting. Some that were in a doubting state when we were there in June have become fully established in the whole truth. . . . If they keep humble the Lord will keep them, and, we trust, add to their numbers. . . . Sister Bates, the wife of our faithful Bro. Bates, is strong in the present truth. The deceptive influence of some who professed to preach the true advent faith, blinded her mind, and prejudiced her against the truth. Bro. Bates persevered, and for years, yes, all through the scattering time [following 1844], has kept the Holy Sabbath alone. But when the gathering time came, and God began to reach out his arm to recover his precious "jewels" from beneath the "rubbish," sister Bates was led to examine the truth for herself. And now, she and her husband are walking in ["?]all the commandments and ordinances of the Lord." Praise the Lord for what he is doing for the trusting remnant.

[James White?]

Fairhaven, Mass., Nov. 4, 1850

[Dear Brother White—]

Perhaps, a brief sketch of my tour in Vt. and N. H. after I parted with you at the general conference in Sutton, Vt., may be interesting to you and also to the little flock.

You know Bro. Stephen Smith was anxious for me to go with him to Lebanon, N. H., to visit Eld. Joseph Baker, who was one of God's strong men, in the judgment hour cry, and fall of Babylon. Bro. Baker, and his companion, received us kindly. Our meeting commenced in the evening. After a while, I said, I fear I shall weary you. No, said he, go on brother, I want to hear the whole. I was trying to chain the three angels messages together, making the work of God a straight, clear, perfect, and harmonious history, for the last ten years. The next morning before we parted, said he, *this is the truth;* it has been working in my mind these years. I learned afterwards that his brethren were anxious to see him [come] out with the third angel's message. I trust that God is fitting him to sound this mighty cry.

Our meeting at Waitsfield was blessed of God. Brother and Sister Butler came from Waterbury with Brn. Chamberlain and Churchill. Brn. Hart and Brailey came from Northfield; and those in the place with Bro. Lockwood's family, composed our meeting. . . .

The Lord made it our duty to accompany Brother and Sister Butler to Waterbury. Here at the house that has been open for meetings, so many years, a little company gathered, and Bro. Butler drank deeper into the straight truth. . . .

At Bennington, we met Bro. Smith again, also, our tried Bro. Hastings, son and daughter. . . . [As] the meeting progressed all . . . [grew] stronger, and stronger in the truth.

The two Bro. Martins and their companions, with two others in Bennington, professed their clear convictions of the seventh-day Sabbath, and shut door. So you see, dear brother, that in places where all was dark and dreary, a few weeks since, light is now springing up. Then let all the swift messengers that God has called, and still is calling into the field, to give the loud cry of the third angel, move forward.

Joseph Bates.

[Sources of the above letters: See *The Present Truth,*

99

Windows

Nos. 4-11, 1849-50; *The Advent Review,* Nos. 1-5, 1850.]

Had the early Adventists persisted in their dedication, Mrs. White indicates, Christ could have come in the 1850's. She wrote in 1883:

Had Adventists, after the great disappointment in 1844, held fast their faith, and followed on unitedly in the opening providence of God, receiving the message of the third angel and in the power of the Holy Spirit proclaiming it to the world, they would have seen the salvation of God, the Lord would have wrought mightily with their efforts, the work would have been completed, and Christ would have come ere this to receive His people to their reward.

But in the period of doubt and uncertainty that followed the disappointment, many of the advent believers yielded their faith. Dissensions and divisions came in. The majority opposed with voice and pen the few who, following in the providence of God, received the Sabbath reform and began to proclaim the third angel's message. Many who should have devoted their time and talents to the one purpose of sounding warning to the world, were absorbed in opposing the Sabbath truth, and in turn, the labor of its advocates was necessarily spent in answering these opponents and defending the truth. Thus the work was hindered, and the world was left in darkness. Had the whole Adventist body united upon the commandments of God and the faith of Jesus, how widely different would have been our history! [Ellen G. White, *Selected Messages,* Book One, p. 68, written c 1883.]

for further reading:

Loughborough, John N., *The Great Second Advent Movement* (1905), chap. 21.

* Olsen, M. Ellsworth, *History of the Origin and Progress of Seventh-day Adventists* (1926), chap. 9.

Spalding, Arthur W., *Footprints of the Pioneers* (1947), 234 pages.

――――――, *Captains of the Host* (1949), chaps. 12, 14, 16.

――――――, *Origin and History of Seventh-day Adventists,* Vol. 1, chaps. 12, 14, 16.

White, James (ed.), *The Advent Review,* Nos. 1-5, 1850.

――――――, *The Present Truth,* Nos. 1-11, 1849-50.

Expanding Beyond New England

As the emerging denomination began to actively evangelize outside of the New England region—which had become apathetic toward Adventism following 1844—the state that responded the most was Michigan.

James White told of speaking in a Michigan barn:

> June 18th and 19th, 1853, we held meetings with the brethren in the vicinity of Franciscoville, who met at C. S. Glover's barn, in Sylvan. This was the largest and much the best meeting we held in the State. Several brethren came in from a distance. On the Sabbath the congregation was large. The subject in the forenoon was the commandments and the law of God; in the afternoon it was the Sabbath.
>
> A prayer-meeting was appointed for First-day morning at nine o'clock, and at the hour more than three hundred people were assembled. Two or three prayers were offered, then the time was occupied by different brethren, who spoke to the point, with freedom and power, till half past ten, when we took the stand and spoke nearly two hours on the first and second angel's messages of Rev. XIV, 6-8. It was thought that there were four hundred people present. We never had a better hearing. In the afternoon we spoke about two hours on the third message of verses 9-12, and at the close of our remarks we felt this solemn subject, and the condition of the congregation,

as we hardly ever felt before. [James White, *Review and Herald,* July 7, 1853, p. 28.]

Joseph Bates baptizes in the wintertime:

> In one of the school districts in M[onterey] we commenced a series of meetings on the evening of the 14th [of January, 1857], and continued until the evening of First-day, 18th[;] notwithstanding the extreme cold weather at the time, the most of the church in M. attended every meeting, traveling from six to ten miles out and home. Their prayers, and spirited exhortations, and singing, both before and after preaching, stirred up the people in the district, and some deep and hearty confessions were made, and strong desires to hear and examine more fully this important subject, while some others fully decided to keep the Commandments of God, and the Faith of Jesus.
>
> On First-day morning [mercury 30 degrees below zero], some of the Brn. in the time of service cut and sawed out the ice some three feet thick, and found water of sufficient depth, wherein seven souls were buried with Christ in baptism. The church attended to the ordinances of the Lord's house, and were much strengthened and blessed of the Lord. [Joseph Bates, *Review and Herald,* February 19, 1857, p. 125.]

J. N. Loughborough gets a winter's pay:

> Money [for me] was hard to obtain in the winter of 1857-58. . . .
>
> It was during this winter that I had the use of Elder White's team in visiting the churches in Michigan, as he was detained in the office most of the time. By this means my traveling expenses were considerably diminished. For the labor performed that

103

winter I received three tenpound cakes of maple
sugar, ten bushels of wheat, five bushels of apples,
five bushels of potatoes, one peck of beans, one ham,
half of one hog, and $4 in money. [J. N.
Loughborough, *Rise and Progress of Seventh-day
Adventists,* pp. 213, 214.]

**One of the most influential of the early SDA ministers was
Merritt E. Cornell. James White reported how he worked in
new areas:**

Sister Cornell has well acted her part. The mode of
warfare is something as follows: Bro. Cornell goes out
alone into a new place, perhaps puts up at the tavern,
preaches a few days, when friends appear to invite
him to their houses; and when the work is well under
way, sister C. joins her husband, and labors from
house to house as they are invited. And when Bro.
Cornell's work is done, it is a good place for sister C.
to remain and defend the truth in private
conversation, and bear responsibilities of the work in
the midst of young disciples. In this way both can bear
a part in the good work, which will bring a glorious
reward in the next kingdom. . . .

The inquiry is frequently made, "Why does Bro. M.
E. Cornell have such success?" This question is
worthy the consideration of all our preachers. His
great success cannot be in consequence of superior
talent, or wisdom to direct his labors. The advice of
others has been of great service to Bro. C. And there
is nothing peculiar in his voice or manner of
reasoning to draw the hearts of the poeople. But he is
a special instrument in the hands of God in raising up
church after church [in Michigan]. Why is this? It is
evidently because of his faithful testimony. He
presents the message as though he believed it, and
expected his hearers to believe it also. He opens the
truth as it is in God's word, and hands it to the people

104

in its testing form, and brings them to a decision. And there is another thing very worthy of notice, that these churches generally come out strong, and grow stronger and stronger. [James White, *Review and Herald,* March 8, 1860, p. 124; July 23, 1861, p. 60.]

Fellow minister John O. Corliss also commented about Cornell:

Elder Cornell's methods of labor were ever out of the ordinary. His was rather a whirlwind style, the novelty of which, in some measure, fascinated and drew people toward the truth he presented, or made them bitter enemies. He was indeed a stormy petrel, whose presence was the signal for a rising tempest. He preferred this method, he said, because no vessel could make port in a dead calm. So after presenting the Sabbath claims in his strong way, he did not hesitate to challenge the world to show his position to be wrong. The consequence was that he was sometimes drawn into public discussion with men who were not honorable in their methods of debate.

Laboring with him at one time in Lapeer County, Michigan, I took occasion to question the advisability of his sharp statements. He turned abruptly and said, "Perhaps I don't know how to do it." He was, however, quite equal to emergencies arising from his earnest public utterances, being able to turn any opposition toward the upbuilding of the truth, even though making no direct argument in its behalf. As an illustration of this, one occasion out of many may be cited:

Elder Cornell had held a series of meetings in a schoolhouse at Freeland, Mich., where about seventy persons had taken their stand to observe the Sabbath, when a rabid preacher from Detroit appeared, and made an appointment to "expose Adventism." His

105

Windows

public effort was prefaced by the statement that he had come there to "overturn Adventism."

The following evening Elder Cornell replied to the Detroit preacher. The audience was so crowded together that most of them had to stand. Besides, it was mostly made up of people antagonistic to the truth. Seeing the situation, Elder Cornell began his review by saying: "Our friend said last night that he had come here to overturn Adventism. I want to tell you in the beginning that he, and others, will find Adventism, in one respect, much like a certain stone wall. A man fresh from Erin bought a lot and started to build a stone wall across its front. A neighbor told him that it would be a useless task, because the frost would overturn it. The man stopped for a moment, then said, 'Faith, then I'll build it two feet high and three feet wide, and if it turns over, it will be taller than it was before.' "

This apt anecdote, though having no value as evidence, quieted the people, and made them willing to listen. The review was then entered upon in Elder Cornell's most vigorous manner.

At the close of the discourse, excitement reigned as both sides of the subject were argued throughout the assembly. Soon the surging crowd pressed toward Elder Cornell in an attempt to do him injury. Just then a tall, fine-looking man of commanding appearance, pushed his way to the stand, and locking arms with Elder Cornell, started toward the door. The angry crowd gave way before them. Upon reaching the open, the stranger—for such he proved to be—lifted his charge bodily to the seat of a carriage at hand, and the driver made a quick departure toward a friendly home. The patron stranger, however, vanished in the darkness, never again to be recognized in that vicinity. [John Orr Corliss, *Review and Herald,* October 11, 1923, pp. 11, 12.]

106

Seventh-day Adventist evangelists often debated their opponents. One that took place in Indiana in 1883 is representative:

> We are now in the southern part of the State at Farmersburg, Sullivan Co., laboring in connection with Brn. Thompson and Oberholtzer, who are with tent No. 3. They commenced meetings here six weeks ago. From the first, the turnout was large, and the interest was good, the congregations ranging from two to six hundred. The interest to hear has been wonderful. Near here is a large settlement of Disciples, many of whom came to the tent. Some became deeply interested, and at last several embraced the truth and became quite earnest in it. This aroused the church, and some of the members would arise after meetings and challenge the brethren to debate the Sabbath question and state of the dead. This they did several times. The brethren did all they could to avoid a discussion. At last the Disciples announced that they had secured Eld. Treat, the champion debater of their denomination in Southern Indiana, and that they had secured a grove near town, and on the 17th of July Eld. T. would come on to expose our positions. The laborers with the tent thought under the circumstances it would be best to engage in discussion with them, so dispatched to me [Sands H. Lane] to come immediately. I reached here on the 12th of July. Found the interest wonderful.
>
> Sabbath, July 14, was a good day. Spoke to a congregation of one hundred, some twenty-five of whom had embraced the truth. It was the second Sabbath meeting. Organized a Bible class in the afternoon. On Monday, July 16, Eld. Treat arrived and immediately came to see us in regard to the debate. We met him in the M. E. meeting-house and arranged the questions with him before many of the leading citizens of the place. We demanded of him on

107

our own account, and in behalf of the people, that he affirm some thing for the first day of the week as a day of rest. At first he would not, but we pressed the matter, and when he saw that the people demanded that he should do so, he at last consented; so we arranged to debate four days. I was to affirm for two days the binding obligations of the seventh day, he to affirm one day the obligation of the first day as a day of rest, he also to affirm the consciousness of the spirit of man between death and the resurrection.

We discussed these questions four days in a grove seated for the occasion. The people came in for miles, and our congregations during the four days ranged from seven hundred to one thousand. The cars which run near the ground stopped regularly, and each day brought many passengers to the ground. Eld. Treat is an able man, a lawyer, minister, and has several years been a member of the Indiana State Senate.

From the first, Eld. T. seemed to be confused. He threw much force and bombast and abuse into his speeches, which only served to turn the people against him. On the Sunday question he made such a complete failure that truly we pitied him. In fact, he failed from the beginning to the end. At the close of the debate scores and hundreds came and shook hands, and one after another began to slip bills and pieces of silver into my hand. When the last one had shaken hands, I had received nearly $25. Many of these persons had never heard on the subjects until the debate. During the spare moments, the people would flock around, and listen to the explanation of the truth.

The debate closed Friday. The next day was a good day at the tent. There were about one hundred and twenty-five present. We took a vote to see how many had commenced to keep the Sabbath, when thirty-seven arose to their feet. . . .

We are now visiting from house to house. . . . Some

have embraced the truth as a direct result of the
discussion with Eld. Treat, and many who were
convinced took a decided stand and are now rejoicing
in the cause. The last Sabbath we were with them,
July 28, forty-five voted to keep the Sabbath;
thirty-two have signed the covenant. [Sands H. Lane,
Review and Herald, August 7, 1883, p. 509; August
14, 1883, p. 524.]

**In Illinois, the church did not make much progress until the
establishment of Hinsdale Sanitarium in 1904 and Broad-
view College in 1910. One of the villages preached to in 1862
was Princeville:**

May 20th, 1862

We [Sanborn and Ingraham] are in Princeville,
Ill., and our meeting is in progress. The weather is
cold[,] the season backward, and every body in a
hurry to get in their corn. But our congregations are
large. Last evening closed a discussion on the Sabbath
question which commenced Sunday evening. Our
opponent was Elder Kelly of this place. He is a
M[ethodist] preacher. He took the position that
Sunday was the creation Sabbath and tried to
demonstrate it by chronological calculation. He said
he could prove from Wm. Miller's figuring that we
were one day too soon on the Sabbath question but
before he got through he said Miller's chronology was
incorrect, and I showed that in his figuring on his
plan he had made a sad mistake and it was so evident
to the people, that the Lord's truth triumphed
gloriously. Some begin already to talk about keeping
the Sabbath. The prospect before us is quite
flattering.

109

Windows

June 4th, 1862

We have been in Princeville three weeks to-day. We have labored against much Sectarian opposition, but the Lord gave us much liberty, and truth has triumphed to the glory of God.

Last Sabbath we organized a church of twenty-five members, and to-day more will be baptized. The arguments used against us by Sectarians in Princeville have ranged as follows: First they discussed with us eight evenings, and failed. Then they cut and carried off three ropes, and failed. Then they brought rotten eggs and of course they failed. And when we were requested by the brethren, who own more than half the Christian meeting house, to hold three meetings therein, the Dragon turned the key; but all to no purpose; for a Universalist gentleman in the place having a large hall, opened it to us free, for which he has our thanks. So truth is still triumphing in Princeville. *Praise* the *Lord.*

Since we last wrote you we have preached eight times more at Princeville, and baptized ten, leaving a church there of thirty-five members, besides many who are almost persuaded to obey the truth. May the Lord help them, is our prayer.

The tent is now pitched in Elmwood, about twenty miles south-west of Princeville, in Peoria Co., Ill. We have preached six times, to large congregations, which are increasing every evening, both in numbers and interest. The prospect here for a good work is certainly flattering. [Isaac Sanborn and Wm. S. Ingraham, *Review and Herald,* June 3, 1862, p. 5; June 10, 1862, p. 16; June 17, 1862, p. 21.]

Adventism did better in Wisconsin, especially after it secured footholds among the Scandinavian settlers. Isaac Sanborn campaigned in Cassville, Wisconsin:

110

Expanding Beyond New England

Oct. 21, 1867

Since returning to Cassville, Grant Co., I have held eighteen meetings with a steady increase of interest in favor of the truth, against a very strong sectarian opposition, which finally became so dragonic [sic] in its venom and spite that on the evening after last Sabbath they came up to the school-house when I was about half through my discourse, and threw three stones about as large as a man's fist through the window at me, and snapped one or two caps on a revolver at the same time. The broken glass flew all around me and on the table where I stood. I do not know that a single particle of it touched me. At least I felt none. One of the stones struck a young sister on the head about six feet in front of me, hurting her quite bad. The second struck a man on the side without harm. The third struck a brother on the opposite side of the house from the window, without harm. It was all done at the same instant. I do not think that any stone came within six feet of me. I stood broadside before the window, about ten feet from it; and I think that the angel of the Lord stood by me and delivered me, for which I praise God's holy name. It caused so much excitement among the people for about five minutes that I stopped speaking, till it was ascertained that the young sister that was hit was not seriously injured. Then I proposed that we sing and pray, which we did. I then went on and finished my sermon in peace, having no fear.

The next morning, which was yesterday, first-day, at ten A. M., we listened to Eld. Ball, Methodist local preacher, who again tried to preach down the Sabbath. And although he had been a week preparing for it, I never saw a man worse covered with confusion than he was. I could see his warmest friends blush for him. As soon as he got through, it being the day we had appointed for baptism when I was here before, we

Windows

repaired to the Grant river, a beautiful stream of
water about two miles distant from the school-house,
where twenty-three willing souls were buried with
Christ by baptism into death, and raised with him to
walk in newness of life. There is still quite a company
of others that expect to go forward soon. [Isaac
Sanborn, *Review and Herald,* October 29, 1867, pp.
304, 305.]

**Iowans seemed open-minded to the new preaching. James
White tells of a wintertime visit to the state:**

At Tipton [Iowa] we took a large addition to a cold
we then had, and by the time we reached Iowa City,
we were unfit for labor. We had to give up
Millersburg and remain with the kind friends in the
City over Sabbath. First-day we spoke in the
Universalist church to a few. The brethren are firm in
the faith, but there can be but little done at present in
that community. . . .

At Dayton we held one meeting on the Sabbath,
and two on First-day in a school-house about sixteen
feet by twenty. To say that the house was "crammed"
would not express the true condition of things. About
twice as many people came as could find seats in the
house. Some had to stay out in the cold wind. But as
many crowded inside the door as could get in. When
we went to the place on First-day it was with some
difficulty that Mrs. W[hite] and self could find our
way to the small desk. And from real necessity she sat
in the desk with me, as there was scarcely a square
foot of room besides in the house. After expelling from
the desk a large dog, there was just room in the desk
for us. The windows were raised on one side of the
house so that those outside could hear. We spoke one
hour and three-fourths, and Mrs. W. finished out the
two hours, and our audience, packed in the house and
out of it, seemed to forget their position and listened

112

with all that interest and patience as if occupying cushioned pews in a spacious church. One thing is certain, the people came and stayed to hear, for there was nothing attractive or comfortable in the place of meeting. We hope to reach Knoxville appointments, but to do it, we must ride two or three days in the cold, chilling prairie winds, which is enough to unfit any human being for speaking for several days. But sick or well, wearied or rested, it will be expected that a man will preach. And these changes from a crowded school house with heated air to the chilling prairie winds, afford the greatest liability of getting colds and retaining them that we ever experienced.

But the ears of this people are open to hear the truth, and it must be preached to them. Meeting-houses are few and small in this country, and many of them are closed against the truth, and against the wishes of the people generally. Therefore Tents must run in this Western field. In new places congregations are very large, the interest great, and the success in raising churches is better than in any other field at present. [James White, *Review and Herald,* April 5, 1860, pp. 156-159.]

Former Millerite, Washington Morse, who moved in from Vermont, spearheaded Seventh-day Adventism in the Minnesota territory. At the outset settlers and the Sioux still fought each other, yet Morse and others managed to gain converts. In the following excerpt Morse exploits an Indian uprising:

In 1856 I Emigrated with a family of Eight Children to Illinois, stopping there just Six months[,] then I went on to Steel[e] county Minnesota where we took a quarter sexion of land[.] Here I was appointed post Master by the United States. . . . Here I labored as Clergy for 12 years[.] I with my Dear Wife and Eight Children was one of the first of three families of

113

Windows

7th Adventists that came to the Teritory of
Minnesota. . . .

In 1862 was the Indian Masicure throughout
Minnesota. There wer great many families slautered
in a brutal manner. And a great many fled for their
life. We lived on a large road leading to the
Miss[iss]ippi River, where many people was hurrying
through to get away. But we stoped all that we could
and made them welcom to anything we had, until
there wer nearly one hundred who lodged in the
school House near our house[,] in our House[,] and
stables. These were fearful times[.] My Wife suffered
much from the loss of sleep and carrying for so many.
. . . Meantime we would keep out scouts to give the
alarm should the Savages come upon us. In this way
scores of people made a stand at our place, for some
weeks. Here we found a good chance to do missionary
work and try to set the blessed truth before those who
had been driven from their homes, and some became
so Interested that we made appointments to come and
hold meetings in their Houses and in the coming
Winter we walked long distances to fill such
appointments with marked success. Thus it was that
Even through this great trouble from the Savages the
seeds of present truth was being sowd. Through all
those years we labored hard and suffered many
privations traveling many hundred miles on foot and
some Instances after a hard day work and travel Lay
down by the side of a Hay or Straw Stack to rest my
tired body and that in a season of the year when
several Inches of Snow would fall during the night.
All through those years the cause was In its Infancy
and Exceeding poor. We labored cheerfully and with
much of Gods blessing and not for this Worlds goods,
as up to this date I never Received but 30 dollars for
my labor from the conference of Minnesota[.]

In 1868, We sold our Home in Deerfield Minn and
removed to Estherville Iowa where we Bought a farm

114

on the desmone [Des Moines] River and took up another 160 acres under the Homestead law and built a House and opened up 75 acres and put in a large crop[.] But the grass Hoppers came and harvested all our crop[.] . . . The next year we had a fine crop, and had it all Burned up by prarie fire. These losses brought us much discouragement and we traded both of our farms for 40 acres of land in Mankato township Minn and was glad to take up our quarters upon that small farm in a Log House. . . .

In the year 1874 We was chosen foreman of Building Committee to Build the first S D A church in Minn, as a Lot was donated us in Mankato. In building this church I worked very hard[,] having 12 cows to care for and milk mostly alone and cutting 40 acres of grass 8 miles from home. With all those hardships It was very hard for me. I donated 1 hundred and 25 dollars tow[ar]ds the church and I worked it all out by myself and my team. [After that I was successively and successfully treated at Battle Creek for "rheumatic pains" that paralyzed my right leg, and for eighty-seven "Black Cancers."] I feel that I owe my life to that Sanitarium or to Dr. Kellogg, as he in the hands of God, has brought me through such Dangers and Suffering, and given me such good health and Soundness. [Washington Morse, MS Memoir. Held by the compiler.]

Corn and cattle producers along the Platte River listened to the evangelists' vigorous preaching, and some became members of the young church in Nebraska. Next appear selections detailing how Adventism entered two towns:

From the beginning [at Ft. Calhoun], we were much annoyed by loud and boisterous talking near the tent, and by objects hurled against the tent. On the evening of Sept. 5 [1882], a Mr. David, from Illinois, gave a temperance lecture in the tent. While

115

he was talking, Bro. O. A. Johnson tried to find out who the disturbers were and to restore order, and was struck twice with clubs. The last blow was upon the head, producing insensibility. He was taken to the tent, where he soon recovered, and it is to be hoped that no lasting injury will result. This broke up the meeting for the evening. The parties were arrested, and were fined for disturbing the meeting and for assault and battery. This did not seem to injure the cause, for we found that all sensible people sympathized with us, and condemned the cowardly conduct of these disturbers. [N. Clausen, *Review and Herald,* September 26, 1882, p. 620.]

We pitched our tent here [at Shelton] on the 28th of July. . . . Thirty or more have decided to keep the "commandments of God and the faith of Jesus." . . . A Sabbath-school has been organized consisting of fifty members. . . .

Yet, while there was a class of eager listeners, the effort to present the truth was not without opposition. Some of the popular ministers opposed it, both from the pulpit and privately; and seeing that it was not thus to be cast to the ground, popular sympathy was so incensed against it that they tried to burn the tent by firing burning missiles at it from a distance. But in this way they were not enabled to carry out their designs. A few nights afterward a crowd of thirty or more surrounded the tent, and declared they would tear it down over our heads if we did not leave immediately. They then commenced throwing coal, hard lumps of clay, and pieces of broken casting,—one piece of sufficient size to tear through the tent. . . . They soon realized that many of them were identified, and through the ruling providence of God they were silenced, and we were permitted to continue our meetings very peacefully until the close. [L. A. Hoopes and G. E. Langdon, *Review and Herald,* October 7, 1884, pp. 635, 636.]

116

Expanding Beyond New England

In the Dakotas the churches contained many hardy settlers of German and Scandinavian origin. E. W. Farnsworth reported the earliest inroads of Adventism there:

The tent has been at Elk Point over three weeks [1876]. Nineteen discourses have been given. The Sabbath question is now before the people. Some have concluded to keep all the commandments of God, and more seem about ready to obey. Our hearers are serious. Opposition is strong. There are six ministers in the place, and nearly all of them are on the war path. We [E. W. Farnsworth and F. A. Barlow] hope for good results here. . . .

I [E. W. Farnsworth] returned to Dakota, Jan. 24, [1877], and resumed meetings in a country place about six miles South of Elk Point village, where I had been laboring for several weeks, and where a few had taken a stand for the truth. Sunday, the 28th, we baptized fourteen in the Missouri. We then organized a church of twenty-six to be known as the Elk Point church. A few of these were Sabbath-keepers before. . . .

The first camp-meeting for Dakota [1879] is in the past. And it can truly be said of this meeting that it has been a success. . . .

1. Its location. Sioux Falls, Dakota, is a beautiful village of sixteen hundred inhabitants situated on Sioux River. One-fourth mile from the village is a wooded island of ten acres, formed by the divided river passing on both sides of it, and uniting again. The waters of this river are the purest of any of the rivers and creeks of the North-west, affording delightful opportunities for bathing, and for baptizing. . . . The island is owned by Judge Brookings, who gave the use of the ground.

2. The numbers in attendance. There were not less than two hundred brethren and sisters present on the

ground. Fully one-half of these were Scandinavians. Besides the congregation tent, there were fifteen family tents, and fifteen covered wagons used as sleeping-rooms. . . . Nearly all the Sabbath-keepers in the Territory, excepting the Russian brethren, were present. . . .

3. The services. After our arrival, Mrs. W[hite] and the writer [James White] did most of the speaking. . . .

Monday was a memorable day. Eleven were baptized, and the Dakota Conference was organized. [*Review and Herald,* August 3, 1876, p. 47; February 15, 1877, p. 55; July 24, 1879, p. 36.]

In 1890 one half of the denomination's members lived in the ten upper Ohio-Mississippi-Missouri River Basin states, but by 1929 the proportion had dropped to only about one seventh. There the church pioneered such evangelistic methods as tent meetings, Bible instructors, Ingathering, and systematic benevolence, and had established such institutions as a publishing house, sanitariums, and schools.

for further reading:

* Christian, Lewis H., *Sons of the North* (1942), chaps. 3-10.

Dick, Everett N., *Union: College of the Golden Cords,* (1967), chaps. 1-3.

* Hill, W. B., *Experiences of a Pioneer Evangelist of the Northwest* (1902), 344 pages.

——————, *Experiences of a Pioneer Minister of Minnesota* (1892), 185 pages.

Loughborough, John N., *Rise and Progress of Seventh-day Adventists . . . ,* chaps. 17, 18.

Olsen, M. Ellsworth, *History of the Origin and Progress of Seventh-day Adventists,* chap. 9.

Spalding, Arthur W., *Origin and History of Seventh-day Adventists,* Vol. 1, chaps. 14, 16.

* White, Ellen G., *Life Sketches of Ellen G. White,* chaps. 22, 23, 24, 27.

Battle Creek

Battle Creek quickly became synonymous with Seventh-day Adventism. For decades up to one seventh of the church's membership lived in the small Michigan town. It contained the denomination's main publishing house, its headquarters, its first college, and its first—and world-famous—medical center. From the beginning Joseph Bates and other early Adventist ministers traveled the roads leading away from the city across the state of Michigan and beyond. Laymen such as David Hewitt, Abraham Dodge, and T. O. Lewis helped Bates establish the budding denomination in the village.

In a testimony meeting in Berrien Springs, Michigan, some of the pioneers were relating early experiences. Brother T. O. Lewis, the son of one of the first converts to move to Battle Creek, had lived in and about Battle Creek for more than fifty years. He gave the following account of the beginning of the Battle Creek church:

> About the year 1850 [1852] Elder Joseph Bates came to Battle Creek, Mich., an entire stranger. Going to the post office, he asked the village postmaster if he could give him the name of the most honest man in the place. "Yes," promptly replied the postmaster. "We have a man by the name of David Hewitt, living in the West End, who is commonly called 'Penny Hewitt,' because, as a community peddler going about with horse and wagon, he is noted for his accuracy even to a cent. Whenever he finds he

has made a mistake, no matter how small the amount, or whether in his or his customer's favor, he will immediately go back, even for miles, to make it right."

That was the kind of man Elder Bates found in Battle Creek to whom to present the truth in that old message center. His message was readily accepted by this honest man, Hewitt, and he talked of it more than of his wares from that time on, as long as he lived.

Soon afterward another good old man by the name of Abraham Dodge, a watch and clock repairer, started out to teach the message in this community, as he repaired clocks in the homes of the people. He was a very amiable man, and one who could talk and work at the same time. As he repaired the clocks, he would talk to the people of the second coming of the Lord and the seventh-day Sabbath. His work was mostly among the farmers.

One day he came to my father's farm, near Kalamazoo, where he found a job with which he was busy for nearly a whole week. During this time he lost no opportunity to present the Sabbath question and the coming of the Lord. This faithful clock mender had the privilege of having two more converts (my father and mother) keep the following Sabbath with him. My grandfather Lewis having been a Baptist minister and believing in the personal coming of the Lord, my father readily accepted that teaching, which left all the more time for the clock man to teach the Sabbath and other points, all of which were accepted and immediately put into practice.

Believing the Lord was soon coming, my father sold his farm and moved to Battle Creek, to join the small company which had developed there after Elder Bates' visit. In accordance with his faith in the shortness of time, he build a very small, plain house, a story and a half upright, with a lean-to, all boarded

121

up and down and simply battened, without basement or any present day conveniences. It probably cost less than $500, and he gave all the remainder of his means to the Review and Herald Publishing Association. Being a shoemaker, my father supported his family of five children by working at his trade. As he made shoes, he taught the message to his customers. In those days every convert immediately became a message teacher.

All the houses of Sabbath keepers in Battle Creek were at that time small and cheap, and the believers were plain, economical, earnest message teachers. Whenever a general meeting was called in Battle Creek, the only thing to do was for the Battle Creek members to open their homes to all who came. This usually made it necessary for the Battle Creek members to sleep on the floor, with only the luxury of the then-popular straw-tick. [T. O. Lewis, *Review and Herald,* August 20, 1925, p. 22.]

Battle Creek Sanitarium became famous around the world. Its concept, that of the health spa, stemmed from Europe. The most famous ones in the United States existed at Saratoga Springs and Dansville, New York.

The first advertisement of the Western Health Reform Institute (later the Sanitarium) gives the following information:

THE WESTERN HEALTH REFORM INSTITUTE.

BATTLE CREEK, MICH.

ITS CHARACTER AND OBJECT

This Institution, as indicated by its name, has been established with a two-fold object; First, as a

Battle Creek

place where disease will be treated on HYGIENIC
PRINCIPLES; and second, as a place where
instruction will be imparted both Theoretically and
Practically, to patients and boarders, on the
important subject of so caring for both body and mind,
as to preserve health, or to secure the largest
immunity from sickness and premature death. The
Health-Reform Movement, as we view it,
contemplates the preservation of health, no less than
the recovery from disease. In the treatment of the sick
at this Institution, *no drugs whatever, will be
administered,* but only such means employed as
NATURE can best use in her recuperative work, such
as Water, Air, Light, Heat, Food, Sleep, Rest,
Recreation, &c. Our tables will be furnished with a
strictly healthful diet, consisting of Vegetables,
Grains, and Fruits, which are found in great
abundance and variety in this State. And it will be
the aim of the Faculty, that all who spend any length
of time at this Institute shall go to their homes
instructed as to the right mode of living, and the best
methods of home treatment.

OUR PRESENT FACILITIES

Our Institution will be open for the reception of
Patients and Hygienic Boarders, on the 5th day of
September, 1866. We shall be able to accommodate
from the commencement, from 40 to 50 patients, and
shall increase the number and size of our buildings as
occasion may require.

OUR LOCATION

We have in this respect all that could be desired.
FIRST. We are in a State which has chosen for its
most appropriate motto, "If you seek a beautiful
peninsula, behold it here."
SECOND. We are situated about midway between

123

the East and West, and patients from either section can reach us with equal facility.

THIRD. Our City is easily accessible from all parts of the country, being an important station on the Michigan Central R.R., the Great Thoroughfare between the celebrated cities of Detroit and Chicago, and one of the main arteries of travel between the East and West. The cars running upon this road are the *stillest, best ventilated,* and *nicest* to be found in the country; the Superintendent, Conductors, and Employes, are gentlemanly and accommodating; and a traveling public give this road the reputation of being the *best managed* of any in the United States.

FOURTH. Our Buildings are located on a site of nearly six acres, the highest and dryest of the city, commanding a fine prospect of city and country, within a few minutes' ride of the depot, from which conveyance can be had by omnibus on the arrival of all trains. . . .

Our Establishment will have plenty of Pure, Soft Water, pure air, good moral influences, and a greater amount of sunshine than any other part of the country can ordinarily boast.

OUR PHYSICIANS

Dr. H. S. Lay with a number of competent Assistants for the Male and Female Departments will constitute the Faculty of the Institute. Of the qualifications of Dr. Lay to manage such an establishment, it will be sufficient to say that he has had seventeen years' extensive medical practice, the latter portion of which he has been employed as a physician in one of the best Health Institutions in the United States [at Dansville, New York], by which he has become thoroughly conversant with the latest and most approved Hygie[n]ic Methods of Treating Disease. To those who may see fit to come to this

124

Battle Creek

Institute as patients, we can say with feelings of confidence, that WHATEVER MAY BE THE NATURE OF THEIR DISEASE, IF CURABLE, THEY CAN BE CURED HERE. . . .

THE HEALTH REFORMER

This is the title of a Health Journal, 16 pp. magazine form, issued monthly at the Health Reform Institute. H. S. Lay, M. D., Editor. It is devoted to an exposition of the Laws of our Being, and the right application of those laws in the Treatment of Disease. We design to make it a model Health Journal, interesting in its variety, sound and valuable in its instructions, and beautiful in its typographical execution. *Everybody should have it.* Price $1.00 per year, INVARIABLY IN ADVANCE. [*Review and Herald,* August 7, 1866, p. 78.]

Battle Creek College appeared in the town's West End in 1874. Under the leadership of James White, Goodloe Harper Bell, Sidney Brownsberger, and William Warren Prescott, it molded some 6,000 or more students.

In 1891 a Michigan State Board of Visitors reported their evaluation of Battle Creek College:

Hon. Ferris S. Fitch, *State Superintendent of Public Instruction:*

The undersigned, the Committee of Visitation for Battle Creek College, made our visit on May 8, 1891.

We find the Institution has secured a property worth about one hundred and sixty thousand dollars, which money has been collected, mostly in small sums, by a people poor in the goods of this world. The building of this Institution is an admirable

125

illustration of the result of the persistent giving of small sums by those who have a definite object in view.

In visiting the buildings, especially the College Home, we were impressed with the perfect order and cleanliness of the entire surroundings. This cleanliness itself gave the Home an air of elegance often lacking in many a more pretentious and elaborately furnished building. The work of caring for this Home, we learn, is mostly performed by the pupils. We were pleased with the dignity and conscious self-respect of the pupils we saw engaged in this service; and when afterwards we had the pleasure of hearing some of these pupils discuss the intricacies of logical fallacies, or work out demonstrations in trigonometry, we could not perceive that their manual labor was any hindrance to their mental development.

We would heartily commend the earnest, zealous spirit, manifest among the students as a whole. While the College is making no pretensions of doing a high grade of college work, it is evident to even a casual observer that it is doing a useful work in elevating and broadening the characters of many young men and women who otherwise would have no inspiration. Many acquire here a thirst for knowledge that carries them beyond the course here laid out. The proportion of young men is remarkably large, it seems to us, for schools of this class.

Another feature of the work that interested us is the prominence given to the study of the English Bible. This work in some form is extended through all the grades from the most elementary to the most advanced. It is a feature, so far as our experience goes, that is unique. The problem of how much moral instruction can be given in the schools of the land without trenching upon individual religious belief, is one that, under various forms of statement, is pressing for solution. Like all educational problems,

126

the proper method of solution is by experiment. At first sight it might appear that Battle Creek College is endeavoring to bring the Theological School down into the College and Preparatory School grades. A closer inspection of their experiment may prove that they are solving for us all the questions, How and how much can we teach Christian morals to the youth of the land? It is well worth the study of all educators, how much of the evident high moral and educational enthusiasm observable among the students of all classes in this school is attributable to this daily contact with, and study of, that "well of English undefiled," the too much neglected "Book of books."

The students of this Institution will never learn from their instructors the modern ideas of the power of money. In this respect the School cannot be said to belong to this age. When we learned the meager salaries the Institution could afford to its instructors, we felt that the age of the martyrs had returned.

We would express our pleasure at the cordial, kindly spirit manifested by President Prescott and all the members of the Faculty in our reception and throughout our visit.

Respectfully submitted, R. W. PUTNAM, DAVID A. HAMMOND, LEWIS G. GORTON, *Board of Visitors. [Fifty-fifth Annual Report of the Superintendent of Public Instruction of the State of Michigan With Accompanying Documents for the Year 1891* (Lansing, 1892).]

The fourth Seventh-day Adventist meetinghouse built in Battle Creek—and the most famous—was the Dime Tabernacle. It received its name from a campaign to collect dimes to pay for part of its $26,000 cost. The structure could seat 3,000. Henry Philip Holser, a student and sanitarium employee at the time, recorded the opening and dedication of the church in his diary:

127

Windows

January 18, 1879. Sat. Went to S[abbath] S[chool]
this morning: the children for the first time had their
school in the Dime Tabernacle. Attended church,
E. W. Farnsworth spoke: gave a very affecting
discourse. Had a very interesting [Sanitarium]
H[elpers] S. S. Eld. A[ndrews] asking review
questions. Gave a treatment after the Sab.

March 1, 1879. Sat. Attended S. S. which was held
in the Tabernacle; it was a grand affair; the whole
school being assembled together. Eld. Canright spoke
to a congregation of 800 on the duties on Sabbath day.
Attended Students prayer meeting at 2:30 and opened
our [Sanitarium] S. S. at 4 o'clock; changed the time
from 3:45 to 4. Had a good school. Att. prayers in
Parlor.

April 19, 1897. Sat. Was on duty at the S. S.
Remained to church. Elder Haskell spoke. Was at
church and social meeting in the afternoon[,] Eld
Canright spoke. Had no S. S. at the Sanitarium.
Attended meeting in the evening. $6300.00 were
raised leaving a debt on the Tab of $3,200.

April 20, 1879. Sun. Spent a short time reading
the 28th testimony [of Ellen G. White] then began
work in the bathroom [giving hydrotherapy
treatments] and continued 'til 12:30 then ate dinner,
went to the Dedication of the Tabernacle and aided in
distributing programmes, subscription envelopes, and
tracts and papers. Ran the elevator [at the
Sanitarium] in the evening and let Charlie attend the
praise meeting. [Henry Philip Holser, MS Diary. Copy
held by the compiler.]

The people of Battle Creek applauded the business ventures
of the Adventists, but some Seventh-day Adventists doubted
the wisdom of consolidating so much in one place. They
feared that the church would stagnate and lose its evangelistic thrust. Many wondered if the Battle Creek Adventists had

128

become too materialistic. Uriah Smith and George W. Amadon, tongue in cheek, examined the idea:

> The children all wear copper toed shoes, just the height of fashion and highly popular. The men wear agate shirt buttons! a material which bears the same name as that which adorns the foundations of the New Jerusalem! Oh, how fallen! Many of the church use Bibles with gilt edges; just such gold is forbidden in 2 Timothy 4:18.
>
> Nearly every family of the Battle Creek church have their tables varnished, when good substantial paint would answer every practical purpose.
>
> Many of the sisters wear strings on their bonnets 15 or 20 inches long, when those of 8 or 10 inches would answer every practical purpose. . . .
>
> And in the culinary department, some are running to the same excess of riot. Why, there are some in this church who have spent fifty or eighty dollars for cooking stoves, when they might get an article that would answer to bake our gems and boil our mush for 20 or thirty dollars, and so much would be saved to advance the precious cause of truth, to help raise the pay of the self-sacrificing ministers to $12 per week. Oh, the extravagance and worldly-mindedness of this professed church who ought to be lights and patterns to all. . . .
>
> And we must confess also that there are some in this church who wear "artificials." Three have fallen into that sin. And worst of all, these are brethren! Think of brethren wearing artificials, and it is a fact that Brethren Smith, Lockwood, and Byington all wear "artificials"—Legs. [Uriah Smith and George W. Amadon, "A Record of Some of the Pride and Extravagances of the Church" (ND), as quoted by Richard Julian Hammond in "The Life and Work of Uriah Smith," pp. 67, 68. MA thesis, Heritage Room, Andrews University.]

129

Windows

Two editorials printed in the "Review" suggest the deep concern which eventually developed about so many Adventists and church institutions congregating in Battle Creek:

Of late, so many of our brethren and sisters from the surrounding churches of Michigan and the adjoining States are moving to Battle Creek, that we feel it our duty to say something about it. Of course, we are not master of any individual's actions, but we can give our advice in the matter, since we are acquainted with the circumstances here and elsewhere better than most of our brethren can be.

In some cases it is right, and, indeed, very desirable, that brethren should move to Battle Creek. This is in cases where they have children whom they wish to educate for a few years in our College. Frequently they can do much better to come here themselves, keep house, board their children, and look after them. In such cases there is no objection to their coming, but still we think that these persons should not locate here permanently. In the past, when the church was small, it was necessary to invite leading families to this place in order to have a good influence, furnish homes for students, and hold the fort. But so many have come in during the last few years and others are coming so rapidly, that we fear for the result. There are plenty here now to furnish homes for all the students, and all the helpers in the Office who may be needed here; hence there is no necessity for others to come.

There are at present about seven or eight hundred Sabbath-keepers located in Battle Creek. It is becoming a very serious task for the leading brethren of the church to look after so many. . . .

They think that there is a large body of brethren here, and that it will be an easy place to live; that in the school, Sanitarium, or Office, they will find plenty of work to do, get good pay, and so have an easy time.

130

Battle Creek

This is the real motive which brings many here. God cannot bless any such conduct. But the worst of all is that many irresponsible persons flock in here. They expect to be petted, and looked after, and cared for. They soon get into trial, and bring trial upon others. They exert their influence wholly on the wrong side with students, with patients, and with the hands in the Office. This class is seriously threatening the interests of the cause in Battle Creek. We want no more of them.

Hence, we advise our brethren in the different States and churches around not to move to Battle Creek without first advising with the Conference Committee of their own State, the General Conference Committee, and the elders of the Battle Creek church, according to the action of the General Conference, as reported last week.

Many youths in our ranks are looking toward Battle Creek on account of the institutions located here affording employment or education, and the extraordinary privileges and advantages to be enjoyed in connection with so large a church. From observation, we are free to say that we consider it exceedingly unwise for people to come to this place without a definite object, and a reasonable assurance that they can obtain that purpose. Many are inclined to come here, whether or no, and run their chances of getting hold of something afterward. They are liable thus to inflict great suffering and disappointment upon themselves, and a great burden upon the church. Other young people come here without their parents, and, having no home, proceed to hire a room, and board themselves. This we believe to be one of the most unsatisfactory methods of living, and experience is daily proving it to be exceedingly dangerous to health, spirituality, and even to morals. Every young man and young woman needs the influence of a Christian home, and should be intimately attached to

131

some Christian family; not simply as a boarder, much less as a renter. There is a great responsibility resting upon the members of the Battle Creek church in behalf of the young members in their midst. We cannot say that these responsibilities have all been fulfilled in the past, nor that they are being fulfilled at the present. But we feel it incumbent upon us to warn our youth not to isolate themselves from Christian home influences. We advise them not to set up housekeeping for themselves, nor to hire a room and board at a restaurant. If they are coming to Battle Creek, and cannot bring their parents with them, we say, Be sure to find some other good parents as soon as you get here. If you can't find them, don't come. [S. N. Haskell and D. M. Canright, *Review and Herald,* May 1, 1879, p. 140; Editorial, June 2, 1896, p. 352.]

for further reading:

Battle Creek Daily Journal (files in Willard Library, Battle Creek).

* Hammond, Richard J., "The Life and Work of Uriah Smith" (MA thesis, SDA Theological Seminary, 1944), 164 pages.

Hetzell, M. Carol, *The Undaunted: The Story of the Publishing Work of Seventh-day Adventists* (1967), chaps. 1, 2.

Powell, Horace B., *The Original Has This Signature—W. K. Kellogg* (1956), 358 pages.

* Schwarz, Richard W., *John Harvey Kellogg, M.D.* (1970), 256 pages.

Spalding, Arthur W., *Origin and History of Seventh-day Adventists,* Vol. 1, chap. 15.

* Vande Vere, Emmett K., *The Wisdom Seekers* (1972), Part I.

Church Finances

For centuries in Western Europe the church enjoyed the practice of tithing and the state legislated it. The Protestant Reformation, however, ended such arrangements in many places. In the United States the churches were clearly on their own resources. Like other Protestant churches, the Seventh-day Adventists had to find some way of supporting the movement while avoiding the problems which had troubled the financing of religious activities in Europe.

From 1845 to 1859 ministers received only random gifts or loans of horses and rigs, free shelter and meals, produce, and a little money. John N. Loughborough remembers the leanness of the period:

> For three months' labor [preaching] in Illinois, from January to April [1857], I received my board, a buffalo skin overcoat, which was worth about ten dollars, and ten dollars in cash. On my way home I walked from McGregor to Waukon [Iowa], a distance of about twenty-six miles, with a heavy satchel on my back, so as to have a little money left on reaching home. The following summer, for four months' labor with the tent in Wisconsin and Illinois, I received my board, traveling expenses, and twenty dollars in money. My case was not an exception; other ministers fared equally well, and we were happy in the Lord's work. [J. N. Loughborough, *Rise and Progress of Seventh-day Adventists,* p. 212.]

133

James White also writes of the difficulties of those times:

One of our most acceptable preachers, not long since, visited four of our largest churches within a circle of 200 miles, and in three weeks preached about fourteen times. A brother let him have the use of his team to perform the journey, worth $10,00 and putting the labors of such a man at $6,00 per week (an amount necessary to meet his expenses) with other traveling expenses, the whole amount needed to give the minister a chance to live, is $30,00 for such a tour.

It is proper here to state that a few persons had shown liberality to this brother in past time, and are ready to help him again when they are prepared. But that all may see the need of a system by which *all* may help a little, and the church *always* be ready to sustain those who labor with them, we would say that from the hands of scores, and we may say hundreds who listened with extreme interest to his sermons, he received in all $4,00!! The brother came home happy in God and the truth, and cheerfully engages in labor with his hands, preaching Sabbaths and First-days. Now remember, Nobody is blamed in all this. But is it not time that such evils were remedied among us? . . .

I am tired of seeing statements of want among our preachers and appeals for funds in the REVIEW. I am tired of writing them. These general appeals to everybody, and nobody in particular, do not amount to much besides filling up the paper, and paining the reader. These things hurt the REVIEW, and are a blot on the cause. . . .

Well, what shall be done? These general appeals, and this trying to raise means without form or order, seems to be proving a failure, and something must be done more definite and effectual. [James White, *Review and Herald,* February 17, 1859, p. 104; May 26, 1859, p. 8.]

134

James White pleaded and eventually got a more organized approach to church financing. Styled "Systematic Benevolence," it served as a temporary means until denominational leaders could devise a more effective program. At first the plan encouraged members to pledge and pay some monthly amount no matter how small:

> A systematic Benevolence ledger still in existence, contains the names of nineteen persons belonging to a church in New York. Their weekly pledges ran from 1 to 20 cents. Each paid or overpaid it. The total contributions reached fifty-two dollars, and thirty-four dollars of it the church forwarded to the local conference. How much money reached headquarters at Battle Creek is unclear. [See "Systematic Benevolence Record Book." Heritage Room, Andrews University.]

The plan's defects were so glaring that after 1861 the denomination urged a more complicated one. It called for the individual's giving more proportionally to his true resources.

Rufus A. Underwood, who was then president of the Ohio Conference, explained the new plan:

> The plan of systematic benevolence was just then in its formation. In 1864-65, when I began to observe the Sabbath, the plan had developed more fully, as I will explain.
> Usually at the beginning of the year when we had our annual church meeting to elect church officers, the church treasurer, assisted by the local elder and by a minister, if any were present, would take a census of the value of the property of each church member, and each member was expected to pay annually two per cent on his holdings, into the church treasury for the support of the ministry. For example:

135

Windows

If a man had $2,000 worth of property and had no debts, he would pay two per cent on this amount, or $40. into the "systematic benevolence" fund for the support of the ministry during the year. If he had $5,000 worth of property, and had a mortgage upon it for $2,500, then he would pay two per cent on $2,500, or just one half of the amount, making his "systematic" $50 annually. Much or little, this was called "systematic benevolence." In a case where the member had no property to be thus assessed, such as young persons or those who had never come into possession of real estate or personal property, the member would pledge to give five, ten, twenty cents, more or less, per week, and this was to be paid in at the end of the quarter.

This system of giving for the support of the ministry, in which the funds passed through the hands of the church treasurer to the State [Conference] treasurer, was not based, as is our present system, on one's income, as you will recognize from the above statements. In many cases the sum pledged amounted to much less than the tithe would have been; and in other cases it was more. My good wife served as State conference treasurer and tract society secretary in the State of Ohio for five years. In those days, in writing to the church elder or treasurer, my wife would often speak of systematic benevolence in this way: "Our ministers are depending upon your faithfulness in seeing that 'Sister Betsy' [Systematic Benevolence] is remembered by each member of the church and funds forwarded to the treasury." My wife held this office in Ohio during the years 1872-77. While it was intended that the system should enlist all the members in a plan of paying in a systematic manner toward the support of the ministry, it was far short of the Bible plan of paying tithe on one's income for the support of the gospel ministry. [Rufus A. Underwood, *Review and Herald,* May 1, 1919, p. 10.]

136

Church Finances

Before long, however, Underwood called for an improved approach, and with reason:

> The thing that stirred me up in the first place was this: My wife was treasurer of the Ohio Conference, and in the little church at North Bloomfield we had one good man who had a farm valued at $10,000, and he paid 2 per cent on it, but the farm didn't even pay taxes; and we had another man who was a mason by trade; you know they get good wages. He had a little property valued at $1,500, but to my personal knowledge that man was making from $3,000 to $5,000 a year, but he paid 2 per cent on his $1,500. I said to my wife one day—I shall never forget it; it was in our parlor, and she was going over the books—and by the way, when she wrote to the brethren about conference matters, she would ask them to remember "Sister Betsy" (S. B., Systematic Benevolence), for the preachers were depending on "Sister Betsy."
>
> The thing that stirred me up was the injustice of the systematic benevolence plan. [R. A. Underwood, *Review and Herald,* June 4, 1926, p. 4.]

What Underwood deeply wanted was the adoption of tithing which the Whites had mentioned as early as 1861. Eventually General Conference president George I. Butler and others supported his idea:

> A little later Elder George I. Butler wrote a pamphlet entitled, "The Tithing System." He showed clearly that the priests and Levites of the old dispensation were supported from the tithe of the people, and used arguments to show that the same system was brought over into the New Testament. His book did not enter into the moral obligation as to *why* we should pay tithe. His pamphlet . . . led many people to adopt the plan of paying tithe. [R. A. Underwood, *Review and Herald,* May 1, 1919, p. 10.]

137

Windows

Not until 1876, however, did the General Conference in session adopt such a concept:

> Resolved, That we believe it to be the duty of all our brethren and sisters, whether connected with churches or living alone, under ordinary circumstances, to devote one-tenth of all their income from whatever source, to the cause of God. [*Review and Herald,* April 6, 1876, p. 108.]

Shortly, Underwood felt that tithing involved more than simply an ancient practice revived. He continues:

> Later I prepared a pamphlet for circulation in the conference over which I presided, entitled "Will a Man Rob God?" I sent this pamphlet to all the members of the conference. It took up the subject from a little different standpoint than that from which Elder Butler had discussed it. The subject was treated from the standpoint of God's ownership of all things, and of man's stewardship; and I endeavored to show that when we paid the tithe to Christ we were not only acknowledging his ownership, but acknowledging that Christ was our Redeemer and that he had purchased us and all that we possessed,—that the tithe paid was a recognition of God's ownership of all things, and that we had been bought with the precious blood of Christ and were simply stewards over the goods he had given us. The General Conference asked my permission to publish this tract, or pamphlet, which I freely gave, and this pamphlet was widely circulated by the General Conference after being reprinted by the Review and Herald.
>
> A little later I was asked to write a series of thirteen Sabbath school lessons on the subject of "God's Ownership, or Our Obligation to Pay Tithe as Stewards of Christ." These Sabbath school lessons were prepared and published, giving one whole

138

Church Finances

quarter to the tithing subject. This gave our brethren
all over the world as far as the message had gone, the
opportunity to study the tithing system from a little
different viewpoint than it had ever been presented
before. In connection with these lessons, in addition to
the tithing system, the subject of offerings was treated
as a grateful recognition of God's blessings. Mal. 3:7,
8. Meanwhile the Testimonies had indorsed the
tithing system in no uncertain terms. This settled the
tithing system among us as a permanent policy for
the support of the ministry. Everywhere, as the cause
has grown, the magnitude of this system and its
utility have demonstrated that it was of divine origin.
[R. A. Underwood, *Review and Herald,* May 1, 1919,
p. 10.]

**Actually, tithing was not giving, since God claimed the
tenth as already His possession. Tithing was a recognition
of God's ownership. Ellen G. White brought the point out
clearly:**

The Lord created every tree in Eden pleasant to
the eyes and good for food, and He bade Adam and
Eve freely enjoy His bounties. But He made one
exception. Of the tree of knowledge of good and evil
they were not to eat. This tree God reserved as a
constant reminder of His ownership of all. Thus He
gave them opportunity to demonstrate their faith and
trust in Him by their perfect obedience to His
requirements.

So it is with God's claims upon us. He places His
treasures in the hands of men, but requires that
one-tenth shall be faithfully laid aside for His work.
He requires this portion to be placed in His treasury.
It is to be rendered to Him as His own; it is sacred,
and is to be used for sacred purposes, for the support
of those who carry the message of salvation to all
parts of the world. He reserves this portion, that

139

means may ever be flowing into His treasure-house, and that the light of truth may be carried to those who are nigh and those who are afar off. By faithfully obeying this requirement, we acknowledge that all belongs to God. [Ellen G. White, *Testimonies,* Vol. 6, p. 386.]

Was there nothing, then, to engender generosity in the church members? There was. The *freewill offerings,* such as giving a second tithe, honoring pledges, making Sabbath School donations, and so on.

Mrs. White had much to say both to the church and to the individual church member about the benefits of systematic contributions. She felt that "disinterested benevolence" was vital to character development. Some representative statements follow:

I was shown that God requires his people to be far more pitiful and considerate of the unfortunate than they are. "Pure religion and undefiled before God and the Father is this, To visit the fatherless and widows in their affliction, and to keep himself unspotted from the world." Here genuine religion is defined. God requires that the same consideration which should be given to the widow and fatherless be given to the blind, and to those suffering under the affliction of other infirmities. Disinterested benevolence is very rare in this age of the world. [Ellen G. White, *Testimonies,* Vol. 3, p. 516.]

God requires his people to be tender in their feelings and discriminations, while their hearts should be enlarged, their feelings should be broad and deep, not narrow, selfish, and penurious. Noble sympathy, largeness of soul, and disinterested benevolence are needed. [Ellen G. White, *Testimonies,* Vol. 3, p. 519.]

140

Church Finances

I point you to the life of Jesus as a perfect pattern. His life was characterized by disinterested benevolence. . . . Heaven will be cheap enough if we resign every selfish interest to obtain it. [Ellen G. White, *Testimonies,* Vol. 4, p. 218.]

for further reading:

*Andreasen, M. L., *The Faith of Jesus and the Commandments of God* (1939), chap. 24.

Balharrie, Gordon, "A Study of the Contribution Made to the Seventh-day Adventist Movement by John Nevins Andrews" (MA thesis, SDA Theological Seminary, 1949), pp. 19-23.

Spalding, Arthur W., *Origin and History of Seventh-day Adventists,* Vol. 1, chap. 17.

White, Ellen G., *Counsels on Stewardship* (1940), 372 pages.

Health and Seventh-day Adventism

After the denomination had settled the problems of selecting a name and organization, its attention turned to a new emphasis. In 1863 Ellen G. White had a major vision on health which supplemented some she had had before. She began to write an increasing flow of articles and books on the role of health in the Christian's life.

But her interest in healthful living was not unique. For some time the United States had been in the midst of a revolution in health concepts. Writers such as Hitchcock, Mussey, Graham, Jackson, Trall, and others had flooded the country with a torrent of material on how to live better. Some of their ideas were good, some were nonsense, some even dangerous. As Mrs. White began to write on the subject, many wondered what relationship her views on health had with those who had pioneered the new health consciousness. Had her ideas come from them or direct from God?

Mrs. White soon discussed the question of health reform herself:

> It was at the house of Bro. A. Hilliard, at Otsego, Michigan, June 6, 1863, that the great subject of Health Reform was opened before me in vision. I did not visit Dansville till August, 1864, fourteen months after I had the view. I did not read any works upon health until I had written Spiritual Gifts, Vols. iii and iv, Appeal to Mothers, and had sketched out most of

142

my six articles in the six numbers of "How to Live." I did not know that such a paper existed as the Laws of Life published at Dansville, N. Y. I had not heard of the several works upon health, written by Dr. J. C. Jackson, and other publications at Dansville, at the time I had the view named above. I did not know that such works existed until September, 1863, when in Boston, Mass., my husband saw them advertised in a periodical called the Voice of the Prophets, published by Eld. J. V. Himes. My husband ordered the works from Dansville and received them at Topsham, Maine. His business gave him no time to peruse them, and as I determined not to read them until I had written out my views, the books remained in their wrappers. As I introduced the subject of health to friends when I labored in Michigan, New England, and in the State of New York, and spoke against drugs and flesh meats, and in favor of water, pure air, and a proper diet, the reply was often made, "You speak very nearly the opinions taught in the Laws of Life, and other publications, by Drs. Trall, Jackson, and others. Have you read that paper and those works?" My reply was that I had not, neither should I read them till I had fully written out my views, lest it should be said that I had received my light upon the subject of health from physicians, and not from the Lord. And after I had written my six articles for How to Live, I then searched the various works on Hygiene and was surprised to find them so nearly in harmony with what the Lord had revealed to me. And to show this harmony, and to set before my brethren and sisters the subject as brought out by able writers, I determined to publish "How to Live," in which I largely extracted passages from the works referred to [and inserted them among the chapters]. [Ellen G. White, *Review and Herald,* October 8, 1867, p. 260.]

Windows

Dr. David Paulson and Dr. John Harvey Kellogg also commented on Mrs. White's relationship to contemporary medical belief:

> Dr. Kellogg asked me [Dr. David Paulson] in New York City 22 years ago [c 1891] if I knew how it was that the Battle Creek Sanitarium was able to keep five years ahead of the medical profession. I did not know. Then he told me.
>
> He said when a new thing is brought out in the medical world he knew from his knowledge of the Spirit of prophecy whether it belonged in our system or not. If it did, he instantly adopted it and advertised it while the rest of the doctors were slowly feeling their way, and when they finally adopted it he had five years the start of them.
>
> On the other hand when the medical profession were swept off their feet by some new fad, if it did not fit the light we had received [from Ellen White] he simply did not touch it. When the doctors finally discovered their mistake they wondered how it came that Dr. Kellogg did not get caught. ["How Kellogg Kept Ahead," E. G. White Publications. Document File 45.]

Mrs. White urged her readers to study the best publications on the subject:

> Do not . . . feel it your duty to live on an insufficient diet. Learn for yourselves what you should eat, what kinds of food best nourish the body, and then follow the dictates of reason and conscience. . . .
>
> Our workers should use their knowledge of the laws of life and health. Read the best authors on these subjects, and obey religiously that which your reason tells you is truth. [Ellen G. White, *Gospel Workers,* pp. 241, 242.]

144

Health and Seventh-day Adventism

At first Seventh-day Adventists strongly pushed health improvement. Ministers taught health principles everywhere. Members wanted to transform their neighbors. The church set up sanitariums to treat and teach people in the new concepts. Dr. J. H. Kellogg eventually became so influential in the field that many suspected it was he who had devised the healthful way of living.

In 1897 Kellogg spoke on health principles at the General Conference session in Lincoln, Nebraska. One of the things he discussed was meat eating. Kellogg was absolutely opposed to it. The audience desired to learn what they could substitute for animal protein. Kellogg told the delegates:

> [Kellogg]: A great many people say, "If I want to eat meat, that is nobody's business. You have no right to make that a test." Yes, that is perfectly true; a man has a right to eat meat if he wants to, and he has a right to swear if he wants to, and he has a right to violate any of God's requirements if he wants to. The Lord does not say that a man shall not do it, and the Lord keeps a man living while he is violating all of God's laws. . . . The point there, I think, is this: We ought not to eat that which we like, simply because we like it. . . .
>
> *Question.*—What is the price of beans here?
>
> *Answer* [by Kellogg].—About two and a half cents a pound.
>
> *Ques.*—How much would a pound of beef cost?
>
> *Ans.*—About ten cents. Or, one and one-half pounds, fifteen cents. Then beefsteak in the form of beefsteak, costs six times as much as beefsteak in the form of beans. And in addition to that, it is full of poison. Peas are another good thing to take the place

145

of beefsteak. This poison takes away a large
proportion of the nutritive value of beefsteak, so that
a pound of beans has three and a half to four times,
nearly four times the nutritive value of a pound of
beef; in other words, a pound of beans will supply life
nearly four times as long as a pound of beef. . . .

Ques.—Can all stomachs digest peas, beans, and
lentils; and if not, what would you recommend in
place of them?

Ans.—I would recommend the use of nuts. Any
stomach will digest almonds and peanuts if they are
cooked in the way I told you. You can make a
beautiful soup of peanuts, a very rich and wholesome,
extremely nutritious food. In a pound of peanuts there
are about two and one-half pounds of beef, the
peanuts are more nutritious than fat pork. Peanuts
are highly nutritious, and not difficult to digest; pork
is highly nutritious, but it is hard to digest. When it is
said that pork will stick by the ribs, it is literally
true,—it will stick by the ribs and not digest. Now
when the stomach has proper food, it will be digested,
and it will soon be emptied, because the food is so
quickly digested.

Ques.—Should all nuts be cooked?

Ans.—I think all nuts would be improved by
cooking; that they are better by cooking. In nut butter
the nuts are cooked.

Ques.—Are nuts better boiled than roasted?

Ans.—I think they are more digestible. If you
parboil peanuts, turn off the first water, and then
cook them for a long time, you will find that they are
much more digestible than when roasted. If they are
simply roasted and eaten, there are little particles

146

which will not be thoroughly masticated, and these will lie in the stomach undigested. . . .

Ques.—Are eggs good as food?

Ans.—Eggs are not the best of food. But they are not so likely to contain germs as are meat or milk. They are more wholesome than meat or milk. They are likely to overstimulate the body unless eaten very sparingly.

Ques.—Which is preferable, beef or milk?

Ans.—That depends on the individual. Persons who cannot eat milk are in the same situation as regards meat as a rule.

Ques.—Would butter have the same effect that milk or meat does?

Ans.—No Sir, I think it would be better, provided that it is sterilized butter. And yet it is a fact that butter is a very poor food. It does not digest in the stomach at all, because it is a free fat. The best form in which we can get fats in any considerable amount is in nuts. In the almond there is about fifty per cent of fat, and almost the same amount in the peanut.

Ques.—Is the Brazil nut a good nut?

Ans.—Yes, it is a good nut, but its flesh is so hard, like the cocoanut, that it is likely to be swallowed in chunks; and if it is not well masticated, it cannot be well digested. [John H. Kellogg, *The General Conference Daily Bulletin* (1897), pp. 186, 187, 189-195.]

Two years later the Doctor's words at the General Conference in South Lancaster, Massachusetts, reflected his displeasure with those who ignored basic vegetarianism. And he told why he did not want GC sessions to meet at Battle Creek:

> When [originally] I saw the health principles, they looked so beautiful and consistent to me that I at once accepted them. Then I had such a struggle in contending for these principles that I did not love anyone who did not love the principles. Some of the worst conflicts the health work has received have been from the ministers at our General Conferences. It was a great trial to our helpers at the sanitarium to have the ministers of the General Conference come to our tables, and ask the helpers, who had not tasted meat for a long time, to bring them in some stewed chicken or beefsteak. We got so that we dreaded to have a General Conference there [at Battle Creek]; and in order to avoid the ill effects it had upon the helpers, we arranged to have the ministers eat at the dormitory, where these things could not be had. The helpers had to contend with that influence a long time afterward, and they would offer as an excuse [for eating meat] that some minister who had brought them into the truth used such and such things. Finally I got so I dreaded to see the ministers. I was so suspicious of them; for I did not know whether I could trust them or not. [John H. Kellogg, *The General Conference Daily Bulletin* (1899), pp. 82, 83.]

And four years later at the 1903 Oakland, California, General Conference session, Kellogg protested against those who held to their "flesh pots" and ignored Battle Creek Sanitarium principles:

> There are men on our [sanitarium] committees who believe that it is wrong, that it is a sin, a disgrace to them, to sit down and eat a corpse, and make a coffin of themselves; and there are men on boards and

committees who say that it is as right to eat a chicken
as bread. I feel that if a man wants to gnaw a bone, he
has as much right to gnaw a bone as for a dog to gnaw
a bone; but God calls us to higher living than that. . . .
This is awful loathsome, to me; and to have men who
have not seen this truth, and who are continually
doing despite to these principles, undertaking to rule
our institutions which are standing for this light—I
say I can not submit to that without protest. [John H.
Kellogg, *The General Conference Daily Bulletin*
(1903), p. 80.]

**The drive for healthful living is a continuing crusade—a fact
that Ellen White recognized. Some of her last appeals to the
church involved "faithfulness in health reform":**

On the subject of temperance we should be in
advance of all other people; and yet there are among
us well-instructed members of the church, and even
ministers of the gospel, who have little respect for the
light that God has given upon this subject. They eat
as they please, and work as they please.

Let those who are teachers and leaders in our
cause take their stand firmly on Bible ground in
regard to health reform, and give a straight testimony
to those who believe we are living in the last days of
this earth's history. A line of distinction must be
drawn between those who serve God, and those who
serve themselves.

I have been shown that the principles that were
given us in the early days of the message are as
important and should be regarded just as
conscientiously to-day as they were then. There are
some who have never followed the light given on the
question of diet. It is now time to take the light from
under the bushel, and let it shine forth in clear, bright
rays.

The principles of healthful living mean a great

149

deal to us individually and as a people. When the message of health reform first came to me, I was weak and feeble, subject to frequent fainting spells. I was pleading with God for help, and He opened before me the great subject of health reform. He instructed me that those who are keeping His commandments must be brought into sacred relation to Himself, and that by temperance in eating and drinking they must keep mind and body in the most favorable condition for service. This light has been a great blessing to me. I took my stand as a health reformer, knowing that the Lord would strengthen me. I have better health to-day, notwithstanding my age, than I had in my younger days. . . .

We do not mark out any precise line to be followed in diet; but we do say that in countries where there are fruits, grains, and nuts in abundance, flesh food is not the right food for God's people. . . .

Teach the people that it is better to know how to keep well than how to cure disease. [Ellen G. White, *Testimonies,* Vol. 9, pp. 153-166.]

The indifference which has existed among our ministers in regard to health reform and medical missionary work is surprising. Some who do not profess to be Christians treat these matters with greater reverence than do some of our own people, and unless we arouse, they will go in advance of us. [Ellen G. White, *Testimonies to Ministers,* p. 417.]

for further reading:

Brown, Gertrude M., *I Have Lived* (c 1971), 158 pages.

Clough, Caroline L., *His Name Was David* (1955), 160 pages.

Hansen, Louis A., *From So Small a Dream* (1968), 288 pages.

Pickard, Madge R., *The Midwest Pioneer: His Ills, Cures, and Doctors* (New York: 1946).

* Schwarz, Richard W., "John Harvey Kellogg: American Health Reformer" (PhD dissertation, University of Michigan, 1965), 504 pages.

* —————————, *John Harvey Kellogg, M.D.* (1970), 256 pages.

Spalding, Arthur W., *Origin and History of Seventh-day Adventists*, Vol. 1, chaps. 19-21; Vol. 2, chap. 17.

* Robinson, Dores E., *The Story of Our Health Message* (1943), 363 pages.

* Walker, William B., "The Health Reform Movement in the United States, 1830-1870" (PhD dissertation, Johns Hopkins University, 1955).

White, Ellen G., *Spiritual Gifts*, Vol. 4, chap. 39.

—————————, *Health, or How to Live* (1865), 86 pages.

Wilcox, Francis M., *The Gospel of Health: A Discussion . . .* (1935), 130 pages.

Civil War
Worries

During the American Civil War both the nation and Seventh-day Adventists strove for unity. Usually the Adventists were antislavery, Republican in politics, noncombatant, and nationally minded. And they, too, moved from alarm to anxiety to near despair following the Union defeat at the first battle of Bull Run (Manassas). Was national disintegration imminent? they wondered.

Two days after Manassas James and Ellen White visited the Roosevelt congregation in New York where on August 3 Ellen experienced a vision. From it she concluded that the Union would not collapse. In order to convince her audience that she was correct, she described the battle as she "witnessed" it in her vision:

> It looked to me like an impossibility now for slavery to be done away. God alone can wrench the slave from the hand of his desperate, relentless oppressor. . . .
>
> [But] I had a view of the late disastrous battle at Manassas, Va. It was a most exciting, thrilling, distressing scene. The Southern army had everything in their favor, and were prepared for a dreadful contest. The Northern army was moving on with triumph, not doubting but that they would be victorious. Many were reckless, and marched forward boastingly as though victory were already theirs. As they neared the battle-field, many were almost fainting through weariness and want of refreshment.

Civil War Worries

They did not expect so fierce an encounter. They
rushed into the battle and fought bravely,
desperately. The dead and dying were on every side.
Both the North and the South suffered severely. The
Southern men felt the battle, and in a little would
have been driven back still further. Northern men
were rushing on, although their destruction was very
great. Just then an angel descended and waved his
hand backward. Instantly there was confusion in their
ranks. It appeared [seemed] to the Northern men that
their armies were retreating, when it was not in
reality so; and a precipitate retreat commenced. . . .
Then it was explained, that God had this nation in his
own hand, and would suffer no victories to be gained
faster than he ordained, and no more losses to the
Northern men than in his wisdom he saw fit, to
punish the North for their sin [of refusing to abolish
slavery]. And in this battle had the Northern army
pushed the battle still further, in their fainting,
exhausted condition, a far greater struggle and
destruction awaited them, which would have caused
great triumph in the South. God would not permit
this, and sent an angel to interfere. [Ellen G. White,
Review and Herald, August 27, 1861, p. 101.]

Some aspects of the Civil War, especially in law, deeply troubled the Adventists. Even before fighting broke out, the
Fugitive Slave Law and underground railroad activity had
caused concern. But most of the church members followed
Ellen White's attitude:

The law of our land requiring us to deliver a slave
to his master, we are not to obey; and we must abide
the consequences of violating the law. The slave is not
the property of any man. God is his rightful master,
and man has no right to take God's workmanship into
his hands, and claim him as his own. . . .
Some, I saw, have a prejudice against our rulers

153

and laws; but if it were not for law, this world would
be in an awful condition. God restrains our rulers; for
the hearts of all are in his hands. Bounds are set,
beyond which they cannot go. Many of the rulers are
those whom Satan controls; but I saw that God has his
agents, even among the rulers. . . . A few of God's
agents will have power to bear down a great mass of
evil. [Ellen G. White, *Testimonies,* Vol. 1, pp. 202,
203.]

In March, 1863, Congress enacted the "Enrollment Law" or
military draft. The denomination wondered if it could secure
noncombatant assignments for its pacifist members. Generally, though, the church membership strained their resources by paying $300 for each male to avoid military ser-
vice as the act allowed. But that brought on a crisis, which
the leaders shared with readers of the "Review":

Dear Brethren, scattered abroad: . . .

1. Believing that Christians are prohibited by the
teachings of the word of God from engaging in carnal
warfare, suppose all of our people who are drafted
raise the $300 commutation money, a privilege thus
far granted; this is a draft upon us for means which
cannot long be sustained. The present call for men,
whether a draft takes place, or whether volunteers
are raised by means of large bounties, will cost the
Battle Creek church more than the whole amount of
their systematic benevolence for the past four years;
and the amount that will be required to clear our
brethren generally from the service on this call,
cannot be estimated at less than from twenty-five to
forty thousand dollars. This means is needed in the
cause.

2. If we do not commute, but go into the service in
hospitals or to care for freedmen, our own ranks are
depleted.

154

Civil War Worries

3. Thousands upon thousands who would doubtless hear the truth, and become earnest Christians, are drawn away to the field of carnage, to be mown down in battle, or languish in hospitals or Southern prisons.

4. The mind of the nation is so absorbed in this dreadful contest that it is almost impossible to call attention to religious subjects.

Thus we must inevitably lose means, or lose our own numbers, and lose those who would embrace the truth, and lose the attention of the people. And now suppose this work to go on, and a call for men to come as it almost inevitably would, every five or six months, what could we do? The cause would be crushed. We are thus brought, as it plainly appears to us, to a place where if the war continues, we must stop. We repeat it, The war must stop, or our work in spreading the truth must stop. Which shall it be? . . .

We pray God to arouse the attention of his people to these things. And we would recommend, nay more, earnestly request, all our churches and scattered brethren, to set apart four days commencing Wednesday, March 1, [1865], and continuing till the close of the following Sabbath, as days of earnest and importunate prayer over this subject. Let business be suspended, and the churches meet at 1 o'clock on the afternoon of each of the week days, and twice on the Sabbath, to pour out their supplications before God. These meetings should be free from anything like discussion, and be characterized by humiliation, confessions, prayers for light and truth, and efforts for a fresh and individual experience in the things of God. Let the sentiment of Rev. vii, 3, be the guide to the burden of our petitions. And as among the poor bondmen, God may have many servants, pray that the war may result in good in opening the door of truth to them.

During these days of prayer, we recommend on the part of all a very abstemious and simple diet, Dan. x,

Windows

3, while some may more or less abstain from food, as
their health may permit, or their feelings may
prompt. Labor will be suspended at the Review Office,
and there will consequently be no paper next week,
but one early the week following. . . .
General Conference Committee: John Byington,
James White, for J. N. Loughborough, Geo. W.
Amadon. [*Review and Herald,* February 21, 1865, p.
100.]

**A memoir by George O. States penned in 1906 attempts to
describe the situation Adventists had to live in:**

Conditions were growing more serious. Many of
our people were drafted, and had to go into the war or
pay three hundred dollars. At this time meetings of
counsel were held in the Battle Creek church, and the
leading brethren advised all to pray much and talk
little. In the winter of 1865 large bounties were paid
for substitutes, and it began to look as if some of the
European nations would take sides with the South,
and thus bring about a general war.

Thus matters stood when in the REVIEW of Feb.
21, 1865, there appeared a long article setting before
our people the seriousness of the situation, appointing
a four-day season of prayer for the end of the war, and
urging our people to put away all differences, humble
their hearts, and seek God earnestly. This they did.

Those of us who participated in those experiences
knew what it was to plead with the Lord. Brethren
and sisters who had differences confessed their
wrongs, and as far as possible made matters right. We
all felt that we were doing a special work, and that
God was going to hear and answer our petitions. We
felt that the only way that the work of God could be
carried on was for the war to cease, and so we
earnestly pleaded for that definite object.

Immediately after these four days of fasting and

156

Civil War Worries

prayer the Northern army began to gain victories. Soon the news flashed over the wires, "Richmond is taken, Lee has surrendered, and the war is over." This all took place within a few weeks after God's people fasted and prayed. It was brought about so soon that men of the world were amazed. A peace convention was held, I think in Washington, D. C., and a large banner was stretched across one of the main thoroughfares, with these words, "This is the Lord's doing, and it is marvelous in our eyes," showing how astonished men of the world were at the unexpected termination of the war. God's people, who spent those four days in earnestly seeking the Lord, knew it was in answer to prayer. [George O. States, *Review and Herald,* October 18, 1906, p. 8.]

for further reading:

Davis, Roger G., "Conscientious Cooperators: the Seventh-day Adventists and Military Service, 1860-1945" (PhD dissertation, George Washington University, 1970), 256 pages.

* Eusey, Lee Ellsworth, "The American Civil War: An Interpretation" (MA thesis, Andrews University, 1965), 152 pages.

Robinson, Virgil E., "An Investigation of the Use of the Bible by the Protestant Churches of America in the Slavery Controversy" (MA thesis, SDA Theological Seminary, 1947), 90 pages.

Spalding, Arthur W., *Origin and History of Seventh-day Adventists,* Vol. 1, chap. 18.

* White, Ellen G., *Testimonies for the Church,* Vol. 1, pp. 253-268.

* Wilcox, Francis M., *Seventh-day Adventists in Time of War* (1936), 407 pages.

Seventh-day Adventists and Worship

As Seventh-day Adventists developed a distinctive theology and life-style, so they created their own characteristic worship forms. Because of its emphasis on the Bible, the church stressed public Scripture study. They adapted the Sunday School concept which many American Protestant churches had begun using around 1840. The basic idea had come from Robert Raikes of England, though the Seventh Day Baptists had conducted Sabbath and Sunday schools at Ephrata in Pennsylvania as early as 1740.

The Battle Creek Church pioneered many practices which later became common in Adventist religious services. George W. Amadon depicted some of them:

> Perhaps it will be as well to state our manner of conducting the Sabbath School at Battle Creek. . . .
>
> We have a School here which numbers about fifty members in all—some forty scholars, seven teachers, and a superintendent. We meet after the forenoon meeting at half past eleven, and continue the School one hour. The exercises are commenced by singing some piece in which all can unite, and then follows a prayer, during which, of course, every member of the school kneels. On arising from prayer the teachers immediately commence hearing the classes recite their lesson, which is usually some six or eight verses of the Bible. These are committed to memory, and repeated in order by each scholar in the class—that is,

158

the first scholar repeats a verse, his neighbor the next, and the other the next, and so on: or sometimes we let each scholar repeat the whole lesson, just as thought best. Then the teacher begins to ask questions on what they have recited, taking each verse in order as they come. And the scholars also ask questions if they choose, and after this manner the lesson is disposed of. We will suppose now that about three quarters of an hour have passed off in the school. Next the superintendent announces a change in the exercises, the teachers and scholars all suspend their communications, while he gives out the following lesson, and proceeds to make remarks upon the one already recited. In this way the minds of the whole school travel over the lesson pretty thoroughly. Here is a good chance also to exhort, encourage and interest the School which most certainly should be done. Perhaps some teacher wants to make a remark to the scholars, now is the time to do it; or some one wants light on a passage of scripture, and if there is any [knowledgeable person] in the house he now gets it [explained]. By this time it is half past twelve and the hour is up. A hymn is now sung from the Youth's Collection of hymns, or the larger book—we use both—and the exercises conclude.

This is our manner of conducting the Sabbath School in Battle Creek. [George W. Amadon, *Review and Herald,* February 16, 1860, p. 102.]

Amadon later gave more details of the first Sabbath School at Battle Creek:

The beginning of our Sabbath-school work in this city dates from the autumn of the year 1855. In the month of October of that year the small plant of the Review Office was moved from Rochester, N. Y., to the village of Battle Creek. There were fourteen persons, in all, who then came to this place. Elder

James White's family numbered seven, and there were also Brother J. W. Bacheller and his mother and sister, Brother and Sister Belden (the parents of F. E. Belden), Brother Uriah Smith, and the writer, all of us making the fourteen already mentioned.

At that time there were ten families of Sabbath-keepers living in this place, and in these families there were about twenty children and young persons, who, with their parents, made forty Sabbath-keepers. These, with those who came from the East with the press, constituted the charter members of the original Battle Creek church, as follows:

Cyrenius Smith,	Delphia J. Frisbie,
Louisa Smith,	Zerah Brooks,
William Smith,	Mrs. Z. Brooks,
Martha L. Smith,	David Hewitt,
Lorinda Smith,	Olive Hewitt,
A. A. Dodge,	Walter Grant,
Caroline Dodge,	Nancy Grant,
Henry Lyon,	S. B. Warren,
Deborah Lyon,	Mrs. S. B. Warren,
J. R. Lewis,	J. P. Munsell,
Mrs. J. R. Lewis,	Matilda Munsell,
J. B. Frisbie,	Mrs. Mary E. Tozer.

At that time there was no church building here for believers in "the present truth," and our meetings were often attended by fifty persons or more. This congested condition of the meetings immediately led to the erection of a small chapel, which stood about a dozen feet south of the flat which is now in process of erection on the west side of Cass Street near Champion Street. This small church building, 18 x 24 ft., was put up in the fall and winter of 1855-56, and was without doubt the first meeting-house erected by Seventh-day Adventists.

160

Seventh-day Adventists and Worship

At this early date, and before any place of worship was constructed, the Sabbath-keepers then living here had a Bible class study and a small [unorganized] Sabbath-school. The one brother who had a burden in this matter, and who led out in forming the nucleus of a Sabbath-school, was Brother Merritt G. Kellogg. He was the oldest brother of Dr. J. H. Kellogg, and has long been a faithful medical missionary among the islands of the Pacific. . . .

In 1855 our school numbered fifty persons, divided into ten classes, and Brother John P. Kellogg, the father of Dr. J. H. Kellogg of the Sanitarium, was superintendent. . . .

In the earlier period of this work there were no regular Sabbath contributions as at present, but funds were frequently raised to assist the needy, and to furnish our youth's paper to those unable to subscribe. From time to time more or less of this benevolence was connected with our Sabbath-school work. When Brother G. H. Bell became connected with the Battle Creek Sabbath-school, about 1868, a much greater effort was made to raise funds than previously. . . .

In glancing over the past history of our Sabbath-school in this place, it must not be neglected to state that in no small degree the success of the work depended on the energy of our secretaries. A good system of reporting greatly tended to the upbuilding of the work. And on this point honorable mention may be made of such faithful secretaries as Mary Kelsey White, Mina Fairfield, Jennie Trembley Richards, Winnie Loughborough Kelsea, Maud Sisley Boyd, and very many others. . . .

One more item in this connection it is proper to not pass over, and that is the superintendency of the Battle Creek [unorganized] Sabbath-school. As already mentioned, the first superintendent, in 1855, was Brother M. G. Kellogg. He served awhile, then this mantle of responsibility rested upon his father,

Windows

John P. Kellogg [first superintendent of the organized Sabbath-school]. Later on the writer looked after this interest awhile, and in 1865 [1869] Brother G. H. Bell, in the Lord's providence, was raised up to put his shoulders to the Sabbath-school wheels. As time proved, he was the man for the place. He printed valuable Sabbath-school lessons in our youth's paper, for children and young people, and later, these were carefully revised and placed in permanent book form, and constituted the eight valuable series of lesson books known as the "Progressive Bible Lessons." . . .

As previously stated, our first little schools were held in private homes; then two months later in the humble chapel erected on Cass Street. [George W. Amadon, *Review and Herald,* November 26, 1901, p. 765.]

Seventh-day Adventist worship services could have assumed many forms, ranging from staid ritualism to extreme emotionalism. They especially rejected the emotional approach to worship and religion. Ellen G. White, who had a major influence on the direction Adventist church services took, explained why:

But many of the revivals of modern times have presented a marked contrast to those manifestations of divine grace which in earlier days followed the labors of God's servants. It is true a wide-spread interest is kindled, many profess conversion, and there are large accessions to the churches; nevertheless the results are not such as to warrant the belief that there has been a corresponding increase in real spiritual life. The light which flames up for a time soon dies out, leaving the darkness more dense than before.

Popular revivals are too often carried by appeals to the imagination, by exciting the emotions, by gratifying the love for what is new and startling.

162

Seventh-day Adventists and Worship

Converts thus gained have little desire to listen to
Bible truth, little interest in the testimony of prophets
and apostles. Unless a religious service has something
of a sensational character, it has no attractions for
them. A message which appeals to unimpassioned
reason awakens no response. The plain warnings of
God's word, relating directly to their eternal interests,
are unheeded. [Ellen G. White, *The Great Controversy,* p. 463.]

Religion is not merely an emotion, a feeling. It is a
principle which is interwoven with all the daily duties
and transactions of life. [Ellen G. White, *Testimonies,*
Vol. 2, p. 506.]

**Ellen White cited four main aspects of correct religious
meetings—prayer, music, discourse, and (sometimes) testimony:**

Long praying wearies, and is not in accordance
with the gospel of Christ. Half or even quarter of an
hour is altogether too long. A few minutes' time is
long enough. [Ellen G. White, *Testimonies,* Vol. 2, p.
617.]

As a part of religious service, singing is as much
an act of worship as is prayer. [Ellen G. White,
Education, p. 169.]

[In the Roman Church] the music is unsurpassed.
The rich tones of the deep-toned organ, blending with
the melody of many voices as it swells through the
lofty domes and pillared aisles of her grand
cathedrals, cannot fail to impress the mind with awe
and reverence. [Ellen G. White, *The Great Controversy,* p. 566.]

Theoretical discourses are essential, that people
may see the chain of truth, link after link, uniting in
a perfect whole; but no discourse should ever be
preached without presenting Christ and Him crucified

Windows

as the foundation of the gospel. [Ellen G. White,
Gospel Workers, pp. 158, 159.]

A calm, unhurried, yet earnest manner of
speaking, will have a better influence upon a congregation than to let the feelings become excited, and
control the voice and manners. [Ellen G. White,
Testimonies, Vol. 2, p. 672.]

Ministers in the desk have no license to behave
like theatrical performers, assuming attitudes and
expressions calculated for effect. They do not occupy
the sacred desk as actors, but as teachers of solemn
truths. There are also fanatical ministers, who, in
attempting to preach Christ, storm, halloo, jump up
and down, and pound the desk before them, as if this
bodily exercise profited anything. Such antics lend no
force to the truths uttered, but, on the contrary,
disgust men and women of calm judgment and
elevated views. [Ellen G. White, *Evangelism,* p. 640.]

The sermon should frequently be short, so that the
people may express their thanksgiving to God.
Gratitude-offerings glorify the name of the Lord. In
every assembly of the saints holy angels listen to the
praise offered to Jehovah in testimony, song, and
prayer.

The prayer and social meeting should be a season
of special help and encouragement. All should feel it a
privilege to take part. Let everyone who bears the
name of Christ have something to say in the social
meeting. The testimonies should be short, and of a
nature to help others. [Ellen G. White, *Gospel
Workers,* p. 171.]

for further reading:

Cleveland, Catherine C., *The Great Revival in the West, 1797-1805* (1916), 159 pages.

Cross, W. R., *The Burned-over District* (1950).

Edman, V. R., *Finney Lives On* (1951).

Pease, Norval, *And Worship Him,* 96 pages.

Plummer, L. Flora, *Early History of the Seventh-day Adventist Sabbath-School Work* (ND), 48 pages.

Spalding, Arthur W., *Origin and History of Seventh-day Adventists,* Vol. 2, chaps. 1, 3.

White, Ellen G., "Behavior in the House of God," *Testimonies for the Church,* Vol. 5, pp. 491-500.

_____, "Co-workers With Christ," *Testimonies for the Church,* Vol. 4, pp. 67-83.

_____, "Love for the Erring," *Testimonies for the Church,* Vol. 5, especially pp. 607-613.

_____, "The Minister in the Pulpit," *Gospel Workers,* pp. 147-179.

165

Educational Reform

Educational reform in Western Christendom stemmed largely from the Protestant Reformation and the expansion of commerce and science. In the United States after 1825 educators experimented with vocational education, land-grant colleges, broadened curricula and course elective privileges, coeducation and physical education, and less emphasis on *in loco parentis* or the institution as substitute parent or guardian.

Naturally, therefore, when the Seventh-day Adventists established Battle Creek College on a seven-acre campus in 1874, they attempted to incorporate some of the new trends. But the dominance in the curriculum of the classical languages with their pagan writers checked their hopes. In place of off-campus missionary activities appeared the on-campus "school family" concept. Instead of a manual-labor-influenced program there developed gymnastics and games. Yet the Battle Creek College faculty did mold their charges, and considerable maturation and acculturation occurred within the influence of its school family.

Ruth Haskell Hayton later extolled her years at Battle Creek College:

> It is a late September day in the year 1887. A young girl from Denver, Colo., sits on the steps of West Hall, the girls' dormitory of our oldest college, in Battle Creek, Michigan.

166

Educational Reform

There must be tears in her eyes or sadness on her face that attracts the attention of W. C. Sisley as he passes on his way. . . .

"Homesick, little girl? Cheer up, for you will soon be happy when you see what a nice home this is going to be. . . ."

Feeling more at home by this time, May goes on to the trunk room, and begins to fill a clothes basket with the contents of her trunk. The array is not large, and is very simple. . . .

When the basket is ready, she calls her roommate, Kate, a bright sparkling girl from New York, with dark curly hair and pretty clothes. May is too loyal to father and mother to be ashamed of her own outfit. . . . By the time the dinner bell rings they have the bureau drawers and the clothes closet divided and their room cozily settled.

As they walk into the dining room, they see the windows hung with dotted mull curtains and filled with flowering plants. . . . Twenty-five tables fill the floor space, with eight places at each table. . . .

Soon all are seated, and are immediately united in a congenial family atmosphere. After grace is said, all are ready to do justice to a steaming bowl of creamy soup, served by the hostess. Two waiters are chosen from each table to change courses. May is placed next to the matron. She feels a little nervous lest she slip on the highly polished floor, as the matron motions to her to remove the bowls. When she returns from the kitchen with the side dish, the matron kindly and quietly whispers to her, "It is nicer never to put the spoon in the serving dish until it is placed on the table." So embarrassed was May over what seemed to her a serious mistake that she never forgot the lesson about the spoon.

One of the red letter days in the program of the dining room is changing places at the tables and reading from the "Don't Book" by President W. W.

167

Prescott. It is noticeable what a great improvement in the handling of table cutlery and the conveying of food to one's mouth follows these talks. Occasionally the author will include more than the dining room "good form," and with dignified humor suggests to the young men that they do not advertise their hair lotions on the walls of their parlor; and quotes to the young ladies one of Shakespeare's sayings about women: "Her voice was ever soft, gentle, and low, an excellent thing in woman," putting a little extra stress upon *excellent*.

Before West Hall dormitory was opened, those who were to have it in charge spent some time in visiting Eastern colleges. The history of the founding, the character of the founder, and the spirit and religious atmosphere of Mount Holyoke Seminary appealed to them. As a consequence the home life at West Hall is influenced much by the ideals held and worked out by Mary Lyon.

There is morning and evening worship. The evening worship is followed by a "silent time" for each student alone in the room. The evening prayer for the young ladies often includes helpful talks from the Preceptress, Miss Ida Rankin. She gives her lessons in a practical and straightforward manner.

"No girl can be winsome and truly womanly, who does not keep her room and her person scrupulously clean," is frequently impressed. . . .

Evening worship is occasionally taken by Mrs. Sadie Prescott, wife of the president. To the young Western girl she is the embodiment of all the culture and refinement of a New England education. A blue wrapper with gold-colored collar and cuffs, which she wears to worship on Friday evenings and Sabbath mornings, and her soft hair in a becoming coil, is a lesson in tasty and appropriate dress. One such evening she takes for her reading Ephesians 2, and places the emphasis on the thought that "in the ages to come" God is going to "show the exceeding riches of His Grace in His kindness toward us through Christ Jesus."

Often when May reads the verses after many years, she thinks of the one who gave the lesson that Friday night at college, the one who "being dead yet speaketh.". . .

The physical life of the young ladies is fostered in a well-equipped gymnasium conducted by Mrs. Counselman, who very efficiently trains them to control of muscles and graceful poise and carriage of the body. Every student is expected to do at least one hour's domestic work a day, aside from the care of one's room. . . .

Interesting, inspiring, and far reaching as eternity are the chapel talks given by the president.

"Sow a thought, reap an act; sow an act, reap a habit; sow a habit, reap a character; sow a character, reap a destiny," is a lesson he frequently tries to impress. He introduces to his students, men and women who have achieved great and noble work for God and humanity. He reads morning by morning of men of faith. . . .

He tries to connect the profession which many make at the much-enjoyed Friday evening prayer meetings, with their daily life, through such books as J. R. Miller's "Week-Day Religion." He rejoices over their spiritual growth. He is away at an annual Week of Prayer, but he sends this telegram: "3 John 4: 'I have no greater joy than to hear that my children walk in truth.'"

The noon hour prayer meeting will last only fifteen minutes, but how much may be learned in that time! The singing of the hymn, "What a friend we have in Jesus, all our sins and griefs to bear," attracts the attention. . . .

Scattered over all parts of the earth are gray-haired men and women who look back with

Windows

gratitude to the help they received from Battle Creek
College, and sometimes when Friday evening comes
and they fold their earthly cares away, they dream of
their youth. [Ruth Haskell Hayton, *Review and
Herald,* August 1, 1929, pp. 23, 24.]

A major failure was the lack of a permanent vocational education program:

This meeting [13th annual session of the SDA
Educational Socicty] convened at Oakland, Cal., Nov.
17, 1887. The President, Geo. I. Butler, in the
chair. . . .

A. R. Henry, the Treasurer, gave a detailed
statement of the workings of Battle Creek College the
past year. He spoke of the different divisions of the
Manual Training Department; the millinery and
dressmaking room, the carpenter shop, the
printing-office, and tent-making loft are in successful
operation. The school is considered in as promising a
condition now as at any previous time.

W. C. Sisley spoke of the additional buildings
which have been furnished, of the erection of which he
has had the superintendence. . . .

The work of the boarding-hall is performed by the
students themselves. They spend one hour each day in
this work, and one hour and a half each day in the
Manual Training Department. The students enter
cheerfully into the work, and the outlook was never
more encouraging than it is at the present time. . . .

D. H. Lamson spoke of the objections which arise
at the homes of the students, upon the part of parents,
to the Manual Training Department, and to their
children being put to work; and requested that some
light might be given concerning how to obviate this
difficulty.

A. R. Henry referred to the same objection, also to
the disadvantage of having a constant repetition of

170

the objections and difficulties presented by students, consequent upon continual change of students as new-comers enter the school. . . .

J. H. Kellogg spoke with interest upon the subject under consideration. The main reason, he said, why objections are raised against the Manual Training Department, is that people do not understand its object. It is not to get work out of the students, but it is to secure for them physical culture, and the development of mechanical knowledge and experience. The new building [the south addition] is necessary to the carrying on of this department. He regarded the knowledge obtained here of more practical value than that of Greek and Latin.

E. W. Farnsworth stated that he thought that objections to the labor department upon the part of students were diminishing. . . . The speaker gave a brief account of the method of carrying out the domestic labor.

Sister White said that in comparing the profit and loss of the Manual Training Department, we should not estimate it upon a mere money basis, but in the light of the Judgment. Then this enterprise will appear on the side of gain, not of loss. The importance of a symmetrical education was set forth in an impressive manner. The constant exertion of the mental faculties, to the neglect of physical exercise, results in nervous difficulties which terminate in evil. The Manual Training Department is second in importance and value to no other part of the College education. Parents should not be permitted to have their children excused from physical labor. To neglect education in the practical duties of life is to wholly unfit the individual for the responsibilities of homemaking. The speaker exhorted the Society to retain their hold upon manual labor; and parents would come to realize the value of physical training.

Windows

The physical must be taxed, as well as the mental. The dealings of God with the children of Israel were used to illustrate the importance of the subject of careful training in the practical duties of life. Exalt the Bible in our schools as the oracle of God. The great work before us is to educate. ["Thirteenth Annual Session of the SDA Educational Society," *Seventh-day Adventist Year Book for 1888,* pp. 78, 79.]

Ellen G. White struggled to shape Seventh-day Adventist education, as we can see from Percy T. Magan's report of the first denominational educational convention which met in 1891 at Harbor Springs, Michigan:

When the precious light of righteousness by faith was breaking . . . there was held at Harbor Springs . . . the first general gathering of Seventh-day Adventist teachers for the purpose of studying Christian education.

At that time the words "Christian Education" were unknown. . . . The meeting was a remarkable one, and the definite beginnings of the work of an educational reformatory movement owe their birth to this gathering. In those days the subjects of reform which were for the most part studied and discussed were the elimination of pagan and infidel authors from our schools, the dropping out of long courses in the Latin and Greek classics, and the substitution of the teaching of the Bible and the teaching of history from the standpoint of the prophecies.

Sister White was present, and I remember well that she read Testimonies relative to our schools and their work which she had written at the time of the conception of our first college. . . . This gathering closed with a song of triumph. [Percy T. Magan, *Review and Herald,* August 6, 1901, p. 508.]

172

Educational Reform

After the Harbor Springs convention Ellen White left for a nine-year tour of mission service in Australia, where she attempted a revolutionary thing: the establishment of a missionary training school, like the "schools of the prophets." We know it today as Avondale College.

Arthur G. Daniells, then head of the church's organization in Australia-New Zealand, depicted the rise of Avondale around 1897:

> It was not long after Mrs. White's arrival in Australia, however, that a message came from her to the Conference Committee, stating that she was instructed by the Lord to tell us that we should establish a school. . . . But all this time we were being counseled through the spirit of prophecy that this place in the city [of Melbourne] was not suitable for a permanent school. . . .
>
> At last we found a block of about fifteen hundred acres, located at Cooranbong, about seventy-five miles north of Sydney. It was offered at a very low price,—about three dollars an acre. The price seemed alluring, but the land itself was disappointing. Most of it seemed to be poor, sandy, and hungry. We were disappointed, and were divided in our judgment in regard to its purchase.
>
> On May 24, 1894, Mrs. White went with the committee to examine the property. . . . Of this Mrs. White wrote at the time to her son, J. E. White:
>
> "There was perfect unity in making the decision to purchase the fifteen hundred acres of land at the price of four thousand five hundred dollars."—E. G. White Letter 82, 1894.
>
> But the doubts entertained by some returned to disturb them—and us. The counsel of land experts who were consulted was disquieting. . . .
>
> Even after we had made the first payment on the land, we were advised by the Assistant Secretary of

173

Windows

Agriculture that to forfeit the deposit would be a small loss in comparison with what we should suffer were we to locate on this block of land. . . . .

It was only the firm, unwavering counsel that came from Mrs. White that finally led the committee to proceed with the enterprise. When the unfavorable report of the Government fruit expert was received, W. C. White and I were requested by our associates to inform Mrs. White. This was a painful and embarrassing task, but we endeavored to do our duty. When we had made our statement, she calmly said: "Is there no God in Israel, that ye have gone to the god of Ekron for counsel?" She reminded us of the experience of prayer and healing [of Brother McCullagh] on the occasion of her visit to the place, and assured us, that from that time she had felt no anxiety.

On one occasion she quoted words from the heavenly messenger spoken for her assurance, "They have borne false witness against the land." Repeatedly she assured us, "God will spread a table in the wilderness." . . .

It fell to my lot to lead out in raising money for the land we had secured. My own courage was at a low ebb. . . .

Then in August, 1896, we learned that Mrs. White had borrowed $5,000 from a personal friend, and had lent it to the school for the erection of buildings. . . . From that day forward, our faith, courage, and zeal in and for that school never wavered. . . .

Our first unit consisted of two buildings—a small dormitory, and a dining hall and kitchen. We were so short of funds that in finishing the dormitory we were obliged to call for volunteers to give free labor. Work was continued into the night, some holding lighted candles while others drove nails. Only those who were on the ground and passed through the struggle can realize how great it was.

174

Educational Reform

When these two buildings were finished and furnished, the first term . . . was begun. On the first day of our new school (April 28, 1897), we realized our need of the admonition, "Despise not the day of small things," for we opened the term with four teachers and but ten students. The long delay, the perplexities, and the discouragements in getting the location and in providing the buildings and equipment had caused our people to lose heart. But when it became generally known that Mrs. White was encouraging the enterprise, and that the school had really opened, a new interest was awakened, and before the term closed there were fifty or sixty students in attendance. . . .

Miracles were wrought for us. In a few weeks our people in Australia raised in gifts and loans all that was required to meet all our obligations. . . .

Land was cleared and placed under cultivation. Fruit trees and grapevines were planted. A dairy was provided; carpentry, painting, and printing became important industries; and a small factory for the manufacture of health foods was installed.

God's blessing rested signally upon the field and orchard at Avondale. I remember at one time, while connected with the school for a short period, I went into the vineyard, lifted up some of the heavy vines, and brought to view large bunches of the most luscious grapes I have ever seen. From the ten-acre orchard I have helped the boys carry to the school kitchen large baskets of peaches, oranges, lemons, and apples, as fine as could be grown. . . .

Some years later a practical demonstration was given by Prof. C. W. Irwin, then principal of the college, of the fulfillment of the assurance, "God will spread a table in the wilderness." As a large number of people surrounded long tables laden with many varieties of choice fruit grown on the property, the

175

providences of God in the establishment and growth of the school were rehearsed. . . .

Hundreds of those who have had these advantages [at Avondale] are now devoting their lives to the advancement of the cause for which the school stands. [Arthur Grosvenor Daniells, *The Abiding Gift of Prophecy*, chap. 28.]

Ellen White personally emphasized practical education when at the age of seventy-seven she volunteered to be one of the incorporators of Madison College—the only institutional board she ever served on. Some of her last appeals were for Madison, its support, and its potential:

The Lord has directed Brethren Sutherland and Magan, men of sound principles, to establish the work at Madison. They have devised and planned and sacrificed in order to carry the work there after God's order; but the work has been long in coming to completion. It is the privilege of these brethren to receive from any of our people whom the Spirit of the Lord impresses to help. They should have means—God's means—with which to do the Lord's work. . . .

The Lord selected the farm at Madison, and He signified that it should be worked on right lines, that others, learning from the workers in Madison, might take up a similar work and conduct it in like manner. Brethren Sutherland and Magan are chosen of God and faithful, and the Lord of heaven says to them, I have a work for these men to do in Madison, a special work in educating and training young men and women for missionary fields. The Spirit of the Lord is with His workers. He has not restricted the labors of these self-denying, self-sacrificing men.

The school at Madison not only educates in a knowledge of the Scriptures, but it gives a practical training that fits the student to go forth as a

176

Educational Reform

self-supporting missionary to the field to which he is called. In his student days he is taught how to build, simply and substantially, how to cultivate the land and care for the stock. All these lines are of great educational value. To this is added the knowledge of how to treat the sick and care for the injured. This training for medical missionary work is one of the grandest objects for which any school can be established. . . .

If many more [students] in other schools were receiving a similar training, we as a people would become a spectacle to the world, to angels, and to men. The message would quickly be carried to every country, and souls now in darkness would be brought to the light. These men under the special light of the Lord, . . . are not to be hindered in any way, for the Lord is leading them.

It would have been pleasing to God, if, while the Madison school has been doing its work, similar schools had been established in different parts of the Southern field. . . .

There is plenty of land lying waste in the South that might have been improved as the land about the Madison School has been improved. The time is soon coming when God's people, because of persecution, will be scattered in many countries. Those who have received an all-around education will have the advantage wherever they are. . . .

To all who would mark out a certain definite course for their brother to pursue, the Lord says, Stand out of the way. . . . God's workers are to come into line, to pray together, to counsel together. And whenever it is [physically] impossible for them to gather for counsel, God will instruct through His Spirit those who sincerely desire to serve Him. [Ellen G. White letter "To Those Bearing Responsibilities in Washington and Other Centers," January 6, 1908. Letter 32a, 1908, White Estate.]

177

for further reading:

Beardsell, Derek C., "George Royal Avery—A Rich Poor Man" (MA thesis, Andrews University, 1967), 153 pages.

Cadwallader, E. M., *A History of Seventh-day Adventist Education* (1958), 314 pages.

* Cady, Marion E., *The Education That Educates* (1937), 260 pages.

Dick, Everett N., *Union: College of the Golden Cords* (1967), 441 pages.

Eddy, Edward Danforth, Jr., *Colleges for Our Land and Time* (1957), 196 pages.

Gardner, Elva Babcock, *Southern Missionary College —A School of His Planning* (1962), 240 pages.

Lamb, Wallace Emmerson, "George Washington Gale, Theologian and Educator" (PhD dissertation, Syracuse University, 1949), 292 pages.

* Neff, Merlin L., *For God and C.M.E. A Biography of Percy Tilson Magan* (1964), 341 pages.

Purdon, Rowena Elizabeth, *That New England School* (1956), 148 pages.

Spalding, Arthur W., *Origin and History of Seventh-day Adventists,* Vol. 2, chaps. 5, 6, 19; Vol. 3, chap. 3.

* Sutherland, Edward A., *Living Fountains or Broken Cisterns* (1900), 427 pages.

* _____, *Studies in Christian Education* (ND), 117 pages.

Thurston, Claude, et al., *60 Years of Progress—Walla Walla College* (1952), 400 pages.

Utt, Walter C., *A Mountain—A Pickax—A College* (Pacific Union) (1968), 160 pages.

* Vande Vere, Emmett K., *The Wisdom Seekers* (1972), 288 pages.

Moments
in Missions

Although the nineteenth century saw the worldwide spread of foreign mission activities among the Protestant churches, Seventh-day Adventists were slower in taking up the gospel challenge. In 1848 Ellen White saw that Adventist doctrines, if printed, would be "like streams of light that went clear around the world," yet her husband wrote and published for English-speaking Americans only.

In a way the Seventh-day Adventist Church was pushed in spite of itself into entering Europe. Through the efforts of Michael Belina Czechowski, a former Catholic priest who had had contact with Adventists in the United States, a few small groups of Sabbath observers formed in Europe.

Czechowski was a controversial figure, difficult to get along with, but his activities began Seventh-day Adventism in Europe. A number of descriptions of him follow:

> Very early in the labors of Elder M. E. Cornell, he was called to hold a series of meetings in western New York, which resulted in bringing into the ranks a Polish priest by the name of M. B. Czechowski. He was quite highly educated, and for a time gave promise of being a valuable addition to the working force of those days.
>
> But this man's talent did not seem suited to the peculiar work of presenting the detail of the message among Americans, and he soon requested to be sent to open a mission in Europe. He was not, however,

179

considered well adapted to such a calling, and so
received no encouragement in his chosen work. The
result was that he drifted away, and sought
employment among the First-day Adventists. By
them he was sent to Switzerland in behalf of their
work. But (as he afterward confessed) his conscience
would not permit him to give up the Sabbath, and as
he knew of no other way to present the importance of
the Lord's coming but that which first impressed him,
he preached the Sabbath message in the Swiss
mission.

About fifty intelligent persons embraced the
message under his labors in that field. But in time
they came to feel that he was not a safe leader in
financial matters, and by degrees they became
alienated from him. [J. O. Corliss, *Review and Herald,*
November 10, 1904, p. 9.]

An enthusiastic lay missionary from the United
States preached in the Waldensian valleys of the
Piedmont, and in particular in Torre Pellice. As a
result, J. D. Geymet, a resident, became interested . . .
and accepted. . . . He was baptized in the Angrogna
River, the first [SDA] to be baptized in Europe. . . .

One day in 1863[?], as J. D. Geymet returned
home from his job in a factory he was attracted by a
group of people listening to an extemporaneous
speaker. The man was speaking of the prophecies of
Daniel and, using a series of pictures representing the
beasts of the prophecies, was talking about the return
of Christ to earth.

Mr. Czechowski, the man who was speaking, was
not very successful in his preaching, but Mr. Geymet
felt a great interest in his explanations, and for a long
time he continued to study the Word of God. He was
particularly interested in the Sabbath question, and
kept studying until one day he decided not only to
observe the day of the Lord but to help Brother
Czechowski in colporteur work. He had tried to get

the Sabbath off at the factory, but without success.

Sister Catherine Revel and her husband also were convinced of the truth through the preaching of Brother Czechowski, but Mr. Revel could not gather the courage necessary to meet the problems that would follow a decision to keep the Sabbath. His wife had to wait several years until he was baptized, but from 1864 onward she observed the Sabbath and thus became the first to do so in Europe.

It hardly seems mere coincidence that the first two Seventh-day Adventists on the European continent were representative of the Vaudois people. [Enrico Long, *Review and Herald,* August 5, 1965, pp. 16, 17. Based on interviews with descendants of Geymet and Revel.]

His [Czechowski's] sympathy was somewhat withdrawn from the S. D. Advent people in consequence of some unfortunate circumstances which arose some little time before his departure to Europe. The most of the trouble was caused by mutual misunderstanding. We have no severe censure to place on Eld. C., nor do we wholly exonerate ourselves from blame. We should have taken greater pains to explain things that were misunderstood by him, and should have had greater interest in this noble-hearted man. Yet we were not wholly without reason for being perplexed at his course of action, and for finally leaving him to do whatever he pleased, without attempting to influence him.

Eld. M. B. C. felt deeply for Europe. . . . It was, therefore, much to our surprise that we learned, some two or three years since, that Eld. C. was not only adhering to the Sabbath, but that he had raised up a body of Sabbath-keepers in Switzerland.

About two years ago these brethren opened communication with us by letter. The last spring we invited Bro. Albert Vuilleumier, elder of the church, to attend our General Conference, pledging ourselves

181

to meet the expense. As he could not come, the Swiss brethren made choice of Bro. James Ertzenberger to come in his stead. He arrived at Battle Creek June 15. He was able to converse fluently in German and French, but wholly unable to speak English. We have become very deeply interested in this dear brother. . . . He has made great progress in learning the English language. It seemed very necessary that he should remain in this country long enough for this, that he might prepare himself to translate our works into German and French.

We learn that the office of publication established by Eld. M. B. C., in Switzerland, or, more properly speaking, the building which he erected on a lot of land purchased by him near Lake Neuchatel, is mortgaged for nearly all it is worth. This must be paid up, or the property will pass into the hands of worldly men, the first of next January. Eld. C., from financial embarrassment, has suspended the publication of his paper, and is in Hungary. His family is still occupying a part of this building. We think this property, which serves as printing office, chapel, and dwelling-house for Eld. C.'s family, should not be lost [if we can honorably redeem it]. [James White, *Review and Herald,* November 30, 1869, p. 181.]

What makes the work [in Europe] appear still more remarkable and providential, is that it has been accomplished independent of our agency and help. It has even been carried forward by those who take the greatest pains to oppose Seventh-day Adventists. While they were doing this, our people had not the least idea that they were raising up a body of Seventh-day Adventists. And while we acknowledge the hand of God in this, we feel humbled in view of the probabilities in the case, namely: that in consequence of our fears to trust money with Bro. Czechowski, and our lack of care to patiently counsel him as to its proper use, God used our most decided opponents to carry forward the work.

And while we acknowledge the hand of God in this work, in which we took no part, and feel that we have cause for humility on account of our past unfaithfulness, let us see to it that we come fully up to present duty. Gladly Mrs. W[hite] and self risk $100 in the effort to help the cause in Europe. And when our people fully learn the facts in the case, and also their duty, there will be hundreds of them pressing into the enterprise with their hundreds, their fifties, their twenty-fives, and their tens. [James White, *Review and Herald,* January 11, 1870, p. 22.]

John Nevins Andrews and George I. Butler later commented on both the value and the hindrances of the start Czechowski had made in Europe:

For a time Eld. M. B. C. published a paper, but he long ago departed from God. His case has given me great pain. He has been for several years a resident of Roumania, a province of the Turkish Empire. His course has been such that I know of no way to help him. In fact, though he is a very unhappy man, I have no reason to think that he is in a state of mind in which he would accept faithful counsel, however tenderly given. Though he accomplished good in this country and in Italy, yet he eventually brought much pain and sadness to the people of God. Nor have our people recovered, even yet, from the discouragement which he brought upon them. . . .

It is my conviction . . . that the good accomplished in Europe by Eld. M. B. C. was largely due to the wise counsel and valuable assistance of sister A[nnie] E. Butler, at that time a member of his family, but now sleeping in death at Tramelan. Her services as translator and general assistant were such that he could not have done without them. Indeed, when her labor ceased and other helpers took her place[,] the

183

work of Eld. C. soon ended in sorrow to the people of God. It will give pain to those who knew the family in America to learn that Ludomir, the eldest son, died the past week. He was accounted one of the best printers in the city of Neuchatel, but I fear that he had no interest in religion. . . . I have learned that Eld. M. B. C. has recently lost the sight of one eye, and his hearing in part. [J. N. Andrews, *Review and Herald,* September 23, 1875, p. 92.]

Tramelan is one of the first places in Switzerland where M. B. Czechowski preached the Sabbath some fifteen years ago. Several families came out then and have kept it ever since. Here my sister, Annie E. Butler, spent the last year of her life, and she sleeps in hope in the little cemetery in the village. [George I. Butler, *Review and Herald,* April 29, 1884, p. 282.]

The Sabbath was preached in Torre Pellice [Italy] some eighteen years ago by Eld. M. B. Czechowski. It was the first place in Europe where he labored. He was not sent to Europe by our people, not being at the time in union with us, though he believed most of the doctrines held by us. The First-day Adventists assisted him with means for some reasons that it is not necessary for me to mention. Hence I suppose we as a people are under some obligation to them for helping establish the Sabbath truth in Europe. [George I. Butler, *Review and Herald,* May 6, 1884, p. 297.]

We found a company of seven [in Piteste, Roumania] who observed the Sabbath of the Lord, and quite a number of others who are much interested, some of whom we trust will soon keep God's commandments. They first became acquainted with some of the doctrines of our faith through M. B. Czechowski, who spent the latter portion of his life in this section of the country. He preached some, and taught French to support himself; for he was at the time very poor, his First-day Adventist friends in

Moments in Missions

America having withdrawn their support. There was nothing in his course of life particularly calculated to draw people to the truth; but the principles of the truth which he taught took hold of some hearts. [George I. Butler, *Review and Herald,* May 20, 1884, p. 328.]

Ellen G. White had a major role in fostering a sense of missions, both through her writings and through actual mission service herself. The years 1885 to 1887 she spent in Europe. She went there upon invitation from European Adventists. While there she helped develop the church on the continent and urged Adventists as a whole to broaden their horizons on how far they must take the gospel:

This visit will never be forgotten. The spiritual influence and godly instruction of Mrs. White won the people in every land. A large number of her many addresses were printed,—some of them in English, and they are among the best contributions from her pen. To very many it was an object lesson of untold value to see the deep insight Mrs. White had into European needs, conditions, and racial mentalities, together with her rare tact, firmness, and wisdom in helping all. There was danger of formalism and of a hard, condemnatory spirit in our work in certain sections of Europe. In meeting this, Mrs. White's work was most helpful. All her instruction led to love, unity, faith in the message, and a deeper zeal for souls.

The advent movement in Europe would never have been the same if it had not been for her visit. For many, many years our members and their children in England, Switzerland, Norway, Denmark, and Sweden never tired of telling about Mrs. White. . . .

In Europe the genuineness of the spiritual gift of Mrs. White was put to an entirely new test,—a test that was watched by some with the keenest interest.

185

Windows

In America, God had shown her the lives of many, and revealed to her what human wisdom alone could never know. But these people, though often unknown, were of her own country and language. It was sometimes said that the things she told had been reported to her by others. In Europe, all this was changed. She was in strange lands, and among people whose mentality, customs, and language she did not understand. But in those countries, too, God told her hidden things concerning Adventists in lands she had never even seen. And the things He revealed to her were of the character and lives of people whose language she did not understand, and which their friends could not possibly have reported to her. Yet, in regard to persons of those countries, she had as clear light as she had had in the testimony she bore about her own kith and kin in America. . . .

The question of Sabbathkeeping . . . was a difficult one. The idea was entirely new in those lands. Not only had the people begun to observe another day, but they had to be taught that the Sabbath was not to be kept in the same way of pleasure and worldliness as was Sunday. . . .

The labors of Mrs. White in the interests of health and temperance also meant much to our work in Europe. . . .

As everywhere, and always so in Europe, Mrs. White pleaded for larger things. [Lewis Harrison Christian, *Pioneers and Builders of the Advent Cause in Europe* (1937), p. 37f.]

As we go from these [Waldensian] valleys, it is with mingled feelings of joy and sorrow,—of joy because there ever existed a people who were not afraid, even many years before the first gleamings of the Reformation, to stand in defense of Bible truth; of sorrow because so few of their descendants manifest a desire to continue to walk in the light as it shines

186

Moments in Missions

from the word of God. We feel confident, however, that the Lord will again work for this people, and restore to those who will come to the light, their former purity and fidelity to his service. The clear light of the third angel's message will yet be reflected from the honest-hearted in these valleys. The light in them which has grown dim will be brightened.

The angel that joins the third angel is to lighten the earth with his glory. There will be many, even in these valleys, where the work seems to start with such difficulty, who will recognize the voice of God speaking to them through his word, and, coming out from under the influence of the clergy, will take their stand for God and the truth. This field is not an easy one in which to labor, nor is it one which will show immediate results; but there is an honest people here who will obey in time. The persecutions which their fathers endured have made them apathetic and close-mouthed, and they look upon strangers and strange doctrines with suspicion. But the miracle of God's mercy, working with man's human effort, will yet cause the truth to triumph upon the very soil where so many have died to defend it. Knowledge will be increased, faith and courage will revive, and the truth will shine as the light of the morning all through these valleys. The old battle field will yet be the scene of victories now unseen, and the adoption of Bible truth will vindicate the past fidelity of their fathers. [Ellen G. White, "Visit to Northern Italy," *Historical Sketches of the Foreign Missions of the Seventh-day Adventists* (1886), p. 249.]

After foreign-born Ole Andres Olsen was elected as president of the General Conference in 1888, Seventh-day Adventists' outreach across the world intensified. A ship's carpenter, John I. Tay, had converted the entire population of Pitcairn Island in 1886, and the event inspired the denom-

ination to build the 100-foot, two-masted ship *Pitcairn* to
evangelize the South Pacific islands from 1890 to 1899.

**Edward Harmon Gates, leader of the 1890-1892 expedition,
prepared "Pitcairn's" log, which contained the following
entries:**

November 25, 1890, Tu. Lat. 25° 4′ S.

At a little after 4 in the morning I got up and went
on deck. It was beginning to get a little light, and we
could plainly see Pitcairn. . . .

But we waited till 8.40, when suddenly the mate
said the boat was coming, when just a little way off
we saw a large whale boat with several men in it. It
was strange to us that we did not see them sooner.

In a little while the boat came up, and we found
that it contained Bro. McCoy, the magistrate of the
island, and seven other young men. Never were we
more glad to see men. They were soon on deck, and a
general hand shaking took place.

They brought us oranges, bananas, and pine
apples, and we thought we never tasted anything so
good, as we had not tasted any fresh food for weeks.
. . . About 11 oclock we got into their boat and started
for land, feeling sad to leave our floating home. The
men were strong, able bodied sailors and their first
strokes with the oars gave us confidence in them.
Their dark hair and skin revealed their Tahitian
blood, though they were generally fine looking men.
The island is simply a beautiful one seen from the sea,
and we could not repress our words and expressions of
admiration.

When we got into Bounty Bay, the magistrate who
sat at the stern, gave the order to stop the boat while
he carefully scanned the water to see if it was safe to
go through the rolling surf which dashed on the
precipitous rocks in a sheet of foam. After a few
moments he gave the order to "lay to," and the men as

if by clock work bent to the oars, and we were rushing through the boiling waters like a race horse.

It was an exciting moment to us; but in a few moment[s] we passed out of the rolling surf, between the sharp rocks, into a quiet little cove. In a moment the strong men lifted the ladies [Ms. Gates, Read, and Tay] and carried them bodily and placed them on a large flat rock. The men did this apparently as easily as though the ladies had been babes.

Nearly all the people of the island were out to meet us. We were taken to the house of Bro. James McCoy, the former magistrate of the island, and told to make ourselves at home. But we did not stay long indoors; there were too many beauties to be seen outside. . . .

The people had been looking for us for a month or more, having heard from a Cal[ifornia] ship that our vessel [at San Francisco] would soon be done. A meeting had been appointed for 5 oclock, before they knew of our coming, to study the subject of baptism, none of the people having been immersed. Bro. McCoy gave a [Bible] reading. . . .

After writing in my journal I went to bed and enjoyed the best sleep I had since leaving Cal.

November 27, 1890, Th. . . .

Another sail was seen [offshore], which was a vessel from San F. which left the same day as we, but was 4 days behind us. This was remarkable, as it was a full rigged ship of 1800 tons burden. . . . Went down to the rocks to see about a place to baptize. At night all came to Bro. McCoy's to sing.

November 28, 1890, Fri. Did a lot of writing about the trip. . . . Bro. [A. J.] Read spoke on the 26th vs of Rom. 3. . . .

November 29, 1890, Sat. . . . At 10:30 I preached from 2 Pet. 1:4. . . .

December 5, 1890, Fri. At the early social meeting there was good freedom, and at its close several more were examined for baptism, among them Edward Christian. The leading brethren then were called together to ascertain if they favored the baptism. After breakfast another meeting of these brethren was held to talk over some special cases. At 5 P. M. we went to the pools, and Bro. Read and myself baptized 64 precious souls. . . . The occasion was a blessed one.

December 6, 1890, Sat. At 6 A. M. had a social meeting and at 8 Sabbath school, which we organized. We took charge of the school to show them how to conduct it. At 11:30 a meeting was held to organize a church. Sixty four entered the organization. . . . We all came together again at 5 P. M. to celebrate the ordinances. It was a precious season, and many wept as the Saviour's sufferings and death were rehearsed to them.

December 7, 1890, Sun. At the morning meeting we had a report of the committee on nominations, and then elected the officers [of the church]. . . . At the close of the meeting the elders and deacons were ordained by the laying on of hands. . . .

December 10, 1890, Wed. Had a meeting in the morning and talked to youth & children about their duties as Christians. At the close called forward those who desired baptism. Sixteen responded, and were examined. . . . When 5 P. M. came we baptized 18 more precious souls at the pools. . . . I administered the [baptismal] ordinance. [E. H. Gates, MS Pitcairn Log Books (1890-1892). Heritage Room, Andrews University.]

The A. J. Reads, a young ministerial couple who accompanied Gates, chose to go to Tahiti. In the estimation of the Adventists, the Tahitians were only quasi Christians:

When we arrived at the island, we found a peculiar state of affairs. We found that all the English missionaries had abandoned the island, because of being so circumscribed by French laws. They found it impossible to carry on their work and so they had left and gone to other fields. French missionaries then took up the work. There are at this time about seven Roman Catholic priests and a large number of Catholic sisters of mercy and other helpers laboring there. The French Protestant Society has also sent out three missionaries to take charge of the Protestant interests on the island, but these are inadequate to instruct so many people in the way of righteousness.

During our first visit to the island, I became acquainted with a native pastor, who invited us to attend his services. So one Sunday morning we went early and attended his services throughout the day. The services were after the same form as they are in this country. There were a few benches, but most of the people were obliged to sit on the floor cross-legged in the native fashion; in the congregation there were also quite a number of dogs, and children playing, all oblivious to their surroundings. But some of the people were paying good attention to the service and taking notes of all that the pastor said in his sermon. When the services were over, the pastor invited us to stop and visit him and attend the evening prayer meeting, which was to be a review of all the services of the day. His meeting-house was made of bamboo poles, and had a thatch roof.

As we entered the building for the prayer meeting, we saw the native people sitting upon the floor and just preparing for the opening service. As they began the opening hymn, they rolled little native cigarettes and lighted them, the women as well as the men participating in the general smoke, and passing the cigarettes from one to the other; they smoked and sang and repeated passages of Scripture throughout the service until the room became quite thick with tobacco smoke. This meeting continued until about

191

half past ten, and then they had an intermission, during which refreshments were served, consisting of hot coffee and white bread. Most of them buy their bread of the Chinese dealers, but some make it themselves. After the refreshments, the meeting continued, as the pastor told us, until half past one in the morning. We left the service before it was over and went to the pastor's house to retire. The pastor has his house a little more like the European houses. He had it partitioned into three or four rooms. While we were sitting, talking to the pastor's wife, we noticed some black thing crawl out between the thatch and fall on the floor. On investigation we found to our horror that it was a centipede. We felt a little uncomfortable at the prospect of sleeping there, but concluded to make the best of it. The next morning we had a talk with the pastor in regard to his service, and suggested that it might be a little more spiritual and beneficial if they would leave out some of the tobacco. During our visit, also, we had occasion to instruct him in several things which he desired to know. One thing was that Mrs. Read . . . [teach] his wife how to make bread. Their only apparatus for bread making was a piece of an old coal-oil tin for a pan and a hole in the ground paved with stones for an oven.

We had a very pleasant visit during the week, and left him quite interested in reading some of our books, for he had learned to read a little English before we met him.

While we were away from the island, the native pastor felt very much impressed with what had been said. On the return of the "Pitcairn" in September, 1892, we found an improved condition of things. There was beautiful shrubbery growing in the yard, he had a nice little garden, and walks laid out, everything was clean about the place, the pigs had been dispensed with altogether, he had a nice little

192

pine-apple patch planted, his bread-fruit trees were doing nicely, and he even had his house whitewashed; and among other things, he had bought a stove.

We also found that the native pastor had begun to study the book "Bible Readings," which we had sold him. He liked the book particularly because there were references to passages of Scripture, and he could see what they were by looking them up in his native Bible. And so week after week, he would take subjects, and look up all the passages in the Scripture upon them. And when we came back, we found him and others of his people obeying the truth of God.

But the pastors are all government employees. So as the native pastor was teaching doctrines that the government did not consider catholic, they decided that he was not fit any longer to be a pastor of that people, and took away his pastorate. But his people had learned to love the truth. And they came day after day to gain instruction from him from the word of God. So when the "Pitcairn" arrived in September, 1892, we found quite a little company of people that were professing to live up to the light of the truth of God. But they still continued the use of tobacco to some extent in their prayer meetings. After our arrival and the establishment of our mission there, we had occasion to give them some instruction in regard to these things, and it was not long until the tobacco had disappeared altogether from the meetings.

One thing in regard to the natives of this island is that they need line upon line, precept upon precept, and so we have to give them the simple truth of the gospel over and over again, and often we find them very dull in grasping spiritual truth. But notwithstanding all the difficulties that we have to meet in laboring among these people, and all the discouragements when we find it so hard for them to appreciate the wonders of God's truth, yet there is one consolation,—we have the assurance that it is the

193

Windows

MIGHTY GOD that has spoken to the ends of the
earth; it is he that has called the earth from the rising
of the sun to the going down thereof, and we know
that his truth will find a place among these people.
[A. J. Read, "Tahiti and Other Islands," *The General
Conference Daily Bulletin* (1895), pp. 180, 181.]

**Again Ellen White left the United States to serve as a mis-
sionary, this time going to Australia, where she lived from
1891 to 1900. Arthur G. Daniells evaluated the impact she had
on the developing church there:**

We in Australia have been slow to grasp the
meaning of God's providence in keeping his servant,
Sister White, in this country. When she came, we all
thought she was making us only a brief visit. She
thought so. But the Lord knew better. He placed her
in this land, and does not cause the cloud to lift and
move elsewhere.

Ever since she came, God has been instructing her
regarding the work here. He has pointed out the
mistakes in our methods of labor. He has caused
another mold to be placed upon the work throughout
the entire field. He has constantly admonished to "go
forward," to break forth on every side. All the time he
is directing us to enlarge our work. He has given his
servant a great burden regarding the educational
work. The struggle it has taken to carry out what God
has plainly revealed should be done, has been terrible.
Satan has contested every inch of the ground; but God
has given us many victories. He has planted the
Avondale School, and we have the plainest evidence
that he will be glorified by it. He has given minute
instructions regarding its location, object, and
management. Now he is telling us that if we will walk
in the light he has given, Avondale will become a
training-ground for many missionary fields. . . .

We have some remarkable experiences this

summer in connection with the four camp-meetings we have held.

God has sent us the multitudes, and has given his Spirit to reveal to them the message for this time. Night after night, and during the day as well, hundreds have flocked to the tent. . . . We have never witnessed the like before. In every place persons have taken their stand for the truth. . . .

The Lord has been blessing us of late in our endeavor to bring our medical work to the front. We have two physicians and fifteen nurses. These workers find far more than they can do. Their work is wholly self-supporting.

The Lord is truly blessing the sanitarium at Sydney. . . .

Can you help us more? Can you assist us to secure the teachers, physicians, and helpers we need? . . . We have an army of intelligent young men and women, anxious to fit themselves for the work of God. We believe that in a short time we shall be able to furnish a large number of valuable workers for various mission fields under the British flag. The Lord is revealing this to us through the Spirit of prophecy, and he will bring it to pass. [A. G. Daniells, "Report from Australasia," *The General Conference Daily Bulletin* (1899), pp. 141, 142.]

In Australia Mrs. White stressed the evangelistic potential of manufacturing dietary meat substitutes, both as a way of attracting and reaching certain kinds of people, and as a means of producing funds to support other activities:

These foods should be made in the different countries; for to transport them from one country to another makes them so expensive that the poor cannot afford them. It will never pay to depend upon America for the supply of health foods for other countries. Great difficulty will be found in handling

195

the imported goods without financial loss. . . . In many places industries for the manufacture of these foods are to be established. . . . The profits on these foods are to come principally from the world, rather than from the Lord's people.

In all our plans we should remember that the health food work is the property of God, and that it is not to be made a financial speculation for personal gain. It is God's gift to His people, and the profits are to be used for the good of suffering humanity everywhere. [Ellen G. White, *Testimonies,* Vol. 7, pp. 125, 126, 128.]

Australia followed her suggestions, and the country supplied and supported numerous and effective missionaries, especially to the islands of the South Pacific. The Sanitarium Health Food Company eventually generated finances that supported not only missions, but also nearly half of the general administrative expenses of the Australasian Division.

In the United States Adventists became increasingly interested in mission service. Ruth Haskell saw evidence of the enthusiasm at Battle Creek College:

[The young men of South Hall of Battle Creek College] organized as the Young Men's Foreign Mission Band. . . .

Not long afterward, eight or ten of the young ladies met in the teachers' parlor of West Hall, and organized with a similar object, calling it the Earnest Endeavor Band. . . .

In the autumn of 1894 the young men's band and the young women's united, and held their meetings together.

The remembrance of the prayer season, the

consecration hymn sung on bended knees, and the inspiration received from many who counted not their lives dear unto themselves, will ever be sweet and sacred to every band member. The Sunset Watch was the time our members were urged to remember one another. . . .

In the few years since they have been organized, our members have been so scattered over the world that the light and influence from their lives seem to meet and commingle. Members of our band have crossed many waters and entered many lands; but the chain which binds us can never be broken. [Ruth Haskell Hayton, "The First Seventh-day Adventist College Mission Band," *Review and Herald,* June 19, 1924, pp. 18, 19.]

During the 1890's General Conference president Ole A. Olsen pleaded for more church members to volunteer for foreign service and for more funds to expand the mission program as follows:

The first missionary sent . . . was Elder J. N. Andrews, in 1874; later, others were sent to different countries, and while the number was comparatively large, yet previous to the year 1893, it did not reach one hundred. During the year following the important General Conference of 1893, sixty-two missionaries were sent forth, and in 1894, sixty-five persons were sent to twenty-three different fields. . . .

But the number sent out the present year is so much greater than that of any previous year, that a comparison scarcely need be made. But consider: Since the close of the General Conference last March, one hundred and forty persons have gone forth to extend the knowledge of the gospel in other lands. . . .

We are in immediate need of funds to meet the demands on our treasury. A long winter is before us. . . . Beloved brethren and friends, while you are taking pains to make your families and homes comfortable for the winter, can you with ease and complacency cherish the thought that our missionaries who have left home and friends, and gone to far-off lands, where, at the best, many privations and hardships have to be met, have to endure increased hardships because they cannot be supplied with the funds with which to meet their necessities? Rather let us deny ourselves. . . .

We ask our friends to give this subject immediate and thoughtful attention. . . .

We make this call with confidence, being assured that our friends will respond both promptly and liberally. Soon, if faithful, we shall hear, "Well done," spoken from the lips of the Master. [O. A. Olsen, *Review and Herald,* December 10, 1895, pp. 792, 793.]

for further reading:

Balharrie, Gordon, "A Study of the Contribution Made to the Seventh-day Adventist Movement by John Nevins Andrews" (MA thesis, SDA Theological Seminary, 1949), 146 pages.

Graybill, Ronald D., *Mission to Black America; the True Story of Edson White and the Riverboat Morning Star* (1971), 144 pages.

Hagstotz, Gideon D., *The Seventh-day Adventists in the British Isles, 1878-1933* (1936), 231 pages.

McCumber, Harold O., *Pioneering the Message in the Golden West* (1946).

Robinson, Ella M., *S. N. Haskell, Man of Action* (1967), 256 pages.

Spalding, Arthur W., *Origin and History of Seventh-day Adventists,* Vol. 2, chaps. 10, 11, 16; Vol. 3, chaps. 6, 19, 20.

Spicer, William A., *Our Story of Missions* (1921), 372 pages.

White, Ellen G., et al., *Historical Sketches of the Foreign Missions of the Seventh-day Adventists* (1886), 294 pages.

198

Canright

Few will doubt Dudley Marvin Canright when he said in 1877, "It is no new thing for any cause to have apostates, and it is nothing against the cause either" (*Review and Herald,* May 31, 1877, p. 173). Canright himself defected from Seventh-day Adventism a number of times, permanently leaving in 1887. He attacked his former church by publishing *Seventh-day Adventism Renounced* (1889) and *The Life of Mrs. E. G. White* (1919).

Though Canright served as a minister for about twenty years, his colleagues did not understand him inasmuch as he suffered attacks of tic douloureux, a nervous disorder affecting the head. (See Carrie Johnson, *I Was Canright's Secretary,* p. 124.)

What sort of ailment is tic douloureux? Standard works on neurology describe it as a spasmodic neuralgia in the area of the trifacial nerve. A degeneration of or pressure on the trigeminal nerve results in neuralgia or pain of that nerve. It occurs most commonly in high-strung individuals. Pain strikes in recurrent attacks, usually with increased frequency until the victim is exhausted mentally and physically and pleads for relief or death. Frequently there is depression and occasionally suicide.

Among Canright's associates few strove more to help him than Ellen White and General Conference president George I. Butler. Ellen wrote at least four letters attempting to help

Canright "find himself."* He repaid her by charging in his 1919 book that she was a fraud. For instance, to support the idea that the people around her manipulated her, he printed a letter written to him by James White on May 24, 1881—a few months before the latter's death:

> Battle Creek, May 24 [1881]
>
> Bro. Canright:—The *Review* will tell of our plan. We shall depend on you to help us. . . . We hope you can join us in our labors. There will be efforts made to get you to Wisconsin, to have you go here and there. . . . I hope we shall all see our way out and be able to labor in union. . . . Elder Butler and Haskell have had an influence over her [Ellen] that I hope to see broken. It has nearly ruined her. These men must not be supported by our people to do as they have done. . . . It is time there was a change in the officers of the General Conference. I trust that if we are true and faithful, the Lord will be pleased that we should constitute two of that board. (Signed) James White. [Quoted in D. M. Canright, *The Life of Mrs. E. G. White* (1919), pp. 63, 64.]

What was the background of White's letter? Was Ellen misled by Butler and Haskell? A letter by George I. Butler to Dr. Kellogg bears on the questions. Butler explained:

> She [Ellen] spoke out very strongly and said, "That will never do—Go and call my husband." We [Haskell and Butler] called him up there, and she told him, right straight off, very decidedly, that that would never do in the world. He made no reply, but walked away, and so he walked down to the street, and there he was getting into his buggy. As chairman of the Committee, I went up to him and said, "Your wife

---

* Ellen G. White, *Selected Messages,* Book Two, pp. 162-170; *Testimonies,* Vol. 3, pp. 304-329; Vol. 5, pp. 516-520, 621-628.

Canright

states that Elder Haskell and I ought to be on that Committee," and that he hadn't ought to be on it. The Elder took it very gracefully and that was carried out at the meeting a half hour later. [George I. Butler letter to Dr. John H. Kellogg, May 10, 1904. John Harvey Kellogg Papers. The Museum, Michigan State University.]

How did Canright's close friend George I. Butler privately regard him after his departure from the faith? Butler's letters to Dr. Kellogg written in 1904 go a long way to reveal his opinion of Canright:

Over and over did I try to save Canright, who was once a power in the Cause; a lecturer, and a debater. He was one of those who could not endure hardship. When everything went to suit him, he was cutting a big swath, but when he got into a place where the thing went hard, he would "fly the track." Four times I helped that poor man back into the light, but the fifth time he went. It is enough to look into his face now, and see what kind of a wreck he is left. He could do great things when God was with him, and the Spirit was with him, but after he moved out, the Spirit did not go with him; he was left in his own spirit and that of another power, and that has been the trouble with all those who go away from the [Adventist] body. [George I. Butler letter to Dr. J. H. Kellogg, May 10, 1904. John Harvey Kellogg Papers. The Museum, Michigan State University.]

At least four times I labored with Elder Canright, and got him to retrace his steps, and look at things in a different light; I loved the man, and did my very best to save him, but it would seem that my confidence in him had been misplaced; and yet I have never regretted the effort I made. The poor man can never come up in the Judgment and say that he was not carefully and faithfully warned of his dangers.

201

Windows

[George I. Butler letter to Dr. J. H. Kellogg, May 13, 1904. John Harvey Kellogg Papers. The Museum, Michigan State University.]

The man stands in an awful danger. Canright thought he was going to do just that way; he was going to preach good revival discourses; never was going to do anything that Snook and Brinkerhoof [apostatizers in Iowa] did, and was going to be awful good. His farewell remarks at Otsego [Michigan], which I went up there purposely to hear, when he talked half or three quarters of an hour, the tears ran down his face as he told what he was going to do, and he felt it just as clearly and fully as a man could, and thought he was going to be awfully good, but when he got over into the Baptist Church, withdrew [from us], and the Spirit of God ceased its influence upon him largely, he became the most bitter, wicked antagonist we have ever had since the Denomination started. His book against Seventh-day Adventists is full of sneaking falsehoods. I do not say that he realizes they are such, but they are such. They are perversions of truth. I pity the man, from the bottom of my soul, when I think of what he is coming to, and where he has brought himself, but a man can no more control himself, after he goes off there [outside the denomination] and takes his stand away from the truths he has well known than a man could [control himself] in a boat a few rods above Niagara Falls.

[George I. Butler letter to Dr. J. H. Kellogg, June 9, 1904. John Harvey Kellogg Papers. The Museum, Michigan State University.]

Evidently by 1904 George I. Butler had become convinced that Dudley M. Canright was confused.

for further reading:

Branson, William Henry, *In Defense of the Faith; The Truth About Seventh-day Adventists; A Reply to Canright* (1919), 398 pages.

Butler, George I., *Replies to Elder Canright's Attacks on Seventh-day Adventists* (1895), 209 pages.

* Johnson, Carrie, *I Was Canright's Secretary* (1971), 191 pages.

Spalding, Arthur W., *Origin and History of Seventh-day Adventists,* Vol. 2, chap. 14.

Straw, Walter E., "D. M. Canrightism Versus Seventh-day Adventism" (ND). Heritage Room, Andrews University).

White, Arthur L., "The Story of Two Men," *The Youth's Instructor,* May 3, 10, 17, 1966.

Eighteen
Eighty-Eight

It is a human characteristic for man to let the center of religion drift from God to man, for Christianity to shift emphasis from Christ to the Christian. Man becomes concerned with his role in salvation, what he should do and believe and preach, and forgets that everything is dependent upon God. The Lutherans, for example, exalted salvation in Christ "by faith alone," but then slipped into an obsession with creeds, with the correct statement of doctrine by itself. Calvinists wandered into quibbling over such issues as predestinarianism. Seventh-day Adventists did not escape the danger. Almost from the outset they focused upon doctrine, polemics, and debating. Their evangelistic approach became, in the words of Ellen G. White, "as dry as the hills of Gilboa."

Adventists had forgotten that the core of Christianity is righteousness by faith—that salvation is absolutely dependent in every possible way upon Christ. Christ died to free man from the bondage of sin and death, and Christ reshapes His believers' characters so they may live with Him in a world remade perfect. The Christian's responsibility is to let Christ rework his life. What Christ does is not abstract theory or doctrine, but practical reality. The danger, though, is to equate Christianity with correct knowledge, right doctrine. Instead Christianity is Christ and what He does for and with the Christian. Seventh-day Adventists had to relearn this fact.

The 1888 Minneapolis General Conference session

struggled with the problem. It brought to a focus events which had begun some time earlier. One issue which led up to the session was Ellet J. Waggoner and Alonzo Trevier Jones' disagreement with George I. Butler's interpretation of the position of the Book of Galatians on the law. In 1886 Butler published at Battle Creek a book titled *The Law in the Book of Galatians*. From Oakland, California, Waggoner issued a rebuttal under the title *The Gospel in the Book of Galatians*.

Mrs. White became disturbed over the public controversy, and on February 18, 1887, she wrote to Jones and Waggoner:

> Letters came to me from some attending the Healdsburg College in regard to Brother E. J. Waggoner's teaching in regard to the two laws. I wrote immediately protesting against their doing contrary to the light which God had given us in regard to all differences of opinion, and I heard nothing in response to the letter. It may never have reached you. If you, my brethren, had the experience that my husband and myself have had in regard to these known differences being published in articles in our papers, you would never have pursued the course you have, either in your ideas advanced before our students at the college, neither would it have appeared in the *Signs* [*of the Times*]. Especially at this time should everything like differences be repressed. These young men are more self-confident and less cautious than they should be. You must as far as difference is concerned, be wise as serpents and harmless as doves. Even if you are fully convinced that your ideas of doctrines are sound, you do not show wisdom that that difference should be made apparent.
>
> I have no hesitancy in saying you have made a mistake here. You have departed from the positive

205

directions God has given upon this matter, and only harm will be the result. This is not in God's order. You have now set the example for others to do as you have done, to feel at liberty to put in [print] their various ideas and theories and bring them before the public, because you have done this. This will bring in a state of things that you have not dreamed of. . . . These questions are not vital points. . . .

To bring these differences into our general conferences is a mistake; it should not be done. There are those who do not go deep, who are not Bible students, who will take positions decidedly for or against, grasping at apparent evidence; yet it may not be truth, and to take differences into our conferences where the differences become widespread, thus sending forth all through the fields various ideas, one in opposition to the other, is not God's plan, but at once raises questionings, doubts. . . .

Elder Butler has had such an amount of burdens he was not prepared to do this subject justice. Brother E. J. Waggoner has had his mind exercised on this subject, but to bring these differences into our General Conferences is a mistake; it should not be done. . . .

My husband had some ideas on some points differing from the views taken by his brethren. I was shown that however true his views were, God did not call for him to put them in front before his brethren and create differences of ideas. While he might hold these views subordinate himself, once [they are] made public, minds would seize [upon them] and just because others believe differently would make these differences the whole burden of the message, and get up contention and variance.

Elder J. H. Waggoner has loved discussions and contention. I fear that E. J. Waggoner has cultivated a love for the same. We need now humble religion. E. J. Waggoner needs humility, meekness, and

206

Brother [A. T.] Jones can be a power for good if he will constantly cultivate practical godliness that he may teach this to the people. . . .

But how do you think I feel to see our two leading papers in contention? I know how these papers came into existence, I know what God has said about them, that they are one, that no variance should be seen in these two instrumentalities of God. They are one and they must remain one, breathing the same spirit, exercised in the same work, to prepare a people to stand in the day of the Lord, one in faith, one in purpose. . . .

I do not think that years will wipe out the impressions made at our last Conference. I know how these things work. I am satisfied that we must have more of Jesus and less of self. If there is difference upon any parts of the understanding of some particular passage of Scripture, then do not be with pen or voice making your differences apparent and making a breach when there is no need for this. [Ellen G. White letter to E. J. Waggoner and A. T. Jones, February 18, 1887; Letter 37, 1887, White Estate, Compare E. G. White, *Counsels to Editors* (1939), pp. 51-55; *Counsels to Writers and Editors* (1946), pp. 75-82.]

The meetings at Minneapolis were difficult and frustrating ones. Even eight years later Mrs. White still clearly recalled the pressure she had been under:

I shall never, I think, be called to stand under the direction of the Holy Spirit as I stood at Minneapolis. The presence of Jesus was with me. All assembled at that meeting had an opportunity to place themselves on the side of truth by receiving the Holy Spirit, which was sent by God in such a rich current of love and mercy. But in the rooms occupied by some of our people were heard ridicule, criticism, jeering,

207

laughter. The manifestations of the Holy Spirit were attributed to fanaticism. . . . The scenes which took place at that meeting made the God of heaven ashamed to call those who took part in them His brethren. [Ellen G. White, *Special Instruction Relating to the Review and Herald Office, and the Work at Battle Creek* (1896), pp. 16, 17.]

To get an idea of what Waggoner presented to the ninety delegates, one must rely on his 96-page pamphlet, "Christ and His Righteousness" (1890). As Waggoner presented the climactic appeal of his studies, he implored:

Let the reader try to picture the scene. Here stands the law as the swift witness against the sinner. It cannot change, and it will not call a sinner a righteous man. The convicted sinner tries again and again to obtain righteousness from the law, but it resists all his advances. It cannot be bribed by any amount of penance or professedly good deeds. But here stands Christ, "full of grace" as well as of truth, calling the sinner to Him. At last the sinner, weary of the vain struggle to get righteousness from the law, listens to the voice of Christ, and flees to His outstretched arms. Hiding in Christ, he is covered with His righteousness; and now behold! he has obtained, through faith in Christ, that for which he had been vainly striving. He has the righteousness which the law requires, and it is the genuine article, because he obtained it from the Source of Righteousness; from the very place whence the law came. And the law witnesses to the genuineness of this righteousness. It says that so long as the man retains that, it will go into court and defend him against all accusers. It will witness to the fact that he is a righteous man. With the righteousness which is "through the faith of Christ, the righteousness which is of God by faith" (Phil. 3:9), Paul was sure that he

208

would stand secure in the day of Christ. . . .

It is true that God will by no means clear the guilty; He could not do that and still be a just God. But He does something which is far better: *he removes the guilt,* so that the one formerly guilty does not need to be cleared,—he is justified, and counted as though he never had sinned. . . . The new heart is a heart that loves righteousness and hates sin. . . .

Many people hesitate to make a start to serve the Lord, because they fear that God will not accept them; and thousands who have been professed followers of Christ for years are still doubting their acceptance with God. For the benefit of such I write, and I would not bewilder their minds with speculations, but will endeavor to give them the simple assurance of God's word. . . .

For most wonderful of all, He bought you for the very reason that you were not worthy. [Ellet J. Waggoner, *Christ and His Righteousness* (1890), pp. 62, 63, 64, 66, 69, 70, 72.]

From Minneapolis Ellen White, Jones, Waggoner, and others carried the message of righteousness to as many as they could in camp, church, institutes, and colleges.

One who heard Jones speak to the congregation in Battle Creek later recalled:

A. T. Jones: A tall awkward man with the features of a frontiersman; self-educated, a tenor voice, a wonderful gift of language, a wonderful scholar in history and Bible. As a public speaker he had no equal in the denomination up to his time. He could quote whole chapters from Romans and Galatians and Hebrews and Revelation in a way to give you a new vision of the beauty of the Bible. At the close of one sermon he quoted the lovely hymn, "There's a

Windows

Wideness in God's Mercy" all through to the end. It was the most wonderful elocutionary effort I have ever heard. The audience (1500) was so deeply moved that for 2 hours they stood up and made confessions and reconsecrations. It was not a mass movement but an individual movement. God spoke thru Jones mightily in those days. [Sanford P. S. Edwards letter to the compiler, April 27, 1956.]

Soon it became more popular to expound righteousness by faith. Where before many had been suspicious of Waggoner and Jones, now the two men found themselves in demand as speakers. As a consequence, Ellen White warned:

They [the rejecters in 1888] take step after step in the false way, until there seems to be no other course for them except to go on, believing they are right in their bitterness of feeling toward their brethren. *Will the Lord's messenger* [Waggoner and/or Jones?] *bear the pressure brought against him?* . . . Should the Lord's messengers, after standing manfully for the truth for a time, fall under temptation, and dishonor Him who has given them their work, will that be proof that the message was not true? No, because the Bible is true. [Ellen G. White letter to O. A. Olsen, September 1, 1892. Letter 19d 1892, White Estate. Italics supplied.]

for further reading:

Bourdeau, Daniel T., *Sanctification or Living Holiness* (1970), 144 pages.

Bunch, Taylor G., *The Exodus and Advent Movements in Type and Antitype* (1937), 185 pages.

Daniells, Arthur Grosvenor, *Christ Our Righteousness* (1926), 165 pages.

Froom, Leroy Edwin, *Movement of Destiny* (1971), 700 pages.

* Olson, Albert Victor, *Through Crisis to Victory, 1888-1901* (1966), 320 pages.

* Pease, Norval F., *By Faith Alone* (1962), 248 pages.

——————————, "The Minneapolis Conference of 1888," *Review and Herald,* August 11, 1969.

——————————, "After 1888," *Review and Herald,* September 18, 1969.

——————————, "1926 and Beyond," *Review and Herald,* September 25, 1969.

Spalding, Arthur W., *Origin and History of Seventh-day Adventists,* Vol. 2, chap. 15.

Steinweg, Bruno William, "Development in the Teaching of Justification and Righteousness by Faith in the Seventh-day Adventist Church after 1900" (MA thesis, SDA Theological Seminary, 1948), 108 pages.

Waggoner, Ellet J., *Christ and His Righteousness* (1972), 96 pages.

——————————, *The Glad Tidings: Studies in Galatians.*

The Church
at the Turn
of the Century

A number of tides and currents swept and surged through the Seventh-day Adventist Church at the turn of the century. One of them involved a desire to consolidate the various denominational institutions, such as the publishing houses. On a purely business management level, putting all the publishing houses together, or merging the sanitariums under one controlling board did seem to have economic and efficiency advantages. But Mrs. White felt that those proposing such plans overlooked the most important element —fallen human nature.

Putting anything under the leadership of a few would result in its being molded into their likeness. Publishing houses, for example, under the direction of a few managers or editors would publish only those things that appealed to them. And also, fallen human nature continually groped for power. Thus she wrote:

> During the year 1890, much thought had been given by leading men connected with the management of the Review and Herald Publishing Association, to a proposal for the consolidation of the work of the publishing houses under one board of control. The proposed union of the publishing interests was advocated as a means of securing unity, economy, and efficiency. At the same time the hope was expressed that at no distant day all the sanitariums might be brought under one ownership

and control. By the same ones who advocated
consolidation of the publishing houses and the
medical institutions, the theory was advanced that
the surest way to establish confidence in the work
that Seventh-day Adventists were doing was to
strengthen the institutions at headquarters, by
providing them with large and substantial buildings
and with ample facilities. . . .

The General Conference for 1891 was held in
Battle Creek March 5-25. Sunday forenoon, March 15,
the committee of twenty-one appointed at the
preceding General Conference to consider the
consolidation of the publishing interests, presented its
report. The committee spoke favorably of the objects
to be gained by consolidation, but advised that the
Conference move cautiously. They then proposed that
the General Conference Association be reorganized,
with a view to its eventually securing control of all
the publishing work of the denomination. [Ellen G.
White, *Life Sketches,* pp. 311-313.]

Mrs. White fought such ideas:

In the weakness of human judgment, men were
gathering into their finite hands the lines of control,
while God's will, God's way and counsel, were not
sought as indispensable. Men of stubborn, ironlike
will, both in and out of the Office, were confederating
together, determined to drive certain measures
through in accordance with their own judgment.

I [Ellen G. White] said to them, "You cannot do
this. The control of these large interests cannot be
vested wholly in those who make it manifest that they
have little experience in the things of God, and have
not spiritual discernment. The people of God
throughout our ranks must not, because of
mismanagement on the part of erring men, have their
confidence shaken in the important interests at the

213

great heart of the work, which have a decided
influence upon our churches in the United States and
in foreign lands. If you lay your hand upon the
publishing work, this great instrumentality of God, to
place your mold and superscription upon it, you will
find that it will be dangerous to your own souls, and
disastrous to the work of God. . . .

No confederacy should be formed with unbelievers,
neither should you call together a certain chosen
number who think as you do, and who will say Amen
to all that you propose, while others are excluded, who
you think will not be in harmony. I was shown that
there was great danger of doing this. [Ellen G. White,
Life Sketches, p. 321.]

We have failed, decidedly failed, in allowing so
much to be done in one place. Everything is not to be
brought under the control of one institution. Such an
effort, carried out, results in placing an open door on
temptation before the man at the head of the principal
institution. [Ellen G. White to Arthur G. Daniells,
Letter 190, August 27, 1903.]

It is not His [the Lord's] plan to centralize power
in the hands of a few persons, or to bring one
institution under the control of another. . . .

It is burden-bearing that gives strength and
development. And for the workers in different
localities to be largely freed from responsibility [by
consolidation] means to place them where their
characters will remain undeveloped, and their powers
will be repressed and weakened. . . .

When so great power is placed in the hands of a
few persons, Satan will make determined efforts to
pervert the judgment, to insinuate wrong principles of
action, to bring in a wrong policy; in so doing he can
not only pervert one institution, but through this can
gain control of others, and give a wrong mold to the
work in distant parts. Thus the influence for evil
becomes widespread. Let each institution stand in its

214

moral independence, carrying on its work in its own
field. . . .

There should be no rivalry between our publishing houses. If this spirit is indulged, it will grow
and strengthen, and will crowd out the missionary
spirit. . . .

Never should the managers of our institutions
attempt, in the slightest degree, to take advantage of
one another. Such efforts are most offensive to God.
Sharp dealing, the effort to drive sharp bargains with
one another, is a wrong He will not tolerate. Every
effort to exalt one institution at the expense of
another is wrong. . . .

Each worker must give his own branch [his own
institution, his very] special effort. . . .

Not consolidation, not rivalry or criticism, but
co-operation, is God's plan for His institutions. [Ellen
G. White, *Testimonies,* Vol. 7, pp. 171-174.]

Like everything else, the denomination suffered from the
financial panic and monetary crisis of the time. Politicians
agitated that changing national monetary policy would improve the American economy. If the economy improved, so
would the church's financial condition. A number of Adventists in Battle Creek plunged into politics. The current political controversy became an obsession to many members. It
soon drew their attention away from their church and religious duties.

**Again Ellen had to remind them of the church's mission. She
told the General Conference of 1897:**

I supposed our own people would step softly, and
move very guardedly, and keep themselves aloof from
all these new issues in regard to the circulating
currency [in 1896]. This is not the devising of

Windows

God—the changing of the circulating currency. What
will it effect? It will cause a state of things that will
bring oppression to the poor, and create great distress
[by inflation?]. . . . I have been [in vision] where I
heard conversations from those in positions of trust in
our institutions, and there was great warmth in
controversy over the different positions taken. The
light given me was, This is the policy Satan has
arranged to bring distress.

Would we know how we may please the Saviour?
It is not engaging in political speeches, either in or
out of the pulpit. . . .

I was surprised as I saw men who claim to believe
the truth for this time all excited in regard to
matters—which relate to the Lord Jesus and eternal
interests? No; but they seemed to be wonderfully
excited in regard to the currency. Some ministers
were distinguishing themselves by weaving these
subjects into their discourses. They were excitably
involving themselves, taking sides in regard to these
questions that the Lord did not lay upon them the
burden to engage in. These persons seemed to have a
large share of self-sufficiency. [Ellen G. White,
Testimonies to Ministers, pp. 331, 332.]

In 1898 she urged:

Keep your voting to yourself. Do not feel it your
duty to urge everyone to do as you do. [Ellen G.
White, *Selected Messages,* Book Two, p. 337.]

And to teachers and managers of SDA schools in 1899, she declared:

The Lord would have His people bury political
questions. On these themes silence is eloquence. . . .

They [Christ's followers] will not wear political
badges, but the badge of Christ. . . .

216

The Turn of the Century

> What are we to do then?—Let political questions alone. . . .
>
> The tithe should not be used to pay any one for speechifying on political questions. Every teacher, minister, or leader in our ranks who is stirred with a desire to ventilate his opinions on political questions, should be converted by a belief in the truth, or give up his work. . . .
>
> It is a mistake for you to link your interests with any political party, to cast your vote with them or for them. . . .
>
> Is it their [our] work to make enemies in the political world? No, no. . . .
>
> [But] on the temperance question, take your position without wavering. [Ellen G. White, *Gospel Workers,* p. 391f.]

Just before the turn of the century a number of movements seeking to reform conditions in the Adventist institutions swept Battle Creek. They particularly concentrated in the college under the direction of Edward A. Sutherland, but the sanitarium, under the leadership of Kellogg, also participated. Alonzo T. Jones attempted to change conditions in the church through his position as editor of the *Review and Herald.* Some of the proposed changes were good, others tended to extremes or were even dangerous.

The following excerpts hint at the activity going on in Battle Creek at the time and the impact it had on some:

> The changes which have taken place in Battle Creek during the past term thus securing the co-operation and influence of the Sanitarium and the Review Office will undoubtedly draw a larger number of students from the general field than heretofore for this school [Battle Creek College]. [Joseph H.

Haughey letter to R. C. Porter, August 2, 1897.
Haughey letter books. Heritage Room, Andrews
University.]

The [Battle Creek] College here is expecting a
larger attendance the coming year, which they no
doubt will have, as the result of the new order of
things, and in connection with the fact that the
influence and co-operation of the Sanitarium and
Review Office is now strongly exerted in favor of the
present administration. [J. H. Haughey letter to M. B.
Mattson, August 2, 1897. Haughey letter books.
Heritage Room, Andrews University.]

The Battle Creek College and Sanitarium faction
were tied together . . . because of common beliefs on
some matters and preponderance of control by
sticking together, made the Sutherland-Magan and
the Kellogg-Jones combination a hard nut to crack for
Elder Daniells when he was newly elected to office in
1901. The College-Sanitarium combination was the
reformer group and the rest of the denomination was
the conservative group. The college group was
primarily for Educational reform but stood with the
San[itarium] or Jones & Kellogg against the form of
organization for the denomination that was adopted
at the 1901 G[eneral] Conf[erence]. Organization was
the issue with Kellogg and Jones. . . . The
combination was not broken until the Berrien Springs
Council in . . . [1904], when Sutherland and Magan
resigned and left E[mmanuel] M[issionary] C[ollege]
and went on their own, independent of G. C. control.
[Sanford P. S. Edwards letter to the compiler, March
21, 1956.]

**The expectancy that the Second Advent of Christ might
occur around 1900 in part spurred the reformers on. Ellen
White wrote a number of times that the eternal world was
near:**

218

The Turn of the Century

The end of all things is at hand [1881]. . . .

I have been shown that we are standing upon the threshold of the eternal world. [Ellen G. White, *Testimonies,* Vol. 5, pp. 16, 18.]

We are now [1890] upon the very borders of the eternal world, and stand in a more solemn relation to time and to eternity than ever before. [Ellen G. White, *Testimonies to Ministers,* p. 147.]

The end of all things is at hand [c 1894]. The Lord is soon coming. Already His judgments are abroad in our land.

The Lord is coming. Oh, the time is short. [Ellen G. White, *Testimonies to Ministers,* p. 187.]

When asked why she wrote so urgently, Ellen explained:

The angels of God in their messages to men represent time as very short. Thus it has always been presented to me. It is true that time has continued longer than we had expected in the early days of this message. Our Saviour did not appear as soon as we hoped. But has the word of the Lord failed? Never! It should be remembered that the promises and threatenings of God are alike conditional. [Ellen G. White, *Selected Messages,* Book One, p. 67.]

Soon after 1900 a few Seventh-day Adventists started what some called the "New Theology." Church leaders generally, however, spurned the new ideas and used "Review" articles and editorials in their counterthrusts. Mrs. White evaluated it thus:

The enemy of souls has sought to bring in the supposition that a great reformation was to take place among Seventh-day Adventists, and that this reformation would consist in giving up the doctrines which stand as the pillars of our faith, and engaging in a process of reorganization. Were this reformation

219

Windows

to take place, what would result?—The principles of truth that God in His wisdom has given to the remnant church would be discarded. Our religion would be changed. The fundamental principles that have sustained the work for the last fifty years would be accounted as error. A new organization would be established. Books of a new order would be written. A system of intellectual philosophy would be introduced. The founders of this system would go into the cities and do a wonderful work. The Sabbath, of course, would be lightly regarded, as also the God who created it. Nothing would be allowed to stand in the way of the new movement. The leaders would teach that virtue is better than vice, but God being removed, they would place their dependence on human power, which, without God, is worthless. Their foundation would be built on the sand, and storm and tempest would sweep away the structure. [Ellen G. White, *Special Testimonies,* Series B, No. 7, pp. 39, 40.]

A "Review" article responded to the New Theology:

In this time of "new light," and "new thought," and "new experience" there has been a great departure from "the old paths." There is now a "new theology" which calls for a new definition of God, a new view of inspiration, and a new adjustment of ideas all around. The old experiences of the men of faith are discredited. The old-time manifestations of God's power in conversion are not believed for, and are not wanted. The old-time testimony of men walking with God is consequently lacking. Is it not time for a call to return to the old paths? Is there not a demand for such a revelation of the way of the Lord as shall offer hope and comfort to weary, storm-tossed souls? What is the meaning of this advent movement if it is not to be "a restorer of paths to dwell in"? . . .

220

The Turn of the Century

These old paths are ever new, and these old experiences are ever new, and they are both eternally new as we serve in the newness of the Spirit, and in the freshness of the endless life, but we never substitute human inventions for the eternal truth. We have new views of the old truth, and new experiences in the old paths, but we do not find it necessary to discard the old truth and to depart from the old paths of righteousness. Let us stand in the old paths. [Editorial, *Review and Herald,* March 24, 1903, p. 3.]

for further reading:

* Gordon, Paul A., "To Vote or Not to Vote," *Review and Herald,* September 12, 19, 1968.

Neff, Merlin L., *For God and C.M.E.* (1964), chap. 5.

Olsen, M. Ellsworth, *A History of the Origin and Progress of Seventh-day Adventists,* chap. 33.

Schwarz, Richard W., *John Harvey Kellogg, M.D.* (1970), 256 pages.

Spalding, Arthur W., *Origin and History of Seventh-day Adventists,* Vol. 3, chaps. 1, 2.

* *The General Conference Daily Bulletin* (1897; 1899; 1901; 1903).

Vande Vere, Emmett K., *The Wisdom Seekers* (1972), 288 pages.

Conflict
Over Control

Organizationally, the denomination in 1895 consisted of a cluster of separate, individual bodies, all ambitious to expand and sometimes overlapping in what they did. The struggle to correct the situation altered Seventh-day Adventist history. It cost the church its biggest institution, Battle Creek Sanitarium, and the San's head, Dr. John Harvey Kellogg.

The sanitarium developed solidly under Kellogg's leadership from 1876 until he began to reject the advice of Mrs. White. One of his key points of controversy with the church involved denominational control with the side issues of management and finances.

Former General Conference president George I. Butler, who intimately knew the people involved, spelled out the problems with Kellogg and implored him to change his course of action:

> She [Ellen White] stood by you through all those long years when you were tugging away for your dear life, and I have at times, in view of the testimonies drawn nearer to you than I should have done otherwise, because I did believe the testimonies. And all this time you were becoming strong and influential, and a man who could carry your points, and scarcely anybody wanted to try pulling sticks with you. You were growing up in a way that you did not like to have anybody oppose you. You did not talk

222

Conflict Over Control

very kindly of them if they did. . . .

I am so anxious to see you take the right view of yourself. If you do, you will have to stop talking in a way to break faith in the Testimonies. [George I. Butler letter to J. H. Kellogg, September 4, 1905. John Harvey Kellogg Papers. Museum, Michigan State University.]

I did think, for many, many years, that you were one of the strongest believers in the Testimonies I knew of. I could not say it to-day, and why? On what ground could I base this difference? Well, I will venture to suggest, Most everybody believes the Testimonies very strongly as long as they favor them, and sustain them, and stand up for them, and fight their battles. The time when they become questionable about the Testimonies is when the Testimonies begin to reprove them, and present before them certain faults, and wrong courses, or methods or motives of action. Then is when faith begins to ooze out at the finger ends. [George I. Butler letter to J. H. Kellogg, March 7, 1906. John Harvey Kellogg Papers. Museum, Michigan State University.]

Kellogg seemed especially aggressive following the re-charter of the Sanitarium in 1897-1898 and the purchase of the institution for a sum equal to its debts.

Understandably the fifteen hundred employees of the General Conference organization resented the two thousand people of the Kellogg-led sanitarium complex looking down on them, and vice versa. A few paragraphs from the 1901 "General Conference Daily Bulletin" indicate some of the attitudes prevalent at the time:

Criticisms began to abound, and every movement originating at the Sanitarium was passed under the

223

microscope of human judgment, and the storm-center
rested upon those who were thought to be responsible
for the movements. Medical missionary work was
regarded as absorbing too much energy and means;
the methods employed in conducting that part of the
work were complained of; those who were at the head
of that branch were thought to be employing
disintegrating tactics. Everything, in fact, that would
tend to neutralize the efforts of all concerned, was put
into the minds of the people, and the severest
strictures were passed from lip to lip, to the evident
delight of him who would destroy the work of God.

All this was talked over among fully three
hundred of the brethren, to the satisfaction of all.
After it was made plain that the evil rumors in
circulation were without foundation, by one united
hearty amen, all agreed to drop all these things from
their conversation, and to do all in their power to
correct the false impressions which have already
gained a footing in the minds of brethren throughout
the field.

If this shall be done, suspicion will be allayed,
dark hints of covert wrong will cease to be given, and
even remote allusion to that which would create
suspicion will soon become a thing of the past. . . . In
this condition of things, the ministry will recognize
the medical missionary work as an essential factor in
evangelizing the world, preparatory to the Lord's
return to claim his people. Not only will the medical
branch be recognized, by the ministry, but it will be
fostered, and upheld in its laudable work. May God
speed that day. [*The General Conference Daily
Bulletin,* April 18, 1901, Vol. IV, Extra No. 14, pp.
305, 306.]

However, the brotherly posturing of 1901 did not outlive
1902, a break coming when General Conference president

Conflict Over Control

Daniells opposed Dr. Kellogg's plan to buy some sanitarium property in England contrary to a "no debt" policy adopted in 1901.

Daniells' account of the rupture, though written long afterward and phrased to put himself in the best possible light, still hints at the two men's feelings:

> We reached London early in the morning, and Dr. Kellogg was waiting at the publishing house for me. He stepped up to me and said, "I want to have a little talk with you before we go into the council."
>
> He took hold of my arm, and we walked down [the] street, and he told me what he had found, a nice building nicely located, that would cost $25 or 30 thousand dollars. He believed that the British brethren would raise 5 thousand or ten thousand, and the American brethren 20 thousand, and we could get our institution.
>
> I did not say anything in opposition, for I thought I would wait until I could get into the committee, and let him make the proposal to them all there.
>
> We went into the committee. Dr. A. B. Olsen was there, and W. C. Sisley, and a number of our British men.
>
> After prayer we invited Dr. Kellogg to tell us what he had asked us to come over for. He then made this proposition that the General Conference would assume 20 thousand dollars, that the British committee assume 5 thousand dollars, and then there would be so little left, it could carry the debt of five thousand if necessary. . . .
>
> I do not know whether I was the first to speak up. Very likely I was. I said, "Doctor, that would be creating a debt here of twenty-five thousand dollars?"
>
> "Yes, it would be assuming an obligation to raise that money."
>
> "And," I said, "you are aware that we have been

225

working night and day for two years with 'Object Lessons' to roll away the reproach of debt from the schools?"

"Yes," he knew that.

"Now, Doctor, all the people who are working so hard to do that understand that we are not going to roll on another burden right on the heels of what we are trying to clear. I do not see how we can obligate the American brethren to the amount of twenty thousand dollars without their approval. We have not a right to do it."

He began to get fretful and snappish, and some of the others broke in,—two men that he hated like poison, Flaiz and Shultz. We had been together nearly an hour, when he just flew into a rage. He hit the table with a terrible bang, and said, "You do not want to have any medical work done in England. You are blocking everything, and I am going to say Good day to the whole of you." He grabbed his hat and went out.

I said, "Boys, you can see we are in a crisis now with the Doctor."

Dr. A. B. Olsen was anxious to get that sanitarium, and wanted us to go ahead.

I said, "Couldn't we do this? You folks assume the amount of five thousand dollars, and then go at it and raise it. And let us go back to Battle Creek, get our committee together, lay it before them and see if they will undertake, by one means or another, to produce that twenty thousand dollars, and when we have got the money, buy this institution."

We all agreed on that, because that would be paying cash. We went and had lunch, and came back, and were putting this into shape when there was a knock at the door. Brother Sisley answered. He said to me, "The Doctor wants to see you." So I stepped out. He said, "Look here, Elder, we have worked together too long and too well, to have a break here."

I said, "That is exactly my sentiment."

226

Conflict Over Control

"But I want to talk over this new policy you have formed."

We went into the washroom of the printing house, and he pushed me in. He came in and shut the door and stood against it. Then he began to tell me that we had never had such a policy since we began our work, that we had always assumed obligations and worked them out and raised the money.

I said, "I know we have always assumed, but we have never paid up yet, and we are in debt heels over head everywhere, the Pacific Press, the Review and Herald, all our schools, everything we have got is just buried with debt, and we are paying out interest enough to purchase an institution. I am pledged to my committee and to our people, not to go on any longer with this borrowing policy."

Then he went at it. He wept, and he stormed, and he told me that Sister White would roll me over in the dust if I took such a stand as that.

I said I would rather land in Timbuctoo than to break my pledge with the people. I could not do it.

Well, then he would go on again. He kept me there nearly two hours, until I was so nervous it seemed I would jump out of the window. The committee were still waiting. We had to catch a boat. The men were all outside and I could see they were talking a bit, and they were displeased. Finally I just stepped right up to him, and I raised my hand and pointed my little finger.

"Look here, Doctor. It is no use for you to say another word. I am set. My conscience is in this, and I will not violate my conscience. You can stop right here, for I will never consent to this thing, until I have the approval of Sister White and of the General Conference Committee."

He just settled his eyes on me like a dark shadow falling over me. Then he said, "Well, sir, I will never work with you on this cash policy. I will see you in

America. Good day." [Arthur G. Daniells, "How the
Denomination Was Saved From Pantheism."
Stenographically reported statement, March 12,
1935.]

The General Conference at Oakland, California, in
April, 1903, intensified the tug over control. The support-
ers of Daniells asked for an amended constitution that
would strengthen the General Conference presidency and
also a resolution requiring that a conference control any
and all property pertaining to the denomination. The
Kellogg group opposed them at length, but both pieces of
legislation passed.

**Ellen White pleaded for harmony between the two factions,
but her call little moved Kellogg. In fact, the doctor un-
equivocally declared his independence:**

[Ellen G. White]: My brethren, clear your souls
before God. Cease your criticizing and faultfinding.
. . .

God wants His servants to stand united in
carrying that [medical missionary] work forward.
Because one man is one-sided and another man is
one-sided, this does not show that the work of God is
to be one-sided. . . .

Because men have made mistakes, they are not to
be uprooted. The blessing of God heals; it does not
destroy. . . .

God wants His institutions to stand in fellowship
with one another just as brethren in the church
should stand in fellowship. [*The General Conference
Daily Bulletin* (1903), pp. 58, 86.]

[Dr. John H. Kellogg]: I expect you will pass it [the
resolution on properties]; but I want you to know that
I object to it, and do not expect to be bound by it in

228

anything I have anything to do with. [*The General Conference Daily Bulletin* (1903), p. 78.]

Kellogg claimed that certain leaders raided his institutions at Battle Creek by urging as many Seventh-day Adventists as possible to work elsewhere. At a Lake Union Conference meeting at Berrien Springs in May, 1904, he almost capitulated all disputed matters—except control of the sanitarium.

Dr. Sanford P. S. Edwards, who was present at the meeting, later sized up the confrontation:

At the 1904 meeting Kellogg was desperately pressed from two sides. He needed the denominational influence to supply money to buy bonds to pay for his new building. The bonds were a drug on the market without denominational approval and Sr. White condemned them. That hurt Kellogg awfully. The medical school was deteriorating for lack of students as were his nursing classes. Kellogg was ready to surrender along theological lines but not on *control*. It was on *control* that he had his backing. Jones, Magan, Sutherland, and others I could name, some conference officers and many ministers feared *centralization of power*. That was the real issue all along. [Sanford P. S. Edwards letter to the compiler, July 28, 1957.]

After the Berrien Springs meeting it seemed that reconciliation was never as possible again. On November 10, 1907, after two elders of the Battle Creek Church had talked with Dr. J. H. Kellogg for seven hours, the church in business meeting disfellowshiped him.

A record of the church proceeding follows:

Minutes of Adjourned Business Meeting of the
S. D. Adventist Church,
Held in the Tabernacle [Battle Creek],
November 10, 1907.

The Chairman, Elder M. N. Campbell, opened this
meeting at 7:30 [P.M.]. . . .

The cases of four young men were then brought up
and acted upon, and the Clerk then called the name of
Dr. John H. Kellogg. Elder Campbell then arose and
made the following remarks:

"This name, which ought to have been considered
some time before, has been delayed for various
reasons from time to time, until it now comes before
us. There are a number of reasons why it is now
necessary to deal with the case of Dr. Kellogg. In the
first place, Dr. Kellogg, although he lives within easy
access of the church, never meets with us there. We
never find him in our meeting. When the Lord's
supper is celebrated and the children of God are
invited to meet around that table, this brother has not
been present for many years. When we come together
to show our regard for each other in the ordinance of
feet-washing, Dr. Kellogg is not with us. He has not,
for a number of years, paid any tithe in for the
advancement of God's cause, the Third Angel's
message, or has he paid a penny toward the carrying
on of the work of this church, the church expenses,
and his interest seems to be absolutely lacking in any
phase of the work represented by this church. Again it
is a regrettable fact, but a fact nevertheless, that Dr.
Kellogg has been devoting himself largely for a
number of years past, and especially the last three or
four years to the work of bitterly opposing those who
have been appointed as leaders in this cause, and
particularly the ministers of the gospel. The ministry

230

has been held up before the young physicians and those associated with him, as unworthy of their confidence, and has been set forth in a ridiculous light. We have an abundance of evidence along this line. It is, I am sorry to say, quite evident that Dr. Kellogg has not only given up his faith in the Spirit of Prophecy, but he has come out and taken a decided stand in opposition to it. We do not discipline persons for cherishing unbelief in the Testimonies, but when they come out in open opposition to them, that is an altogether different matter. Again, it is evident that Dr. Kellogg has allied himself with those who are putting forth their best efforts to overthrow the organized work for which this church stands. Now, I do not wish to say anything in any way derogatory to the character of this brother. That is not my mission; but viewing it from the standpoint of a fellow member, it seems that this case requires attention at the hands of this church.

Before taking this matter up in a public way, a committee of brethren, who had known him for many years, and entertained friendly feelings towards him, was appointed to visit him at his home. These brethren did so, and spent considerable time talking over the issues at stake at the present time. This committee, consisting of Brethren Amadon and Bourdeau, are here to-night and will render their report. I will now call upon Brother Bourdeau for his report.

[Elder A. C. Bourdeau]: "We had an interview with Dr. Kellogg, which lasted more than seven hours. . . . He spoke against some of our leading brethren whom we consider men of God, and our sister that we consider the servant of the Lord, as stating things that were as 'false as sin.' . . . I would make a motion that the name of Dr. J. H. Kellogg be dropped from the records of this church."

Elder Campbell then called on Brother Amadon to

231

give in his report, which was as follows:

[G. W. Amadon]: ". . . I was not influenced a particle to believe the many statements that he made—very strong, vehement assertions against the brethren leading in this cause, that we regard as God's appointed servants. We receive them and reverence them as men called of God and placed in certain positions in the church. But brethren, we have an old book here that says, 'How can two walk together except they be agreed?' Now, that means something. If you had heard the scorching words of vituperation uttered against this organization which Dr. Kellogg uttered,—well, it would have set you thinking. I feel very sad, as a member of this church, in regard to the position of Dr. Kellogg, a man that stands upon the crest of popular favor; a man that God has spoke of as He has him—to see him take the position he does is a very sad thing. . . .

"I second the motion made by Brother Bourdeau concerning Dr. J. H. Kellogg, that his name be stricken from our church roll."

[Elder Campbell]: "You have heard the statements of these two brethren who called upon the Doctor. After they returned they immediately wrote out the experience that they had been through so far as they could remember, and we have had it struck off by the stenographer and, having read it, I think they have stated the situation very mildly indeed.

"From the statements of these two brethren, we understood that the Doctor wished to be notified when his case came up. Last week we notified him that his case would come up to-night. If the Doctor is present, it is no more than right that he have a chance to make any statements that he wishes to make."

The Doctor not being present did not respond. The question was then called for and Elder Campbell said: "You have heard the motion: All in favor of this motion will say 'aye.' Opposed say 'no.'" The motion was unanimously carried. [A copy of the "Minutes of Adjourned Business Meeting of the S. D. Adventist Church, Held in the Tabernacle, Nov. 10, 1907." Supplied to the compiler by Malcolm N. Campbell.]

Tradition claims that the Battle Creek Tabernacle expelled many of Kellogg's followers. Whether such stories are true or not we cannot determine. But between 1905 and 1909 the Michigan Sanitarium and Benevolent Association in annual constituency meetings dropped scores of Seventh-day Adventist members because they allegedly failed to correctly represent Sanitarium principles. On July 23 and August 21, 1905, it decided to scrutinize a list of ninety Sanitarium employees to consider their eligibility to become members of the MSBA. The next day, in annual meeting, though only twenty-eight constituent members out of a possible five hundred were present, it admitted twenty-three new members.

Kellogg also explained the necessary termination of the Sanitarium's original thirty-year charter, and how in 1897 the court appointed a receiver who sold the Sanitarium at auction at Marshall, Michigan, to the highest bidder, namely, the Michigan Sanitarium and Benevolent Association. The new association purchased the property of the former association by producing in court all of its obligations. Thus it paid for the property an amount ($782,253.64) just sufficient to pay its debts—nothing more. And why nothing more? Because it could afford to pay no more, and moreover *the original investors were really donors who never expected to get their money back.*

Kellogg assured the meeting, "So this is . . . a private association . . . distinctly said to be non-sectarian and undenominational. And the propriety of this method of organization has never been questioned until very recently."

233

Windows

At a Sanitarium Board Meeting on January 2, 1906, Kellogg stated, "Now I have come to the point where I feel I know pretty well where I am and I know pretty well what I want to do and am willing to do it, and I feel like saying to the Board here if you feel the same way, I am ready to go ahead to work without any reference to things, except so far as they admonish us to do things right and put things on a better basis. And if we all feel that way—that we are ready to go ahead no matter what happens in the fear of the Lord and in the name of the Lord, standing on the principles—I know of no reason why our work should not move on. Let us simply stand for the truth and go ahead, doing our duty as men and saying nothing about backing out or running away or anything of the sort."

On August 21, 1906, the Tenth Annual Meeting of the MSBA with only thirty-seven members present admitted thirty-six new ones. The August 31, 1907, board meeting voted to donate ten dollars to each prospective member —usually a sanitarium employee—as a reward to help him pay his annual membership fee because "it behooves us to increase our membership by taking in such new members as are favorable to our interests."

At the board meeting of July 25, 1908, someone suggested the advisability of purging the membership—of the 680 members allegedly only about 10 percent were in sympathy with the institution. A letter went to the 680 advising of the plan.

The annual meeting on December 30, 1908, brought only thirty-nine present. Kellogg gave a long explanation of the Sanitarium's history since 1867, the legal wording of the charter and by-laws, and the difficulties it had lately suffered. Judge Jesse Arthur moved for further purging in a January meeting.

On January 16, 1909, a board meeting attended by thirty-five members dropped 128 names, such as Andross,

Bourdeau, Colcord, Cottrell, Crisler, Daniells, Fitzgerald, Frances, Froom, Griggs, the Irwins, W. K. Kellogg, Knox, Palmer, Reaser, Russell, Salisbury, Tait, G. B. Thompson, Westphal, W. C. White, Wilcox. [Based on the "Minutes of the Michigan Sanitarium and Benevolent Association," the parent organization after 1897 of the Battle Creek Sanitarium and Hospital. Copy held by the compiler.]

After 1901 SDA constituents in the Michigan Sanitarium and Benevolent Association still comprised a majority, but since it was almost impossible for all to assemble in a constituency meeting, Kellogg had obtained effective control of the sanitarium for decades to follow.

for further reading:

Daniells, Arthur Grosvenor, *The Abiding Gift of Prophecy* (1936), chap. 30.

Powell, Horace B., *The Original Has This Signature* (1956), chap. 4.

Robinson, Dores E., *The Battle Creek Sanitarium: Its Origin, Development, Ownership, and Control* (1943), 64 pages.

———————————, *The Story of Our Health Message* (1943), 364 pages.

Schwarz, Richard W., "John Harvey Kellogg: American Health Reformer" (PhD dissertation, University of Michigan, 1965), 504 pages.

———————————, *John Harvey Kellogg, M.D.* (1970), 256 pages.

Spalding, Arthur W., *Origin and History of Seventh-day Adventists*, Vol. 3, chap. 8.

The General Conference Daily Bulletin (1899, 1901, 1903).

White, Arthur L., "Who Told Sister White?" *Review and Herald,* May 21, 1959.

White, Ellen G., *Special Testimonies*, Series B.

Fires
in Battle Creek

For twenty years Ellen G. White had warned about the dangers of Adventists colonizing in the west end of Battle Creek. (See, for example, *Testimonies,* Vol. 8, pp. 90-92.) Most, unfortunately, ignored her. But some responded, as the examples below illustrate.

Joseph H. Haughey, for many years associated with Battle Creek College and Emmanuel Missionary College, wrote:

> It does almost make my bones rattle to think of the things that are going on and will go on in Battle Creek so long as our people there maintain the idea that all power which comes to this world must in some way pass through that little town, or the institutions, or the organizations, or the people who live there.
> [J. H. Haughey letter to F. W. Howe, March 29, 1898. Haughey letter books. Heritage Room, Andrews University.]
> Matters in Battle Creek are about as we would expect from the varying reports which have gone out all over the country and perhaps all over the world. There are two classes of Seventh-day Adventists, the zealous for purity, holiness, uprightness of life, and the others only apparently so. To distinguish between them, it is only necessary to compare the spirit of criticism, faultfinding, talking about others, complaining that things are not what they should be, trying to put brakes on the wheels or to load them more heavily, thus discouraging those who are really

236

moving on towards the Heavenly City. [J. H. Haughey
letter to W. T. Bland, June 17, 1898. Haughey letter
books. Heritage Room, Andrews University.]

William W. Prescott's reaction:

[Before the Review personnel on February 12,
1902]: You and I know that for some years there has
been a sort of feeling more or less prevalent
throughout the denomination . . . that there is
something wrong about the Review and Herald, until
there has come to be almost a kind of slur connected
with the name. . . .

Now I say, Let us clean out all the dark corners.
. . . It is wicked to do commercial work on a wicked
basis. . . .

But now we face a situation—whether we brought
it or not, no matter. Here is a large institution. . . . We
cannot turn that over [reform it] in a day. [W. W.
Prescott, *Review and Herald,* Feb. 18, 1902, p. 108.]

Then the calamities came. On February 18, 1902, fire
destroyed the Battle Creek Sanitarium and Hospital, the
principal structures of the medical complex.

The "Review and Herald" reported the sanitarium catastrophe to the denomination:

The precise origin of the fire is not known. A few
minutes before four o'clock on Tuesday morning,
February 18, the night watchman, while on his round
of inspection in the main building, found that some of
the electric call bells would not ring, owing to a "short
circuit," which had in some way been set up between
the electric wires in the basement of the building.
While attending to this, the odor of smoke was
detected, coming from beneath the men's bath room.

237

Windows

Summoning assistance from the night clerk's office, a hurried investigation was made, and a fire was found to have started in the basement at a point underneath the massage room. This was in a large wing of the main building, extending eastward. A dense smoke was rising, and the alarm was immediately given from two alarm boxes in the main building, and from the nearest city box, and help summoned from a fire station located close by. But the fire was in a place not easy to get at with the hose, and spread rapidly, running upwards through some ventilating shafts, and breaking out in a few moments' time at the top of the building. By this time doctors, nurses, and other employees and medical students in the building had been aroused, and the energies of all were turned to the task of removing the patients to a place of safety. The nurses had been instructed and drilled in preparation for such an emergency, and the result was shown in the remarkable work that followed. . . .

All were gotten out of their rooms, and carried or led to a position of safety, many climbing down the fire escapes, with which the building was well provided. . . .

The loss on the buildings burned was about $300,000. This loss is a little more than half covered by insurance. [*Review and Herald,* February 25, 1902, p. 126.]

Dr. Kellogg learned of the disaster while in Chicago, and had rough-draft plans for rebuilding in hand when he reached Battle Creek. He wrote in the "Review":

I walked by the ruins this morning, and saw the ashes and smoking embers, and I am glad I was able to say in my heart, "What hath God wrought!" I know God is in it all, because this is God's work, and not man's work. And if God built the house, and permitted the house to burn, it is for some good

238

Fires in Battle Creek

purpose; and the one desire of my heart is to know what that purpose is, and to know what this experience means to me and to the Sanitarium. . . .

Now I know that this [Sanitarium] work has not been altogether understood in Battle Creek. Some perhaps have looked upon the poor instruments that God has been using in this work, and have seen their weaknesses and their mistakes and their frailties, and perhaps have judged the work somewhat by them. Now I beg of you, my friends, forget them if you can. Forget them, and think only of the truth that is represented, and see the truth only. Where I have made mistakes that you have recognized, I ask your forgiveness; where I have made mistakes that you have not recognized, I have earnestly asked God to forgive me. I am full of weaknesses and frailties. I know it. I hope that no one will take me as an example of the truth; but I pray God from this time forward, in all my life, so to cover me with truth that nobody can see me any more. O my friends, I want my life to be such a shining out of truth, of Christ revealed in humanity, that nobody can see me. I do not blame you if you have not understood; you could not help but misunderstand with such a poor interpretation. But when we build our new work and reorganize it,—for I feel that the Lord has given us the opportunity now to reorganize and to do better things than ever before,—I pray that God will give us such wisdom that we may put into every foundation stone, into every brick, and into every part of the structure such Christlike principles and such unsullied truth that those who come here and gaze upon it may ever say, "See what God has wrought." [J. H. Kellogg, *Review and Herald,* March 4, 1902, p. 134.]

As 1902 closed, a fire on December 30 devoured the large east building of the SDA Publishing Association. H. E. Rogers, an office worker in the west building across the street, described it to his family:

I will write you something with reference to the fire which totally destroyed the east building of the Review and Herald, the evening of December 30, 1902. The fire was discovered about 7:30 P. M., and the alarm was given very quickly, by one of the workmen engaged in an adjoining room. The city fire apparatus responded promptly; but before they arrived the fire had spread very rapidly, and three floors were ablaze, forty or fifty feet wide, from top to bottom of the building. At the time the building was comparatively empty, as nearly all the hands left at six o'clock. A few were engaged in different departments, and some of them could not come out the main stairway, but had to come out on the fire escapes. To show the rapidity with which the fire burned, I would state that the night watchman passed the very spot where the fire started but twelve minutes before the alarm was given. He went on his way through the building, and when on the top floor he heard the alarm, and rushed down, but could not get down the main stairway, but had to come down the fire escape.

The fire originated in the dynamo room, or immediately adjoining, or possibly underneath in the basement. At that point there is a large belt connected with the engine that runs the dynamo, which has an opening for the belt to run in clear to the top floor; through this opening the fire was sucked, and thus spread very rapidly to all the floors. Adjoining the dynamo room is the main press room, the floor of which was thoroughly saturated with oil, which caused the fire to become very hot, and so was very difficult to put out when the department arrived. Within ten minutes after the alarm was sent in there were ten streams of water turned on the building,

240

from all sides. It took only a few minutes for one to see that the building was doomed. To show you the rapidity of the fire, I might say that the stenographer in the front office, Mr. W. H. McReynolds, was working there at the time, and on hearing the alarm, started out to notify others in the building; he was gone only a few minutes, and returned to find the office filled with smoke that was stifling. He slammed the safe doors shut, and jumped out. The things that happened to be in that safe were the only records that were saved from the front office. That safe was opened day before yesterday, and everything was found all right, though somewhat scorched. Their smaller safe, containing the records of the Association, and the stockholders' stocks, etc., was also opened, and the things were considerably charred in that.

The heat was very intense. The wind at first blew from the West Southwest, and had it continued in this direction, the entire row of buildings east of the Office, would certainly have gone down. However, the wind shifted to south southwest, and carried the heat and embers into the park, and thus saved those buildings. The building was practically down in about one and one-half hours, though parts of it are burning yet. They kept six streams of water all the first night, and three or four most of the time since the fire.

At first it was feared that the vault doors had been left open, in which case the many thousand dollars' worth of plates of denominational books would have been destroyed; but it was later ascertained that the doors had been shut by some young men after the fire began. . . .

At one time the West Building was in considerable danger from the intense heat. I was there a very few minutes after the fire began. And at once I began removing everything in the General Conference office and putting them in the vault on our floor. I first tried to turn on the electric lights, but found that I could

241

not do so. Elder Daniells was sitting in his room at the time the fire broke out, talking with Elder Evans, the President of the Review and Herald Co., and the first thing they noticed that anything was wrong was that the electric lights went out, and as they did not come on again, they thought something might be the matter, and upon looking out of the window, discovered that there was a fire, and they at once rushed over, and even then they could not get inside of the building on account of the smoke and stifling heat. After taking almost everything out of our desks and putting them in the vault, I went out on the roof over the counting room, and watched the cornices to see if that building was going to burn. Finally, just before the walls of the east building fell, the heat was very intense so that my clothes almost smoked, I noticed the blue smoke begin to start from the roof, and called to some men below to turn on a stream of water, which they did. . . .

There is not a particle of doubt but that the Review and Herald will never again be rebuilt as formerly. If anything is done here, it will be on only a small scale. After the next General Conference, which will be held in Oakland, March 27 to April 13, the General Conference will doubtless be removed permanently to New York City, and it is thought probably that some of the printing that has been done here may be removed to the East and done there where it is near to those populous centers. [H. E. Rogers letter to All The Folks, January 4, 1903. Xerox copy held by the compiler.]

Although occurring two decades later, a third heavy blow fell at Battle Creek in 1922 when fire consumed the Tabernacle. Michigan Conference president, J. F. Piper, and the Tabernacle pastor, A. E. Serns, told "Review" readers about it:

242

Fires in Battle Creek

Sabbath night, Jan. 7, 1922, . . . fire was discovered in the basement of the Tabernacle. Its origin is unknown. Several alarms were immediately turned in, and the fire department was soon there. There was a large volume of smoke pouring from the basement windows, and it soon reached the auditorium and vestries of the building. This prohibited the firemen and friends from taking anything from the burning structure.

Less than an hour before the fire was discovered, the janitor had been in the basement attending to necessary duties, and at the time there was no indication of anything wrong about the building. . . .

At one time during its early stage the firemen thought they had the fire under control; but the flames seemed to burst forth suddenly throughout the entire structure, and in two hours after the discovery of the fire it was a mass of ruins. [J. F. Piper, *Review and Herald,* January 26, 1922, p. 4.]

Almost every one who knew that building, feels its loss keenly. Many of the old pioneers would walk up to the smoldering ruins, and with tears flowing freely, mourn like Israel of old when the temple was destroyed. [Arthur E. Serns, *Review and Herald,* January 26, 1922, p. 5.]

The first two fires shook up the Battle Creek church members. Many took them as a divine sign that they should leave the Michigan city. The publishing house and the General Conference headquarters moved to Washington, D.C. Others, though, felt they should remain. Dr. Kellogg determined to remain and rebuild the sanitarium on "this spot, rendered dear and sacred by more than a third of a century's experiences and memories." He told Adventist leaders:

Several brethren from different parts of the field were in Battle Creek last week, in response to a call

243

for a council to consider various questions relating to the rebuilding of the Sanitarium. . . .

It will not be possible in our limited space to give more than a brief statement of the results of the council. In view of the attitude of the people of Battle Creek toward the Sanitarium and its work, as set forth in another article in this issue, the council advised that the new building should be erected in this city. It was recommended that the East Hall, formerly occupied as a nurses' dormitory, should hereafter be used for patients, and that only one building be built in place of the two which were burned; and that this building should be five stories in height, not to exceed 450 feet in length, and that it should be constructed of stone, brick, marble, iron, steel, and cement. ["A Council Meeting," *Review and Herald,* March 25, 1902, p. 192.]

(Of Battle Creek wishes and of a denominational committee decision): Within a few days [of the fire], messages began flowing in from all parts of the United States, some advising the erection of the new building in another place, but the majority advising to rebuild in Battle Creek, the very name seeming to be dear to multitudes who had here found restoration to health, and knowledge whereby to maintain health and usefulness.

The citizens of Battle Creek took the matter in hand with great earnestness. . . .

[But] the [Sanitarium] board still [after five weeks] felt themselves wholly incompetent for the task of deciding whether or not the Sanitarium building should be reconstructed, and if so, where; and not wishing to take the responsibility of settling this important question in which many thousands are interested, a council of the General Conference officers and Union Conference presidents was called. These brethren convened Monday, March 24, and spent nearly a week in the consideration of this and other matters pertaining to the Sanitarium and its work. The counsel of these brethren was greatly appreciated by the board of managers, and it is proper to say that the steps which have been taken looking toward the erection of the Sanitarium in Battle Creek were by the unanimous advice and recommendation of these brethren and the members of the Medical Missionary Board, as well as the Sanitarium management. . . .

The managers have thought it wise to construct a building which would furnish about three hundred moderate-sized sleeping rooms. If means were sufficient, large, airy rooms would be provided, but the board have felt the necessity of reducing the building to the smallest size possible, hoping that they may be able to furnish accommodations for approximately half of those who come from abroad for treatment. . . .

The building must be severely plain, but dignified, and beautiful in lines and proportions, but without artificial decoration. Even the roof will be utilized as an exercise ground, being made flat for this purpose. A fuller description will be published later, when the plans are more fully perfected.

It is expected that the cost of the new building will be less than the cost of the building which burned, or at least no more, but the construction will be far more substantial and enduring. Brick, iron, stone, and cement will be the materials used, so that the building will be absolutely fireproof. The building will look much larger than the old structure, through the avoidance of wings, the whole structure being arranged in one long building, running north and south, thus furnishing an equal supply of light and air to each room. [J. H. Kellogg, *Review and Herald,* April 8, 1902, pp. 21-23.]

Ellen White did not remain silent about the trends at Battle Creek. In fact, she wrote much both before and after the 1902 fires. In November, 1901, she read a manuscript before the managers of the Review and Herald:

> I feel a terror of soul as I see to what a pass our publishing house has come. The presses in the Lord's institution have been printing soul-destroying theories of Romanism and other mysteries of iniquity. The office must be purged of this objectionable matter. I have a testimony from the Lord for those who have placed such matter in the hands of the workers. God holds you accountable. . . .
>
> He has a controversy with the managers of the publishing house. I have been almost afraid to open the *Review,* fearing to see that God has cleansed the publishing house *by fire.* [Ellen G. White, *Testimonies,* Vol. 8, pp. 91, 92. Italics supplied.]

> To-day I received a letter from Elder Daniells regarding the destruction of the Review Office by fire. I feel very sad as I consider the great loss to the cause. I know that this must be a very trying time for the brethren in charge of the work and for the employees of the office. I am afflicted with all who are afflicted. But I was not surprised by the sad news; for in the visions of the night I have seen an angel standing with a sword as of fire stretched over Battle Creek. Once, in the daytime, while my pen was in my hand, I lost consciousness, and it seemed as if this sword of flame were turning first in one direction and then in another. Disaster seemed to follow disaster, because God was dishonored by the devising of men to exalt and glorify themselves. . . .
>
> It has been asked if I have any advice to give. I have already given the advice that God has given me, hoping to prevent the falling of the fiery sword that was hanging over Battle Creek. Now that which I

246

dreaded has come,—the news of the burning of the
Review and Herald building. When this news came, I
felt no surprise, and I had no words to speak. What I
have had to say from time to time in warnings has
had no effect, except to harden those who heard; and
now I can only say, I am so sorry, so very sorry, that it
was necessary for this stroke to come. [Ellen G.
White, *Testimonies,* Vol. 8, pp. 97, 99.]

**In September, 1903, to those who would rebuild at Battle
Creek, she warned:**

The Lord permitted fire to consume the principal
buildings of the Review and Herald and the
Sanitarium, and thus removed the greatest objection
urged against moving out of Battle Creek. It was his
design that instead of rebuilding the one large
Sanitarium, our people should make plants in several
places. [Ellen G. White, *Special Testimonies,* Series B,
No. 6, p. 53.]

To Kellogg, she declared in 1904:

The Battle Creek Sanitarium was [re]erected
against the expressed will of God. Presidents of
Conferences and others were consulted, it is true, and
they assented to the plans presented, because they did
not desire to differ with the leader of the medical
work when they could possibly agree with him. And
besides, they had not received all the messages that
he had received. Those who had not seen the
testimonies that the leaders in the medical work had
seen, were not responsible for what they did not know.
. . .

When the Lord swept the large Sanitarium out of
the way at Battle Creek he did not design it should
ever be built there again. But in their blindness men

247

went ahead and rebuilt the institution where it now
[1904] stands. . . .

God would not have let the fire go through our
institutions in Battle Creek without a reason. Are you
going to pass by the providence of God without finding
out what it means? God wants us to study into this
matter, and to build upon a foundation in which all
can have the utmost confidence. He wants the
interests started to be conducted in such a way that
his people can invest their means in them with the
assurance that they are a part of his work. [Ellen G.
White, *Special Testimonies,* Series B, No. 6, pp. 25, 26,
33.]

**Among her final communications to the dissident medical
leaders was a lamentation over their willfulness:**

The burning of these two institutions was verily a
judgment from God. And yet men who have been
given wonderful advantages and opportunities, and
who are capable of understanding the dealings of God
with His people of old, have stood up to defy, as it
were, the Holy One of Israel, and to make of none
effect the working of God's providence in His dealings
with His people. . . . Some are filled with a wicked
spirit of resistance and opposition, and this spirit they
will continue to cherish till the bitter, bitter end.
[Ellen G. White, *Special Testimonies,* Series B, No. 7,
p. 9.]

for further reading:

Powell, Horace B., *The Original Has This Signature —W. K. Kellogg* (1956), pp. 56-68.

* Schwarz, Richard W., "John Harvey Kellogg: American Health Reformer" (PhD dissertation, University of Michigan, 1956), 504 pages.

*_____, *John Harvey Kellogg, M.D.* (1970), 256 pages.

Spalding, Arthur W., *Origin and History of Seventh-day Adventists,* Vol. 3, chap. 8.

White, Ellen G., *Testimonies for the Church,* Vol. 8, Section 2.

Pantheism

Though Dr. Kellogg steadily assumed greater and greater control of Battle Creek Sanitarium, as long as it continued to employ church members, the denomination granted him some degree of toleration. But when he began advocating pantheistic theories, many Adventists felt that he had gone too far. For them he no longer was a white-suited knight championing healthful living.

Kellogg appears to have held some kind of pantheistic ideas as early as 1873, about the time he attended Dr. Russell T. Trall's Hygieo-Therapeutic Institute in New Jersey * and moved toward the "Soul Identity" theory which conceived of the body and soul as two "units." Mrs. White vigorously rejected his additional theory of divine immanence.

Anyone who attempts to investigate the origin of pantheism among Seventh-day Adventists must take into account the following interview between Mrs. White and Dr. Kellogg:

> When Dr. Kellogg receives the messages of warning given during the past twenty years; when he is sincerely converted; when he acts as a consistent, level-headed Christian worker; when his energies are devoted to carrying forward medical missionary work

---

* See Schwarz, R. W., "John Harvey Kellogg: American Health Reformer," pp. 24, 388.

after the methods and in the Spirit of Christ; when he bears a testimony that has in it no signs of double meaning or of misconstruction of the light God has given, then we may have confidence that he is following the light. . . .

This subject has been kept before me for the past twenty years, yea, for more than twenty years. Before my husband's death, Dr. Kellogg came to my room to tell me that he had great light. He sat down and told me what it was. It was similar to some of the views that he has presented in "Living Temple." I said, "Those theories are wrong. I have met them before. I had to meet them when I first began to travel." . . .

Ministers and people were deceived by these sophistries. They lead to making God a nonentity and Christ a nonentity. We are to rebuke these theories in the name of the Lord.

As I talked about these things, laying the whole matter before Dr. Kellogg, and showing him what the outcome of receiving these theories would be, he seemed to be dazed. I said, "Never teach such theories in our institutions; do not present them to the people." ["Talk Given by Mrs. E. G. White at General Conference of Seventh-day Adventists, Washington, D.C., 1905." MS-70-05, White Estate.]

Around 1895, however, Dr. Kellogg ended his silence on his theory. A. H. Lewis, editor of the Seventh Day Baptist "Sabbath Recorder," came to Battle Creek as a patient, and he was a guest in Kellogg's home. (The doctor's wife, Ella Eaton Kellogg, was also a Seventh Day Baptist.) Dr. Sanford Edwards, who knew Lewis well, witnessed what happened after Lewis's arrival:

One day a white bearded gentleman came in [to my classroom at Battle Creek College] and took a seat with the class. It was A. H. Lewis, D.D., LL.D., the editor of the Sabbath Recorder, church paper of the

S. D. Baptists. He and his wife were patients at the Sanitarium. I had heard him preach at the Tabernacle, so recognized him. He motioned me to go on with my class as he just wanted to listen. At first I was scared, but a little prayer settled that, and I had the most freedom ever, and the spirit was there. After the class Dr. Lewis came over and shook hands and said, "You gave a wonderful talk to your class. Is this not an unusual approach to a scientific subject like physiology? Where did you get it?" My answer was: "On my knees in the dark room." He tho[ugh]t a minute and then said, "If more of us got our sermons in the same way, we would be better preachers." Then he began a discussion which is why all the above detail. Dr. Lewis asked: "Dr do you not think that you may be stretching a point, in emphasizing the exact features of God's being? He is a spirit. You talk of His hands, His feet and eyes and ears and tongue just like He were a physical being. God is a presence, an essence, He is everywhere; in the trees, in the flowers, the food we eat. Are you not in danger of getting too narrow a view of God?"

After a minute's thought, I answered: "Admitting for the time being what you have said about God, to me He has hands; He holds my hand. He has feet; I walk in His footsteps. He has ears; He hears my prayers. He has eyes; He sees my sins and forgives them, my weakness and gives me strength, my heart yearning and gives me grace. God is a person to me." The discussion ended with my having learned where Dr. Kellogg and George Fifield and W. W. Prescott and M. Bessie DeGraw and E. J. Waggoner got some, if not much of their Pantheism. Dr. Lewis was once Mrs. Kellogg's pastor and President of Alfred University where she got her degree. His paper, the Sabbath Recorder, was steeped in Pantheism. It came regularly to the Kellogg home. [Sanford P. S. Edwards letter to the compiler, April 16, 1956.]

Pantheism

Kellogg attempted to incorporate his ideas in his book "The Living Temple," which he intended to sell to raise funds to rebuild the Sanitarium. Sample paragraphs from "The Living Temple" particularly offensive to the theologians of the church follow below:

There is a clear, complete, satisfactory explanation of the most subtle, the most marvelous phenomena of nature,—namely, an infinite Intelligence working out its purposes. God is the explanation of nature,—not a God outside of nature, but in nature, manifesting himself through and in all the objects, movements, and varied phenomena of the universe. . . .

Suppose now we have a boot before us,—not an ordinary boot, but a living boot, and as we look at it, we see little boots crowding out at the seams, pushing out at the toes, dropping off at the heels, and leaping out at the top,—scores, hundreds, thousands of boots, a swarm of boots continually issuing from our living boot,—would we not be compelled to say, "There is a shoemaker in the boot"? So there is present in the tree a power which creates and maintains it, a tree-maker in the tree, a flower-maker in the flower,—a divine architect who understands every law of proportion, an infinite artist who possesses a limitless power of expression in color and form; there is, in all the world about us, an infinite, divine, though invisible Presence, to which the unenlightened may be blind, but which is ever declaring itself by its ceaseless, beneficent activity. . . .

But the divine Artist not only made man in his own likeness, so that he might reflect in his form and outward appearance the divine symmetry and beauty of the thought of the Master Artist, but after having made him, or in the act of forming him, God actually entered into the product of his creative skill, so that it might not only outwardly reflect the divine conception, but that it might think divinely, and act

253

divinely, and thus fittingly constitute the masterpiece of creative skill. . . .

It is important that we should recognize the fact that God creates every man. We often fall into error by a careless or superficial use of terms,—we say that "nature does this or that," forgetting that nature is not a creator. What we call "nature" is simply the picture of divine activity which we see spread out about us in the universe. God is not behind nature nor above nature; he is in nature,—nature is the visible expression of his power. [John H. Kellogg, *The Living Temple* (Battle Creek: Good Health Publishing Co., 1903), pp. 28, 29, 40.]

Ellen White and William A. Spicer and others perceived theological heresy in "The Living Temple," and so strong was the protest against it that the denomination refused to sell it. Spicer, recently returned from mission service in India, quickly recognized that such concepts would mar the personality of God in SDA thought. Excerpts from his pen reveal his apprehension:

Sitting down with no thought that there could be any difference of a really controversial nature, and with the heartiest of friendly feelings, personally, I was at once in the midst of a discussion of the most controversial questions [with Dr. Kellogg]. Instead of things in the book being inadvertently overdrawn because of employment of scientific terms, unfamiliar to most of us, I learned that the teaching was conservatively stated in the book [*The Living Temple*]; that the teaching was really of intent to signify that God was in the things of nature. "Where is God?" I was asked. I would naturally say, He is in heaven; there the Bible pictures the throne of God, all the heavenly beings at His command as messengers between heaven and earth. But I was told that God was in the grass and plants and in the trees (with

motions to the grass and trees about us, as we sat on
the open veranda). Where is heaven? I was asked. I
had my idea of the center of the universe, with heaven
and the throne of God in the midst, but disclaimed
any attempt to fix the center of the universe
astronomically. But I was urged to understand that
heaven is where God is, and God is everywhere in the
grass, in the trees, in all creation. There was no place
in this scheme of things for angels going between
heaven and earth, for heaven was here and
everywhere. The cleansing of the sanctuary that we
taught about was not something in a far-away
heaven. The sin is here (the hand pointing to the
heart), and here is the sanctuary to be cleansed. To
think of God as having a form in the image of which
man was made, was said to be idolatry.

By any understanding I had of language, I was
listening to the ideas of the pantheistic philosophy
that I had met with in India. In fact, I was told that
pure pantheism, as the early teachers conceived it,
was indeed right—God was in the things of nature. A
personality was in every blade of grass and in every
plant.

Trying to get the import of it all, it seemed to me
these ideas set all earth and heaven and God swirling
away into mist. There was in it no objective unity to
lay hold of. With scripture terms and Christian ideas
interwoven, it seemed the old doctrine of the
Hindus—all nature a very part of Brahma, and
Brahma the whole.

Over against this mysticism I found it good to let
my mind lay hold of the concrete picture of scripture
and of the Spirit of prophecy. I urged that there is a
place called heaven; and there God's throne is, and
there the personal God is as He in person is not in all
places. There is the Garden of Eden, translated to
heaven before the Flood, with trees that once grew on
earth, as real and tangible in heaven as when they

grew rooted in the soil of Eden on earth. The redeemed, in immortal flesh, can walk in the midst of the garden, and go up to the throne and see the Father's face, and they can go from the throne down through the garden. The pictures of little "Early Writings" [by Ellen White], with their concrete descriptions of the verities of heaven and the New Jerusalem, and the scenes as the redeemed first enter there were a blessing to me during that interview.

As I came away, I knew well enough that there was nothing of the Advent message that I could fit into such a philosophy. As I had listened, one light after another of the message seemed to be put out. Religious teaching that to me was fundamental was set aside. [William A. Spicer, "How the Spirit of Prophecy Met a Crisis," pp. 18, 19. Copy held by the compiler.]

Between meetings at the General Conference sessions at Oakland, California, in 1903, Ellet J. Waggoner argued for pantheism, but Ellen White worked to counteract it. Privately she enlisted two doctors, Sanford P. S. Edwards and David Paulson, to talk to their friend Dr. Kellogg.

Immediately following the Oakland Conference, Edwards and Paulson went to Ellen White's Elmshaven home, where she charged them to save Kellogg from pantheism if possible. Edwards writes of her anxiety:

We were taken up to the study and Mother [White] met us with a smile and after we were seated she started on a most interesting story about the events in her life and our lives with which she was conversant. For an hour she entertained us but not a word about "the message." Finally she turned to me and said: "I

256

presume you brethren are wondering about those
[executive] meetings in Oakland. I had a message, but
it was not God's time or place. He took it away from
me and only left my Bible to read from. I love Doctor
Kellogg. He may be lost. I hope and pray not. If he is
lost let him go with you brethren standing by with
your hands on his shoulders trying to save him." She
then sweetly dismissed us, and Doctor Paulson and I
walked up the hill arm in arm: we had a mission and
a commission. We tried to carry it out. We made some
mistakes in our methods. Sister White reproved us.
We tried again. I have her letters of reproof and
commendation. Very precious! . . .

The last time I met Doctor Kellogg, was at a
dinner in the Loma Linda Sanitarium dining room. A
group of us gathered around him. There was George
Thomason, D. D. Comstock, Frank Abbott, Ben Colver
and myself, all doctor friends. We said in parting:
"Are you not coming [towards heaven] with us?" He
answered after a minute of thought, "Perhaps I am
nearer with you than you know." And so he was left
with God, with our hands on his shoulders. [Sanford
P. S. Edwards letter to Francis D. Nichol, July 2,
1955. A copy supplied by S. P. S. Edwards to the
compiler.]

**The General Conference Autumn Council of 1903, convened
in Washington, D.C., quickly confronted Kellogg's theories.
President Arthur Daniells had no effective weapon against
them immediately at hand except for dogged determination.
Daniells describes the confrontation:**

The crisis came in the month of October, 1903. The
headquarters of our denominational work had been
moved from Battle Creek to Takoma Park. We had
appointed a council of our leading workers, and were
hoping to lay broad plans for advance moves. But our
proposed plans were interrupted when a group of

about ten men came to our meeting and introduced points of controversy, which soon focused in a discussion of the teachings to be found in the book to which we have referred, "The Living Temple." It was a painful session to us all.

One evening a prominent worker accompanied me from the meeting to my home. He believed the new views, and was doing all in his power to uphold and to circulate the book which was the cause of our controversy. As we stood under a street lamp on the corner near my home, he said to me, "You are making the mistake of your life. After all this turmoil, some of these days you will wake up to find yourself rolled in the dust, and another will be leading the forces."

To this I replied: "I do not believe your prophecy. At any rate, I would rather be rolled in the dust doing what I believe in my soul to be right than to walk with the princes, doing what my conscience tells me is wrong."

We parted and, with a heavy heart, I entered the house. There I found a group of people who were very happy. One of them said: "Deliverance has come! Here are two messages from Mrs. White."

No one can imagine the eagerness with which I read the documents that had come in the mail while we were in the midst of our discussions. There was a most positive testimony regarding the dangerous errors that were taught in "The Living Temple."

The timeliness of this testimony will be appreciated the more by quoting from two of the documents received. In one of them, we read concerning the book in question:

"Be careful how you sustain the sentiments of this book regarding the personality of God. As the Lord presents matters to me, these sentiments do not bear the endorsement of God. They are a snare that the enemy has prepared for these last days. . . .

"The track of truth lies close beside the track of

error, and both tracks may seem to be one to minds which are not worked by the Holy Spirit, and which, therefore, are not quick to discern the difference between truth and error. . . .

"In the visions of the night this matter was clearly presented to me before a large number. One of authority was speaking. . . . The speaker held up 'Living Temple,' saying, 'In this book there are statements that the writer himself does not comprehend. Many things are stated in a vague, undefined way. Statements are made in such a way that nothing is sure. And this is not the only production of the kind that will be urged upon the people. Fanciful views will be presented to many minds. What we need to know at this time is, What is the truth that will enable us to win the salvation of our souls?' "—E. G. White Letter 211, 1903.

In another of the documents received during this conference occurred this solemn charge:

"After taking your position firmly, wisely, cautiously, make not one concession on any point concerning which God has plainly spoken. Be as calm as a summer evening; but as fixed as the everlasting hills. By conceding, you would be selling our whole cause into the hands of the enemy. The cause of God is not to be traded away."—E. G. White Letter 216, 1903.

The next morning we assembled again for our council. After prayer, I arose and told the brethren that we had received two very important messages from Mrs. White. This aroused the attention of all, and they sat in thoughtful silence while I read the documents.

It would be impossible to find language to state as clearly and as forcefully as I wish I might all the facts relating to the reception, presentation, and influence of these testimonies, and others received during that council. Never had I seen such signal evidences of the

Windows

leadership of an all-wise Being as in connection with
these experiences. Only the divine mind could have
foreseen our condition and our needs, and have sent
us the exact help we needed at precisely the right
moment. We had come to the parting of the ways. It
was evident that we were facing a complete division of
leading men, and soon the people would have been
called upon to choose sides.

As I read to the assembly statement after
statement setting forth the falsity of the teachings in
the book, "The Living Temple," many loud "Amens"
broke forth, and tears flowed freely. From that hour
light came into the council, and the presence of God
was clearly felt through the day. When I had finished
reading, the brethren immediately began to express
their gratitude to God for this clear voice that had
spoken to us. So precisely did these messages point
out the situation that everyone who spoke at all was
obliged to say that it was the voice of God speaking to
us. Before the council closed, the author of the book
stated that he would take it from the market. [Arthur
Grosvenor Daniells, *The Abiding Gift of Prophecy*
(1936), pp. 336-339.]

Dr. Kellogg drifted so far theologically that his former
denomination could not always ignore him. For instance,
because the Battle Creek Sanitarium and Hospital offered
internships to young SDA doctors, Dr. Percy T. Magan,
president of the College of Medical Evangelists in California, believed it necessary to tell Kellogg that the relationship must end.

How Magan faced Kellogg:

Dr. Magan: "Doctor, we do not want, and I
especially do not want, that certain issues between us

Pantheism

shall in any sense be clouded or obscured, and it is
these things [the termination of internships] which I
am anxious in as kindly and brotherly way as possible
to make clear to you. You of course know, doctor, that
you hold certain views in regard to the Bible, and you
express these views very frankly to all and sundry
when it may seem proper to you so to do. You hold the
view that our Lord and Saviour Jesus Christ was not
the divine son of God; that His birth was the result of
ordinary physical relations between Joseph and Mary,
and that he was not born by the direct influence of the
Spirit of God upon Mary's life. You have told me this
a number of times. Whether you really believe it in
your heart or not I have never been able to settle, but
certainly it is that you talk it. Again, you have over
and over expressed to me certain ideas in regard to
the Book of Job, that it is in some respects a very
beautiful but a very tragic poem, but that the alleged
facts related therein never really happened at all. . . .
Again, doctor, you have frequently put various
questions to me which to my mind are altogether
irreverent relative to the personal appearance of the
Deity—His eyes, His form, the appearance of His face,
etc., etc. . . .

"It hurts me to say this to you, but I cannot do
otherwise. I would not be true to myself or to my trust
if I were not perfectly frank. We have the deepest
respect for the health work that you are doing, for the
manner in which you have labored untiringly by day
and night through a long series of years to
promulgate better living. But as long as your views
upon the work of God and ours are so far apart we
cannot enter reciprocal relationships. This would not
be right."

Dr. Kellogg: "Well, Magan, do you really think
that I am around buttonholing people and teaching
them these things? Now I will tell you what I will do.
I will give you leave to go to any of our young people

here in the sanitarium, or any of the older people, and ask them if I ever teach them such things. You have my permission to question them and quiz them any way you want. I will be glad to have you do this."

Dr. Magan: "No, doctor, I have no intention of doing that. . . . I felt I wanted to say the things which I have already spoken to you and in the presence of these men for whom I have the deepest respect. I wanted to have a frank and brotherly talk with you about them."

Dr. Kellogg: "Well, I do not think I teach those things very much. I am sure I do not go around trying to upset people's belief and faith in the Bible. I have no desire to do this, no matter what I may think myself. But, after all, the Bible traces the genealogy of Christ and winds it up in Joseph. What do you do with that?"

Dr. Magan: "I have not come here, doctor, to enter into any theological controversy with you." . . .

Dr. Kellogg: "Well, I think you are all wrong. I do not think you understand these things correctly, and in any event I do not think that I teach these things in a way to upset the faith of any."

Dr. [B. N.] Colver [of the sanitarium staff]: "Now, doctor, I want to talk to you. There is not a man who has been connected with you for a number of years in the past who does not know that you are a rank evolutionist. You have stuffed the college across the road with teachers of evolution. You spend hours over there talking evolution yourself. God only knows what a terrible thing this is for the sanitarium, but as far as the college is concerned I do not suppose we can help ourselves. Nevertheless, to my mind it is a bad, bad business. Again, doctor, you do teach the things that Magan has charged you with teaching. You not only teach them to a few, but you teach them to everybody that you can get to listen to you, and you teach them by the hour." . . .

262

Pantheism

Dr. Kellogg: "Let me ask you a question, Colver."

Dr. Colver: "No, doctor, not yet. I want to say some more. I firmly believe that you are wrecking and ruining the Battle Creek Sanitarium with your doctrines. Many of our doctors have already given up the faith of their fathers and you are more the cause of this than any other one agency. Because of this these men are now giving up our health reform doctrines, and I see nothing but woe and sadness ahead of us if this kind of thing goes on much longer."

. . .

Mr. [M. W.] Wentworth [of the sanitarium staff]: "Now, doctor, you know that I do not make any profession of Christianity, but I want to tell you that I believe Dr. Magan is absolutely right and you are altogether wrong. You have wrecked the faith of a number of our people here, and if this thing keeps up it will only be a few short years until the Battle Creek Sanitarium will be the Battle Creek Sanitarium no more. It will be a worldly hospital. I believe with all my heart that Seventh-day Adventists started this place and they have prior rights here." . . .

Dr. Kellogg: "Magan, let me ask you a question. Do you teach the principles of health which you are teaching, I will grant very faithfully and efficiently, do you teach these because Ellen G. White told them to you?"

Dr. Magan: "I must tell you, I do not understand all these things the way you do from a scientific standpoint, and much of my teaching is based upon the word of God and the spirit of prophecy rather than upon scientific demonstration."

Dr. Kellogg: "Then, Magan, I am very sorry that it becomes necessary for me to tell you that I have a very poor regard for your intellectual capacity and ability. I cannot understand how a man whom I have always thought to have the intelligence which I have attributed to you could do the way you say you do."

263

Dr. Magan: "That is all right with me, John. Your statement does not worry me a particle, and now I must tell you something. If I am an imbecile or a moron, or both, as you intimate, if I am a creature of low intellectual capacity because of my faith and belief in the word of God and the spirit of prophecy, there are two men who are responsible for my present adumbrated condition. One of these is now dead and gone, the one whose name you recently mentioned— S. N. Haskell. It was my privilege to spend quite a period of time with him when I was a lad in this work. I loved him very dearly and respected him very much, and I have always felt, and ever shall feel, that S. N. Haskell had deeper spiritual insight into the meaning of what we term the spirit of prophecy than any other man who ever lived and wrought and walked amongst us. His teachings made a lasting impression upon my mind. The other man who is responsible for my being a moron and an imbecile is a little bustling fellow in a white suit who sits right in front of me at the present time, you, John Harvey Kellogg. I well remember the day when you used to stand on top of a table in the old gymnasium with tears streaming down your face, telling the helpers, of whom I was one, what a wonderful thing God's gift to this people through Ellen G. White was. I have heard you read from her writings by the hour and talk in a most earnest and subdued way about the wonderful spiritual insight that she had and how much it all meant to you. In an earlier day you made deep impressions upon my life."
. . .

Dr. Kellogg: "Well, Magan, whenever I made those statements which you referred to I always qualified them."

Dr. Colver: "No, Dr. Kellogg, you did not always qualify them. You did not qualify them at all. You believed them with all your heart, and there are scores of people who can rise up to witness to that."

264

Pantheism

Dr. Kellogg: "At any rate, Magan, if I should tell the brethren all I know about you you would be in a pretty bad way."

Dr. Magan: "Let me tell you something, John, 'the brethren' know a long way more about me than you do. They have known me intimately now for forty-five years." . . .

The next morning as I was crossing the [sanitarium] lobby to get into Dr. Kretchmar's car and go down to the station and take my train I met Dr. Kellogg. He put his arm around me and led me into his office and seemed very broken and very sad. He told me he felt very badly the way he talked to me the day before and that he would never forget as long as he lived all the sacrifice which he knew I had made in his behalf. It filled me with sadness and pity to hear the poor old man talk. His own chief officials taking sides against him; he realizing that many of his leading doctors have no use for the principles of health for which he has given his life, and the end so soon to close upon him. I could not help but put my arm around him and tell him how broken-hearted I felt over the entire situation, but that I could do no different than I had done. He followed me to the door, got into Kretchmar's car, rode down as far as Champion Street hatless and overcoatless, and then walked back in the rain to the sanitarium, to me a sad spectacle of one who has been very dear to the heart of God and who has wandered very far away. [Percy T. Magan letter to W. A. Spicer, August 6, 1928. Copy held by the compiler.]

If the news media at Battle Creek were knowledgeable about Dr. John Harvey Kellogg's religious ideas at his death in 1943, then his theology had changed even more. The following item appeared at the time of his funeral:

On July 2, 1935, Dr. Kellogg discussed with me

265

some matters of religion, [Pastor Carleton B.] Miller [of the First Congregational Church of Battle Creek] said. The occasion will always remain as a celebrated one to me because of what he said and the way he put it.

At that time he was seriously in doubt as to the immortality of the soul, but as days followed he came to formulate a most beautiful conviction and expression of the golden hope of Christianity. My only reason for quoting him is that his religious faith can help those seeking spiritual light as his biologic creed has brought so many to physical well-being.

"I am formulating a scientific basis for faith," said Dr. Kellogg. "Take prayer. Prayer is a cry for help instinctive to all life. We call for help when we are at the end of our rope. There would be no thirst if there were no water; no hunger if no food. A scientific experiment is a prayer. Ideas, born of silence and concentration, by entering one's inner chamber, are also answers to prayer."

Thus we see how eagerly he followed where truth might lead. Prayer, more than words and lip service, is the soul's sincere desire, the conscious and sub-conscious appeal to the Divine.

Then Dr. Kellogg said: "We have three lives. The somatic self where the cells die sooner or later; the germ self where the cells continue as long as the race exists, and the spirit self. Our personality has voluntary will such as starts muscle action, and involuntary will or a pacemaker. The spirit is the heart, but there is no consciousness apart from the physiological."

I suggested that this does not exclude the fact or truth that spirit abides eternally, that personality survives. The Divine Intelligence is able to accomplish this no less than other miracles and mysteries. Tell me, what question embraces one of the great physical miracles and mysteries? Quick as a

266

flash and with a sparkle in his eye and a joyous smile on his face, Dr. Kellogg replied: "Why doesn't the stomach digest itself? By the same Truth by which God does not permit death to dissolve or destroy the spirit."

Dr. Kellogg has said that "death is not the destruction of life." He added that in Aramaic, "surrender" has the meaning of "peace." "My own peace I give unto you," means "I surrender to you."

In that surrender John Harvey Kellogg has found peace, freedom and victory. ["Funeral Is Held for Dr. Kellogg," *The Battle Creek Enquirer and News,* December 15, 1943, p. 1.]

for further reading:

Reed, Leclare E., "The Concept of God Expressed in the Writings of J. H. Kellogg" (Term paper, SDA Theological Seminary, 1942).

* Schwarz, Richard W., "John Harvey Kellogg: American Health Reformer" (PhD dissertation, University of Michigan, 1956), 504 pages.

* _____, *John Harvey Kellogg, M.D.* (1970), 256 pages.

Spalding, Arthur W., *Origin and History of Seventh-day Adventists,* Vol. 3, chap. 8.

White, Ellen G., *Special Testimonies,* Series B.

* _____, *Testimonies for the Church,* Vol. 8, Section 5.

Moving Out
of Battle Creek

The descendants of the Adventists who had come so hopefully to Battle Creek in the 1850's and 1860's mournfully departed in 1903. As early as 1899, President E. A. Sutherland had scouted the Berrien Springs, Michigan, area with the hope of relocating Battle Creek College there. At a favorable moment in the General Conference of 1901 Ellen White advised moving to a farm. On March 12, constituents, delegates, and congregation voted unanimously to take the college away.

During the next two days, however, many Battle Creek residents became so vocal in opposition to the transfer that to squelch the opposition, Mrs. White insisted:

> God wants the school to be taken out of Battle Creek. Let us take away the excuse which has been made for families to come into Battle Creek. . . .
> Some may be stirred about the transfer of the school from Battle Creek. But they need not be. This move is in accordance with God's design for the school before the institution was established. But men could not see how this could be done. There were so many who said that the school must be in Battle Creek. Now we say that it must be somewhere else. The best thing that can be done is to dispose of the school's buildings here as soon as possible. Begin at once to look for a place where the school can be conducted on right lines. God wants us to place our children where

they will not see and hear that which they should not see or hear. God wants his church to take up the stones, to remove the rubbish, to clear the highway for the coming of the Lord. He wants them to prepare to meet their God. [Ellen G. White, *The General Conference Daily Bulletin,* 1901, p. 216.]

[Battle Creek College, transferred to Berrien Springs in 1901 in advance of the conflagrations, became Emmanuel Missionary College, and later Andrews University.]

Although fire did not consume the General Conference building at Battle Creek, President Daniells and his colleagues determined to move denominational headquarters and the Review and Herald to another location. The 1903 General Conference session delegates agreed, and suggested some site in the Atlantic states. Denominational leaders prepared progress reports of the search for the "Review" to publish:

E. R. Palmer:

From time to time since the burning of the Review and Herald printing office, the Lord has spoken [through Ellen White] to this people in words that could not be misunderstood, directing that the General Conference, Mission Board, and Review and Herald publishing work be removed from Battle Creek. The General Conference in session voted that this should be done; the General Conference Committee resolved to undertake the work; and the stockholders of the Review and Herald, by a strong majority, agreed to the recommendations made by the General Conference so far as they pertained to the moving of the Review and Herald Publishing Association.

A committee was appointed to select the new location, and this committee entered upon its work.

269

Windows

The first efforts were not successful, and the committee returned to Battle Creek without having selected a place. Then the good Lord took this important matter into his own hands, and directed that the general offices be moved to Washington, D. C. Thus the work of the locating committee was simplified to the point of obedience. . . .

The packing was begun Thursday morning, July 30; the carters began moving the goods Monday morning, August 3; and the work was completed Wednesday evening, August 5. Four large cars had been filled with the furniture, fittings, libraries, and supplies of the General Conference, Mission Board, the Review and Herald and *Instructor,* and the personal effects from twelve private houses. The way-bills showed thirty-six tons of goods. The task was a heavy one, but it was accomplished without the slightest delay or mishap; and when the work was done, and the last car was on its way, we fervently thanked God, and took courage. [E. R. Palmer, *Review and Herald,* August 20, 1903, p. 14.]

A. G. Daniells:

Furthermore, we are glad to tell our people that we have met with a warm welcome in Washington. The *Post* speaks of our coming here as one of the most significant and important events of the year. The people of Takoma Park show great friendliness. Our brethren and sisters in Washington have met us at the trains and taken us to their homes, until we could get settled in our own homes. After presenting to our people in Battle Creek the communications we had received from the Lord's servant [E. G. White], and the blessed experiences we had in our efforts to find a location in harmony with the Testimonies, a large proportion of the Tabernacle congregation manifested undoubted confidence in the move, and bade us

270

Moving Out of Battle Creek

farewell with their best wishes and earnest prayers for great blessings. It was hard for many to see the offices go, but they manifested a kind Christian spirit. We shall not forget these dear souls. [A. G. Daniells, *Review and Herald,* August 20, 1903, p. 6.]

In one of the communications that came from Sister White while we were looking for a location for our headquarters in the East, the statement was made that although there was opposition to moving from Battle Creek, yet confidence would be established as soon as the move was made. This assurance gave us much encouragement when it came, but at that time we were not able to form the faintest conception of its real meaning as it has been unfolded since.

From the letters that have come to our office from nearly all our organized conferences and mission fields throughout the world, we have undoubted evidence that the Spirit of God spoke confidence to the hearts of our people everywhere when the move was made. Presidents of conferences, secretaries and treasurers of various organizations, superintendents of distant mission fields, and many humble believers among the rank and file of our people, have written to us, telling of the gladness that came to their hearts when they read the first announcement of our removal to Washington. Some say that they could scarcely refrain from tears, others say that they immediately knelt down and thanked the Lord, and asked that his special blessing might attend this change.

As letters have come from all parts of the world, and from so many who have had no correspondence whatever with one another, all in the most perfect accord, we can see very plainly that the impression all have received has been from one source—the Spirit of God.

We desire to assure our dear brethren and sisters

Windows

everywhere, who have felt so deeply interested in this move, and who have written us so kindly, that we greatly appreciate this beautiful harmony that exists. It sustains us wonderfully in our efforts to make the changes indicated by the spirit of prophecy.

It gives us blessed assurance of a new era in this cause. This has surely set in. The signal blessing of God has attended every step in our removal to Washington, and the efforts to develop the work here.

The good hand of the Lord has been with Brethren Washburn and Sheafe since they came to this city one year and a half ago. At that time there was but one church here; now there are three. [Arthur G. Daniells, *Review and Herald,* December 31, 1903, p. 5.]

W. W. Prescott:

Now in our coming to this place, I do not expect to see so much money expended in the merely material things connected with the work. I do not expect to see so large buildings here. I do not expect to see so much invested, nor so many persons directly connected with it. And so if we are inclined to judge merely from the outward form, that which strikes the mind outwardly, we shall weep over the loss; but, viewing it in the light of God's providences and God's promises, I believe that we shall see that the glory here will far exceed any that we have seen and experienced in the past. [W. W. Prescott, *Review and Herald,* September 3, 1903, p. 11.]

Ellen G. White:

My Dear Brethren: Our people far and near need to ask themselves how the Lord regards their neglect of important centers in America. There are many places in this country in which the truth has never been proclaimed. Many years ago there should have been a sanitarium in Washington, D. C. But men have chosen their way in many things, and the places to which the truth should have found entrance, by the establishment of medical missionary work, have been neglected.

The Lord has opened this matter to me decidedly. The publishing work that has been carried on in Battle Creek should for the present be carried on near Washington. If after a time the Lord says, Move away from Washington, we are to move. We are pilgrims and strangers in this earth, seeking a better country, even a heavenly. When the Lord tells us to move, we are to obey, however inconvenient and inconsistent such a command may seem to us to be. [Ellen G. White, *Review and Herald,* August 11, 1903, p. 8.]

A week ago we took a drive through various portions of Takoma Park, and Sister Daniells showed me the quiet and beautiful settlements near our land, half hidden by the natural forest. These settlements reminded me of Oakland, as it was thirty years ago. We feel thankful that our work can be located in such a place. It seems as if this place has been waiting to be occupied by our working forces. The situation fills me with hope and courage. [Ellen G. White, *Review and Herald,* May 26, 1904, p. 17.]

While General Conference headquarters and Review and Herald buildings were built on land a few miles beyond Washington's suburbs, two more institutions reminiscent of Battle Creek were contemplated, and consummated as soon as possible: the Washington Sanitarium and Hospital, and the Foreign Missionary Seminary, later Columbia Union College.

A number left the church as a result of the upheavals at Battle Creek, but some later returned. In 1904 Hiland G. Butler administrated Dr. Kellogg's food interests and few

were more embittered than he. His obituary suggests the personal and spiritual struggles that colored his life:

> Hiland George Butler died as the result of an automobile collision, October 15, 1929, at the age of sixty-five years. . . . He was in good health at the time of the accident, and but for that might have lived many years. He was one of the twin sons of Elder George I. and Mrs. Lentha A. Butler. His father served for ten years as our General Conference president. . . .
>
> Hiland received his education in Mount Pleasant, Iowa, South Lancaster, Mass., and Battle Creek, Mich. He was early engaged in the preparation and sale of health foods in Battle Creek and for a time in Great Britain.
>
> In January, 1887, he was married to Clara Kellogg. Five children were the fruitage of this union. Breaking from the health food firm in Battle Creek, he purchased a large tract of land in Bitterroot Valley, Mont. Various circumstances combined to turn him from his Christian profession and old associates. His wife secured a divorce. He sought to enlist in the World War, but was too old to be accepted. He joined the Red Cross, and his division was sent to one of the most dangerous fields, the Austrian battle front. . . .
>
> He returned from the war and came to California, purchased a ranch of twenty acres near Dinuba, not far from an old-time friend, Dr. George A. Hare, and started life anew, but unconverted, rough, profane. But God placed the burden of Hiland Butler's soul on Dr. Hare. He bought a piece of land near Butler's, not for any profit he expected from it, but if possible to lead Hiland back to God. Hiland told him he was happy and free, but Dr. Hare knew better. As the time for camp meeting came, the doctor planned room for him, and induced him to go. He went for three days,

Moving Out of Battle Creek

and the presence of God, the association of Christians, broke through his reserve and sin armor, and he was moved. At the end of three days he returned home, and alone with God settled the great life question.

He came clear back, confessed his sins to his neighbors, and they knew the genuineness of the reformation wrought through Jesus Christ. After this the two friends united in an evangelistic effort in the town of Sanger, and twenty-five stable souls united with their Lord in baptism. [M. C. Wilcox, *Review and Herald,* November 28, 1929, p. 29.]

for further reading:

Daniells, Arthur Grosvenor, *The Abiding Gift of Prophecy* (1936), chap. 31.

Hetzell, M. Carol, *The Undaunted* (1967), chap. 2.

Spalding, Arthur W., *Origin and History of Seventh-day Adventists,* Vol. 3, chap. 4.

Vande Vere, Emmett K., *The Wisdom Seekers* (1972), chaps. 10, 11.

Mrs. White Dies

In 1915 Ellen G. White died, having outlived nearly all her contemporaries. She had mothered a young, growing church for more than sixty-five years. Few women have written more than she did.

Non-Seventh-day Adventist historians have appraised Ellen White in various ways:

David Mitchell:

Although Mrs. White herself always refused to accept the designation of "prophet," she did not deny prophetic inspiration. There is strong internal evidence in her writings which indicates more than human insight and understanding. [David Mitchell, *Seventh-day Adventists*, p. 294. Copyright 1958, Vantage Press. Reprinted with permission of the publisher.]

Walter R. Martin:

Many critics of Seventh-day Adventism have assumed, mostly from the writings of professional detractors, that Mrs. White was a fearsome ogre who devoured all who opposed her, and they have never ceased making the false claim that Seventh-day Adventists believe that Mrs. White is infallible, despite the often published authoritative statements to the contrary. Although Seventh-day Adventists do hold Mrs. White and her writing in great esteem, they

Mrs. White Dies

maintain that the Bible is their only "rule of faith and practice." Christians of all denominations may heatedly disagree with the Seventh-day Adventist attitude toward Mrs. White, but all that she wrote on such subjects as salvation or Christian living characterizes her as a Christian in every sense of the term. [Walter R. Martin, *The Truth About Seventh-day Adventism* (Grand Rapids, Michigan: Zondervan Publishing House, 1960), p. 113. Reprinted with permission of Walter R. Martin, Director, The Christian Research Institute, Wayne, New Jersey.]

Booton Herndon:

From that time [1845] the timid and sickly unschooled girl began her development into a poised and eloquent woman, the mother of a church. She lived for seventy more years. She was a loyal wife, and mother of four children. She traveled the world over, even in her seventies addressing meetings of thousands of followers. She wrote an average of 2000 words a day for the rest of her life; her writings total fifty-three volumes plus thousands of articles and letters. Further, they stand up. Her book *Education,* though she herself never completed the fourth grade, is the basis for instruction in the church's 5,000 parochial schools. One of her books, *Steps to Christ,* has sold more than five million [1975, eighteen and one-half million] copies, in seventy-seven [1975, 102] languages. And many of her prophecies, on subjects on which she could have no possible knowledge except that given to her in visions, have been fulfilled to the letter. [Booton Herndon, *The Seventh Day: The Story of the Seventh-day Adventists* (1960), p. 55.]

Two men thoroughly acquainted with Ellen in her declining years made the following evaluations of the "Lord's Messenger":

277

Windows

Arthur G. Daniells:

Those who have been associated with her through all the years that have passed . . . never have had occasion to alter their conviction that the revelations which have come to her through the years have come from God. [Arthur G. Daniells, *Review and Herald,* August 5, 1915, p. 5.]

William A. Spicer:

It was this gift of the Spirit of prophecy, even in the early days when the agent was so young and inexperienced, that pointed out right ways when strong men of larger experience were at a loss to know how to turn. It was exactly this gift that was needed to give the pioneers the faith and courage—little band as they were, men of the Galilean fishermen type, with no money, having spent their all in the former work before 1844—it was this gift, I say, which rallied the courage of these pioneers to lift up their eyes and undertake to carry a message to all the world. Without such a token of a divine call to so great a work, the undertaking of it would have seemed a most reckless adventure. . . .

Critics have criticized and multitudes have ridiculed any idea of the gift of the Spirit of prophecy in the modern church. But none of the critics ever produced the remotest approach, measured by any spiritual standard, to the kinds of volumes that have come pouring forth from the pen of that woman who at seventeen years of age was called in human weakness to bear her part in the Advent Movement.

The writings themselves are their own witness. Their ministry of blessing has gone to the ends of the earth in many languages, and still this ministry goes forward. [William A. Spicer, *Certainties of the Advent Movement* (1929), pp. 198, 208.]

278

Mrs. White Dies

During her terminal illness Mrs. White evaluated her lifework of writing:

> Close beside her chair, on a table, were kept several of the books she had written. These she would often handle and look over, seeming to delight in having them near. Like an affectionate mother with her children, so was she with these books during her last sickness. Several times, when visited, she was found holding two or three of them in her lap. "I appreciate these books as I never did before," she at one time remarked. *"They are truth, and they are righteousness, and they are an everlasting testimony that God is true."* She rejoiced in the thought that when she could no longer speak to the people, her books would speak for her. . . .
>
> "I do not expect to live long. My work is nearly done. Tell our young people that I want my words to encourage them in that manner of life that will be most attractive to the heavenly intelligences." [C. C. Crisler, "Last Sickness" in *Life Sketches of Ellen G. White* (1915), pp. 445, 446, 448. Italics supplied.]

She warned against ignoring and criticizing what she had written:

> God has been pleased to give you line upon line, and precept upon precept. But there are not many of you that really know what is contained in the Testimonies. You are not familiar with the Scriptures. If you had made God's word your study, with a desire to reach the Bible standard and attain to Christian perfection you would not have needed the Testimonies. . . .
>
> And now, brethren, I entreat you not to interpose between me and the people, and turn away the light which God would have come to them. Do not by your criticisms take out all the force, all the point and

279

Windows

power, from the Testimonies. Do not feel that you can dissect them to suit your own ideas, claiming that God has given you ability to discern what is light from heaven, and what is the expression of mere human wisdom. If the Testimonies speak not according to the word of God, reject them. Christ and Belial cannot be united. For Christ's sake, do not confuse the minds of the people with human sophistry and skepticism, and make of none effect the work that the Lord would do. Do not, by your lack of spiritual discernment, make of this agency of God a rock of offense whereby many shall be caused to stumble and fall, "and be snared, and be taken." [Ellen G. White, *Testimonies,* Vol. 5, pp. 665, 691.]

She cautioned against doubting Seventh-day Adventist history:

> In a crisis, he [God] will raise up men as he did in ancient times. Young men will be bidden to link up with the aged standard-bearers, that they may be strengthened and taught by the experience of these faithful ones, who have passed through so many conflicts, and to whom, through the testimonies of his Spirit, God has so often spoken, pointing out the right way and condemning the wrong way. When perils arise, which try the faith of God's people, these pioneer workers are to recount the experiences of the past, when just such crises came, when the truth was questioned, when strange sentiments, proceeding not from God were brought in. . . .
>
> Satan has laid his plans to undermine our faith in the history of the cause and work of God. . . . Shall we allow this to be done, brethren? [Ellen G. White, *Review and Herald,* November 19, 1903, p. 8.]
>
> The very last deception of Satan will be to make of none effect the testimony of the Spirit of God. "Where there is no vision, the people perish." (Prov. 29:18.)

280

Mrs. White Dies

Satan will work ingeniously, in different ways and through different agencies, to unsettle the confidence of God's remnant people in the true testimony. He will bring in spurious visions to mislead, and mingle the false with the true, and so disgust people that they will regard everything that bears the name of visions as a species of fanaticism; but honest souls, by contrasting the false and true, will be enabled to distinguish between them. [Ellen G. White, *Selected Messages,* Book Two, p. 78.]

Warning against attacking the church:

The church of God below is one with the church of God above. Believers on the earth and the beings in heaven who have never fallen constitute one church. Every heavenly intelligence is interested in the assemblies of the saints who on earth meet to worship God. In the inner court of heaven they listen to the testimony of the witnesses for Christ in the outer court on earth, and the praise and thanksgiving from the worshipers below is taken up in the heavenly anthem, and praise and rejoicing sound through the heavenly courts because Christ has not died in vain for the fallen sons of Adam. While angels drink from the fountain-head, the saints on earth drink of the pure streams flowing from the throne, the streams that make glad the city of our God. O that we could all realize the nearness of heaven to earth! [Ellen G. White, *Testimonies,* Vol. 6, p. 366.]

God has a people in which all heaven is interested, and they are the one object on earth dear to the heart of God. . . .

To claim that the Seventh-day Adventist Church is Babylon, is to make the same claim as does Satan. . . .

My brother, if you are teaching that the

281

Seventh-day Adventist Church is Babylon, you are
wrong. God has not given you any such message to
bear. . . . I presume that some may be deceived by
your message, because they are full of curiosity and
desire some new thing. . . .

He is leading, not stray offshoots, not one here and
one there, but a people. . . . The gospel net draws not
only good fish, but bad ones as well, and the Lord only
knows who are his. . . .

Fallen angels upon earth form confederations with
evil men. In this age antichrist will appear as the true
Christ, and then the law of God will be fully made
void in the nations of our world. Rebellion against
God's holy law will be fully ripe. But the true leader
of all this rebellion is Satan clothed as an angel of
light. Men will be deceived and will exalt him to the
place of God, and deify him. [Ellen G. White,
Testimonies to Ministers, pp. 41, 42, 59, 61, 62.]

Encouragement for facing last-day events (written in Waldensian country):

We are standing on the threshold of great and
solemn events. Prophecy is fast fulfilling. The Lord is
at the door. There is soon to open before us a period of
overwhelming interest to all living. The controversies
of the past are to be revived; new controversies will
arise. The scenes to be enacted in our world are not
yet dreamed of. . . .

But God's servants are not to trust themselves in
this great emergency. In the visions given to Isaiah,
to Ezekiel, and to John, we see how closely Heaven is
connected with the events taking place upon the
earth, and how great is the care of God for those who
are loyal to him. The world is not without a ruler. The
program of coming events is in the hands of the Lord.
The Majesty of heaven has the destiny of nations, as

Mrs. White Dies

well as the concerns of his church, in his own charge.
. . .

He watches the furnace fire that must test every
soul. When the strongholds of kings shall be
overthrown, when the arrows of God's wrath shall
strike through the hearts of his enemies, his people
will be safe in his hands. [Ellen G. White,
Testimonies, Vol. 5, pp. 753, 754.]

And she discussed the role of her writings in the future:

Abundant light has been given to our people in
these last days. Whether or not my life is spared, my
writings will constantly speak, and their word will go
forward as long as time shall last. My writings are
kept on file in the office, and even though I should not
live, these words that have been given to me by the
Lord will still have life and will speak to the Church.
[Ellen G. White as quoted in *The Writing and Sending Out of the Testimonies to the Church* (Prepared by the Ellen G. White Publications), pp. 13, 14.]

283

for further reading:

Christian, Lewis H., *The Fruitage of Spiritual Gifts* (1947), 446 pages.

Gilbert, Frederick C., *Divine Predictions of Mrs. Ellen G. White Fulfilled* (1922), 464 pages.

* Jemison, T. Housel, *A Prophet Among You* (1955), 505 pages.

* Noorbergen, Rene, *Prophet of Destiny* (1972), 241 pages.

Shaw, Horace J., "A Rhetorical Analysis of the Speaking of Mrs. Ellen G. White, a Pioneer Leader and Spokeswoman of the Seventh-day Adventist Church" (PhD dissertation, Michigan State University, 1959), 655 pages.

Spalding, Arthur W., *Origin and History of Seventh-day Adventists,* Vol. 3, chap. 16.

* Spicer, William Ambrose, *The Spirit of Prophecy in the Advent Movement* (1937), 128 pages.

* White, Ellen G., *Life Sketches of Ellen G. White* (1915), 480 pages.

World War I

The eruption of World War I found Seventh-day Adventists much less surprised than most people. For decades their church publications had discussed coming conflicts. Nonetheless many church members were embarrassed with their assumed role as forecasters of international events when they erred on a few specifics:

1. For years, they expected the Pope to head an international organization after the war. The pontiff, they reasoned, soon would become "president of a parliament of man."

2. Also, all along they saw Turkey as an indicator of earth's last events.

Certain evangelists used such ideas daringly in their advertising. But their tracing of future details was sometimes presumptuous, and failures meant chagrin.

Almost as soon as they could set type after the war began, the Adventists in "The Signs of the Times" and "The Watchman Magazine" anticipated the behavior of Pope and Turk. Eagerly wrote M. C. Wilcox in September, 1914:

> Naturally, with the world feeling as it does at the present time, he [the pope] would be the very one chosen to act as head of any peace congress which the world itself might call. It is for that that the papacy is longing. It is for that that some of her greatest prelates are working. It is that which they are expecting: It is that very thing which the Bible itself declares will come; for we read in the seventeenth

285

chapter of Revelation regarding the restoration of
that head [the Papacy], and [cooperation of] the
last-day [national] powers which exist under the
symbol of the ten horns. [Milton C. Wilcox, "The Late
Pope and His Anxiety for Peace," *The Signs of the
Times,* September 8, 1914, pp. 3, 4, 8.]

And in August, 1915, "The Watchman" agreed:

The idea has been advanced that the pope is soon
to leave Rome and establish his court temporarily or
even permanently at some other important point,
such as Constantinople or Jerusalem (of course after
the Turk shall have been driven out). . . . We think
there is little probability that the pope will ever
permanently abandon the "Eternal City" as the seat
of papal government. [Editorial, "Will the Pope Leave
Rome?" *The Watchman Magazine,* August, 1915, pp.
339, 340.]

**Each magazine discussed the future of the Papacy about
fifteen times, the conviction being that after the war the pope
would swell to religio-political, or perhaps juridical, domi-.
nance in the world. Quickly, too, "The Signs" set forth an
analysis of "The Eastern Question":**

The Turkish power will come to its end, not when
driven out of Europe [which likely will be soon], but
at the battle of Armageddon, which is to be fought
where some of the great battles of ancient Israel were
fought, on the plain of Esdraelon, in northern
Palestine. After leaving Europe, the Turk will "plant
the tabernacles of his palace between the seas in the
glorious holy mountain; yet he shall come to his end,
and none shall help him." [Daniel 11:45.] Till now, the
Turk has received help from the great European
powers. But the time is near when this help will be
withdrawn, and, driven from Europe, he will come to

286

his end in the final convulsion of earth's powers at Armageddon. . . .

The Turk has not yet come to his end, probation has not closed, and Christ has not begun His eternal reign; therefore the present conflict in Europe, however wide-spread or terrible it may be, is not the Armageddon of the Scriptures. It is undoubtedly the beginning of the gathering of the nations for that final sanguinary world struggle, where all the powers of earth are to be involved, and when they will fall, to rise no more. [E. E. Andross, "This War-Mad World," *The Signs of the Times,* September 22, 1914, pp. 1-3, 8.]

Eleven months later the "Signs" published more about the anticipated trends in the Near East:

Not only does the prophecy [in Revelation] include the nations that have now for many years been so vitally interested in the near East, but the "kings of the earth and of the whole world" are to be gathered, says the prophet. Rev. 16:14. This, then, includes the nations of the far East. In fact, they are very specifically included.

"And the sixth angel poured out his vial upon the great river Euphrates; and the water thereof was dried up, that the way of the kings of the east might be prepared." Verse 12. . . . It is self-evident that such language leads us to apply the prophecy to such nations as China and Japan. . . .

It is difficult to say what the immediate future may bring forth, but it is predicted that sooner or later a close alliance will be made between China and Japan. . . .

Let us imagine China, with her undeveloped resources and . . . her millions of people, united in not merely an alliance, but a partnership with Japan. . . . Can we not then see more clearly what is meant by

287

the "kings that come from the sunrising" in the great
world struggle just before us? [John E. Fulton, "The
Kings of the East in Prophecy," *The Signs of the
Times,* August 17, 1915, pp. 1, 2.]

The "Signs" ran seven articles on the subject by General
Conference president Arthur G. Daniells, beginning April,
1916. He, likewise, insisted that the Turk must move his
government to Jerusalem. Over fifty major articles in "The
Signs" assured that the Turk was destined for Jerusalem,
and for extinction following "a little time of peace."

Turkey driven from Europe, the division of the
Balkan peninsula and Asia Minor among the great
powers, and then another more terrible war over the
spoils. That will be Armageddon. [Arthur G. Daniells,
"The Storm Center of the World's Crisis," *The Signs
of the Times,* April 25, 1916, p. 7.]

When God permits the driving of the Turk from
Constantinople, we may consider that the opening of
the floodgate, to be followed by a stream of significant
events rushing on to break into the great sea of
eternity. [Lucas A. Reed, "The Turk Pitching His
Tents Toward Jerusalem," *The Signs of the Times,*
March 13, 1917, pp. 6, 7.]

"The Watchman Magazine" also placed Turkey in the center
of "the mighty drama of the golden horn." Over forty articles
and editorials bearing on Turkey's rise in Jerusalem and his
demise in onrushing Armageddon appeared. "Keep your
eyes on the fast-flying events in the East," it commanded. In
January, 1918, the magazine printed an article by William E.
Videto giving free rein to his speculations:

The first part of the thirty-eighth chapter of
Ezekiel shows what nations will represent Europe in
the conflict at Armageddon. . . .
"Son of man, set thy face toward Gog, of the land

288

of Magog, the prince of Rosh, Mesheck, and Tubal, and prophesy against him." Ezek. 38:2, R.V. Magog was one of the grandsons of Noah, who peopled all the north of Asia, the land called anciently Scythia, but now Siberia. Tubal, another grandson of Noah, settled in the central part of Siberia which is still called from him, Tobolsk. Mesheck, also a grandson of Noah, settled in the central part of Russia, and his descendants built the city of Moscow, hence the name Moscovites, commonly used to designate the Russian people.

But according to the prophet, the "chief" of all these is the "prince of Rosh" (R.V.), and the word "Rosh" is the root word of "Russians" (Roshians). Russia, now weak and revolution-torn, is yet to act a leading part in Europe. In alliance with her will be "Gomer and all his bands." Verse 6.

Gomer, another grandson of Noah, had a son named Ashkenaz. Gen. 10:3. The Jews have always considered Ashkenaz to be the father of the Teutonic or German race.

The Celts who settled in western Europe are closely related to the Teutons and form another of the "bands of Gomer." Not only Germany, Scandinavia, Holland, and Austria, but France and England are included. We may safely predict that Germany will yet stand shoulder to shoulder with Russia, France, and England; whether willingly or because she has been conquered by them, no one can tell. But the fact that Russia is to be leader is highly significant.

With these nations are to be associated Persia, Ethiopia, Lybia, and Togarmah (Armenia) now mostly under Russian rule.

But most important of all from our standpoint is the fact that at this time all of these nations are to be destroyed to make way for the setting up of Christ's kingdom which shall have no end. [William E. Videto,

"The Great War. Can We Know the Result?" *The Watchman Magazine,* January, 1918, pp. 27, 28.]

When Jerusalem fell to the British in December, 1917, the theorizing ardor dampened, but Adventist writers next had the Balfour Declaration and the Zionists' hopes for the establishment of a Jewish state in Palestine to prod them. Both the "Signs" and "Watchman" magazines rejected the possibility of creating a Zionist state in the Holy Land. The restoration-of-Israel prophecies, they believed, were not meant for genuine Hebrews, but for "spiritual Israel" only:

> We need to study carefully these prophecies of the Bible, in order that we may not arrive at such an erroneous conclusion [as have the Zionists].
>
> The Jerusalem that the student of the Bible is to look to to-day is not the Jerusalem of Palestine. . . . He is to look to the New Jerusalem so graphically described in the book of Revelation. . . . The Old Testament promises of the restoration of the Jews were all based upon conditions which the Jewish nation never met, and therefore those promises will never be fulfilled. We have passed the time for them. The next great event is the second coming of Christ, and Palestine will not be restored to the Jewish nation for them to hold it as they did twenty-five hundred years ago.
>
> However, great political events will culminate in Palestine during these closing years of time, for it is there that the great war of Armageddon is to be waged. [Editorial, "The Taking of Jerusalem," *The Signs of the Times,* January 1, 1918, p. 9.]
>
> The restoration of a Jewish nation in Palestine, composed of the lineal descendants of the people whose apostasy from God resulted in the ruin of their nation, and who are no more in harmony with the purposes of God than were their fathers of Zedekiah's or of Pilate's day, can have no connection with the

290

plans of God. God is planning a gathering of the
spiritual seed of Abraham, the true Israel, who are all
followers of Christ, but not of the descendants of
Abraham through the flesh. [Editorial, "A Jewish
Nation," *The Watchman Magazine,* March, 1918, pp.
12, 13.]

These [Zionist] expectations are doomed to
disappointment. They will never be realized any more
than the expectations of the Jews at the first advent
regarding the appearance of their Messiah were
realized. It can be stated with the greatest
positiveness that there is no prophecy in the Bible,
rightly understood, which would lead any one to
expect that either before or after Christ's second
coming, either in belief or unbelief, the Jewish nation
will be restored to the land of Palestine, and be
converted to Christ. [Carlyle B. Haynes, "Will the
Jews Return?" *The Watchman Magazine,* September,
1918, p. 14f., quotation from p. 15.]

**Certain Adventist writers, however, maintained more sensi-
ble attitudes. They urged caution when explaining prophecy
and denounced the fanciful interpretations. The general
church paper, "The Review and Herald," chiefly edited by
Francis M. Wilcox, held to the conservative line:**

[We need] a sobering sense of our solemn
responsibility.... The Word of God deals for the most
part with great principles. It does not tell us in clear
detail just what we should do in every situation that
may arise. The Lord knew that the dangers
confronting his church would become so complex, so
multitudinous in form, that it would be practically
impossible to instruct his disciples in detail as to how
they should relate themselves to every phase of the
situation. [Editorial, *Review and Herald,* February 22,
1917, p. 4.]

291

Windows

We urge upon our brethren and sisters throughout the field, and especially upon ministers, teachers, and writers, the necessity of safeguarding their public utterances and work from extravagance of speech, unwarranted statements and predictions, and sensational methods. We also caution against the harboring of a spirit of unchristian partisanship. ["Spring Council of the North American Division Conference Committee," recommendation concerning "Public Utterances by Workers," *Review and Herald,* May 10, 1917, p. 5.]

Especially should great care be used when writing or speaking upon subjects of prophetic import. Let us not indulge in too much speculation as to the outcome of many of the great issues in the world. Let us not hazard our reputation as a people for consistency in Bible exposition by making wild statements. . . .

Let us speak where the Word speaks; where it is silent, let us be silent. Let us not seek to be wise above what is written. Let us use sane statements and sane methods, and like wise, sober, level-headed men and women, consistently and considerately give the world the message which God has given us. [Editorial, "Public Utterances by Writers and Speakers," *Review and Herald,* May 24, 1917, p. 3.]

Let us not consider that it is necessary for us to seek to explain every prophetic symbol. We should be far better Bible students and expositors than we are; but if we do not know the meaning of some scripture, it is better frankly to confess it than to place some strange and fanciful interpretation upon it, which does not accord with divine revelation or with sound reasoning. . . .

So long as God in his Word has given us no warrant for forecasting the exact order of events, why should we assume to be wise above what is written? . . . Unless the Lord endows us with the gift of prophecy, and gives us divine enlightenment to fill in some of the details regarding the prophecies of his Word, let us be careful of our forecasts. . . .

The Lord has given us abundant evidence in the great world around us, without our entering the field of idle, fanciful interpretation, thus prejudicing the minds of sensible people against our entire system of prophetic exposition. [Editorial, "Guarded Utterances," *Review and Herald,* September 6, 1917, pp. 3, 4.]

These are days in which we do well not to hazard too much speculation regarding the trend of events in the world. This war has afforded a long and continued series of surprises. The forecasts of the best-informed men have come to naught. It is better for us to await patiently the progress of human history in the unfolding of God's plan, than to run ahead of his providence and make statements which time may demonstrate to have been only idle speculation. [Editorial, "The Fall of Jerusalem," *Review and Herald,* December 20, 1917, p. 24.]

for further reading:

Daniells, Arthur G., *The World War. Its Relation to the Eastern Question and Armageddon* (1917), 128 pages.

Dick, Everett N., "Twentieth Anniversary of Medical Military Training Among Seventh-day Adventists," *The Youth's Instructor,* May 4, 1954, pp. 10, 24.

Herschberger, Guy F., *War, Peace and Nonresistance* (1969), 382 pages.

Spalding, Arthur W., *Origin and History of Seventh-day Adventists,* Vol. 4, chap. 9.

* Spicer, William Ambrose, *The Hand That Intervenes* (1919), 334 pages.

Weeks, Howard B., *Adventist Evangelism in the Twentieth Century* (1969), 320 pages.

* Wilcox, Francis M., *Seventh-day Adventists in Time of War* (1936), 407 pages.

Daniells Decades

The longest and one of the most creative periods of SDA history stretches from 1901 to 1922 when Arthur Grosvenor Daniells served as president of the General Conference. Daniells was an extraordinary leader with vision, vitality, determination, communicative skills, and dedication. He traveled extensively and understood his people. They, in turn, felt they knew him.

In a crisis Daniells did not lose courage. The test that established him in esteem was the Kellogg controversy at Battle Creek. Daniells' fortitude is evident in his remarks at the General Conference of 1909 upon his reelection to the presidency:

> I have never made a speech when my name has been submitted for action on an occasion like this. I do not know how to make an appropriate speech, but somehow I do feel like saying something. I have given this matter a great deal of serious thought, not only since the Conference has been in session, but for many weeks and months before we came here. I would like to tell you in as few words as possible how I feel about this matter. At the Oakland General Conference, in 1903, I felt quite free as to being re-elected, because I felt that the work we had started out to do in 1901 had not been completed. We had not carried the work of reorganization through as was necessary. Two years were not enough time to inaugurate such great changes. Then, again, a fearful

295

controversy had arisen in our midst. We were then in the very heat of a great crisis, and there was a determination to get rid of men who, it was thought, were responsible for the trouble that was on hand; and somehow I did not feel very much like being gotten rid of in that way, and for that purpose. So I said nothing, and I felt somewhat relieved to continue. But I will confess that I fully expected then that that would be enough, that two years more would complete the work, and then I would pass on to some other field. [Arthur G. Daniells, *Review and Herald,* June 10, 1909, p. 14.]

President Daniells was a good administrator. He enlisted others to secure organization and money, to promote education, to plan missions, and to build morale. In so acting he believed he followed "God's plans" as communicated to Ellen White in 1896:

God gave to Moses special direction for the management of his work. He directed Moses to associate men with him as counselors, that his burdens might be lightened. . . .

The president of our General Conference has been left to gather to himself burdens which God has not laid upon him, and the things that he has tried to do could not be done wisely and well. . . .

As a people we should study God's plans for conducting His work. Wherever He has given directions in regard to any point, we should carefully consider how to regard His expressed will. This work should have special attention. It is not wise to choose one man as president of the General Conference. The work of the General Conference has extended, and some things have been made unnecessarily complicated. A want of discernment has been shown. There should be a division of the field, or some other plan should be devised to change the present order of things.. . . .

The president of the General Conference should have the privilege of deciding who shall stand by his side as counselors. Those who will keep the way of the Lord, who will preserve clear, sharp discernment by cultivating home religion, are safe counselors. . . . Counselors of the character that God chose for Moses are needed by the president of the General Conference. . . .

I have the word of the Lord for presidents of conferences. . . . If you will not be burden bearers, but choose to lay your whole weight of responsibilities upon the president of the General Conference, then, week by week, month by month, you are disqualifying yourselves for the work. [Ellen G. White, *Testimonies to Ministers,* pp. 340-343.]

Chiefly because of him the General Conference sessions of 1897, 1901, and 1903 achieved considerable denominational reorganization. Therefore when considering the position of presidency in 1904 (and thus indirectly the church constitution of 1903) Ellen insisted:

God has chosen Elder Daniells to bear responsibilities, and has promised to make him capable by His grace of doing the work entrusted to him. The responsibilities of the [presidential] position he occupies are great, and the tax upon his strength and courage are severe; and the Lord calls upon us to hold up his hands, as he strives with all the powers of mind and body to advance the work. . . .

I know that Elder Daniells is the right man in the place. He has stood nobly for the truth. . . . [Ellen G. White, *Special Testimonies,* Series B, No. 2, p. 41.]

In 1905 Daniells extolled the new organizational plan:

Windows

One of the most weighty educational problems that
Daniells had to face concerned the College of Medical
Evangelists at Loma Linda, California. Would Loma Linda,
the church wondered, duplicate the frustrating experience
at Battle Creek? Would the Kellogg-trained medical staff at
Loma Linda try for independence again?

Daniells Decades

The question of training Seventh-day Adventists along medical lines at Loma Linda developed following the debacle at Battle Creek (the American Medical Missionary College closed in 1910), and continued until the General Conference shouldered CME as the denomination's full-fledged medical school in 1915.

Several selections will acquaint the reader with the agonies of policy making at Loma Linda in 1915:

> The key decision to close or continue came before the constituency of CME at the Autumn Council of the GC Committee held at Loma Linda. Some opposed the required program. But one evening a few [delegates] surrounded President Daniells and reviewed Ellen White's counsels and prayed most of the night.
>
> The next morning Elder A. G. Daniells addressed the members of the delegation. He admitted his own fears and apprehension, which he knew had been shared by others. But in clear, forceful language he now reaffirmed his faith in the counsel that had guided them in their former decisions, and declared his deep conviction that there was only one way to go, and that was forward. This positive stand on his part was a potent influence. . . . After thorough discussion formal action was taken, advising the board of management "to carry on the school in harmony with the counsel given through the servant of the Lord, providing a four-year medical course."
>
> Elder A. G. Daniells, in speaking of this resolution, said: "We must square up to this now. . . . When we pass this recommendation, we commit ourselves to the earnest support of this school. . . . We do not say, Stop. We say, Go on and maintain this school, and make it a success. When I vote for that, I feel in duty bound from this day on to do all I can by my counsel and influence, to help carry the school

299

through successfully, and that I am pledged to do."
[Dores E. Robinson, *The Story of Our Health Message*
(1943), pp. 335, 336, quoting from the "Minutes of the
Constituency of the College of Medical Evangelists,
November 11, 1915."]

**Religion instructor F. M. Burg voiced Loma Linda gratitude
in a thanksgiving convocation:**

This council has also given us reasons for rejoicing
and thanksgiving, by clearing the atmosphere
surrounding the . . . College of the depressing element
of uncertainty. . . . We should appreciate the
magnitude of the problem which presents itself to
those who are responsible for the financial obligations
that are involved in maintaining and providing our
school with the equipment necessary to assure its
success.

Reflection on our part will help us to understand
the reasons for their conservative and careful
deliberation while counseling together as to the policy
that should be adopted and followed. . . . And now the
word may be passed to our young men and women . . .
that Loma Linda College of Medical Evangelists is to
live, with the cooperation and support of this
denomination, and with provisions made for it that
will enable the school to accomplish everything that
was intended in its planting. [F. M. Burg, *Review and
Herald,* December 23, 1915, pp. 17, 18.]

**Colporteur evangelism sprang to life after the economic de-
pression of the 1890's. The newly recruited book salesmen
had instructions not to pass by any house, not to overlook
any fringe settlement. "Camp Life in Canvassing" (1908)
describes the life of a colporteur in Louisiana:**

We have lived in a tent and wagon for about two
years and a half, and find it a pleasant, healthful life.

300

Daniells Decades

My wife often says that she would not trade her tent for any house, although she was raised in the city.

The wagon is our bedroom, and it is long enough for a full-sized mattress for us at one end, and a shorter one for the children at the other. When we get the territory worked for five or ten miles around our camp, we pack our wagon and move to another location. The two-wheeled [horse] cart in the picture is a very crude but practical affair. I do my canvassing and delivering with it. The box will hold a hundred pounds or more of books, and is made waterproof by a covering of heavy black oilcloth. In canvassing it holds my helps, raincoat, etc., and when I can not get the cash for books, I take trade, such as corn, butter, eggs, sirup, chickens, potatoes, and, in fact, anything we can use or sell. Often I take in enough sirup and other supplies, while on delivery, to pay for what feed and groceries we need for two weeks; and make a very successful delivery by being able to take trade when, for lack of cash, the delivery would otherwise be a failure.

We have as good a living and as much clothing as we ever had, and are able to have a part in spreading the message in thinly settled territory, where the living preacher is never likely to go. When we were working for ourselves or others, we always had something that kept us away from camp-meeting; but now that we are working for the Lord, we can travel to camp-meeting, even if it is two hundred miles away. We can take orders going, and deliver coming back, and make our trip pay. [Charles L. Collison, *Review and Herald,* June 11, 1908, p. 16.]

During 1912-1915 a number of evangelists emerged who specialized in large cities. They pioneered the "Bible in the Hand" program, correspondence lessons, and press release techniques. The principal leaders were O. O. Bernstein, E. L.

Cardey, Charles T. Everson, R. E. Harter, Carlyle B. Haynes, J. W. McCord, Peter Gustavus Rodgers, K. C. Russell, and J. S. Washburn. Accounts of such evangelistic efforts follow:

J. W. McCord in San Jose, California (1913):

This series has lasted twelve weeks and has been the longest and the most successful in the ministry of the workers [here]. Up to date, sixty-five have taken their stand for the Lord and his Sabbath, and the harvest is not yet finished. . . .

While our Sunday night attendance varied from five hundred to six hundred, the general average for the eighty-five meetings of the series amounted to above three hundred a night. . . .

We wish to speak of the perfect unity that has prevailed among the workers. This blessed unity; the hard work and the faithful attendance of the local church; . . . the help of the [city daily] papers so readily given in publishing a daily synopsis of the sermons; and the all-sufficient grace of the Holy Spirit have made this success possible. [J. W. McCord, *Review and Herald,* December 4, 1913, p. 16.]

O. O. Bernstein in Minneapolis (1912-1915):

There are thirty adults keeping the Sabbath as the result of the summer's work [1912], ten of whom were recently baptized. Another baptism is soon to follow. The influence of the tent-meetings has been felt in various quarters of the city. . . .

A second effort of six weeks began Sunday, November 10, in the Nicollet Avenue and Fifteenth Street Baptist church, which we have rented. . . . The opening night every seat in the auditorium, galleries, and anterooms were taken early, so that chairs had to be placed in the aisles, and then scores who were unable to get in went away. . . .

302

Daniells Decades

During the past seventeen months [1913-1914] eighty persons have been baptized and added to the church as a result of the work in this city. A large number of others are keeping the Sabbath and preparing for baptism.

Last summer's tent effort was only of six weeks' duration. Although interfered with by intense heat and swarms of hungry mosquitoes, the meeting was a success.

The Lord blessed the two years and four months [prior to July, 1915] which we spent . . . in . . . Minneapolis, Minn., where four evangelistic efforts were conducted, with upward of 125 souls who were added to the Lake Street church by baptism. [O. O. Bernstein, *Review and Herald,* December 12, 1912, p. 17; January 1, 1914, p. 16; July 29, 1915, p. 15.]

J. S. Washburn in Philadelphia (1914-1915):

We began our tent meetings in West Philadelphia, Sunday, July 19, with the largest attendance for the opening night and with the best interest I have ever known [in thirty years]. . . . Our large tent was packed, and a great number stood outside. . . . We have the help in this campaign of a large choir of thirty voices from the West Philadelphia church. . . . This has been a great help. . . . Our tent is brilliantly lighted with electric lights, and the streetcar facilities for reaching the tent are good. . . .

Our tent is pitched this year [1915] in a part of West Philadelphia. . . .

In the work in the large cities, it is sometimes difficult to get the names and addresses of those who attend the meetings, yet this year we have secured the names and addresses of nearly two hundred interested families. At our Sunday night meetings we ask how many would be glad to receive the twenty-eight numbers of the Family Bible Teacher, free. We distribute pencils and slips of paper to all who will give us their names and addresses. We then mail to each one these four-page leaflets in installments of about seven numbers at a time. This accomplishes two objects: the interested ones appreciate and study these valuable condensed Bible readings, and, second, we secure in this way the names of those who are already truly interested. Their names are filed in order, and when literature is sent or visits made, this too is recorded. We have found this system an excellent one, enabling us to get in touch with the people. . . .

At this tent meeting we are following the plan of holding a short responsive Bible reading at the beginning of each meeting. . . . By this plan we have been able to get many of the people to bring their Bibles, and thus to look up many of the texts when read. This is a help in making the truth plain to the people and in starting them to study the Bible for themselves. . . .

The truth seems more fresh than ever before, and after thirty-one years of preaching the message, it seems to me that I am just beginning to learn how to hold tent meetings and to teach the people this wonderful saving truth. The end hastens. Soon we shall hold our last tent meeting. [J. S. Washburn, *Review and Herald,* August 6, 1914, pp. 14, 15; October 7, 1915, p. 18.]

One of Daniells' main interests was missions. A confirmed missionary with experience in Australasia (1886-1901) he determined to embed the idea in the denomination and to mount a vaster program overseas. He traveled in all parts of the world, he studied the problems he found, and he took hundreds of pictures for stereoptican projection.

Soon scores of youth coveted overseas assignment as "the highest service" they could do for the church.

Few so well exemplified the spirit of mission expansion as William Harrison Anderson (1870-1950). These diary entries of 1904 find him northwest of Bulawayo, Rhodesia, scouting for a future mission station:

August 9: We made a very early start, and traveled a long distance. The country is covered with scrub brush. Signs of big game are abundant. I saw hart[e]beest and wild hogs; also the fresh tracks of buffalo.

August 10: We could not travel far on account of the boy who had fever. He was some better, and the other carriers took most of his load. There was still plenty of game and birds. As we were short of food, I killed four guinea-fowl at one shot, and the boys ate them. The country is more open as one climbs the plateau.

August 11: After a short walk in the morning we came to a nice pool of water, where we had a bath and did our washing. It was very refreshing. One has to be careful where he bathes in this country, as many of the deep pools contain crocodiles. We came out on the open prairie at noon. The soil is quite good here. There are also herds of big game.

August 12: We arrived in Kalomo. I was soon comfortable at the home of Mr. Rangely, the magistrate. We had entertained him at our home in Southern Rhodesia, and he was glad to return the favor. He arranged for me to see the administrator the next day.

August 13: I saw the administrator at 11 A.M. He said that the government had decided to give each missionary society a particular part of the country. . . . They offered us the country to the north and east among the Batokas or the Batoka and

305

Mashukulumbwe to the north. I decided to visit both places.

August 14: I had a long visit with the district commissioner, whom I met two years ago. He gave me much information about the people and the Batoka country. I was glad to find a letter from my wife at the post-office. We left Kalomo in the afternoon, and made our camp about ten miles out. We were very short of food, as we came to no native kraals.

August 15: We had our usual Sabbath service. In the afternoon we had a long talk on the experiences of David and Saul. We walked ten miles after the Sabbath.

August 16: We had a long walk of sixteen miles. We could get no food, as there are no native kraals on the road. I shot some birds for the boys. We came to a white man's camp in the evening, and I bought some food for the boys, which they ate with a relish. The natives here live a long way off the road. A native does not like living on a main road. There are too many demands on him for food. He does not like to refuse a hungry man food, as he is naturally very hospitable. But if he sees hungry men every day, his scanty store is soon exhausted. He seeks a remedy in moving four or five miles away.

August 17: The carriers had no food, so we went on to a native kraal before breakfast. I was told that it was about eight miles to the village, but I found that it was twenty. We saw the fresh tracks of a herd of elephant that had crossed the road just ahead of us. We arrived at the kraal at 1 P.M., and were able to get a little food, but the water was bad. We rested three hours, and went on again in the evening. We traveled six miles, and made our camp for the night. We had no dinner, so we went to bed hungry.

August 18: I awoke at three in the morning with severe cramps in my bowels, and a very bad attack of dysentery. I could sleep no more, so we started on again at daybreak. I soon came up with a donkey wagon in charge of Mr. Maddocks, a geologist for the Northern Copper Company. He kindly gave me a ride in his wagon to the next river, eight miles ahead. I was suffering intensely, and by noon I had a very high fever. I ate very little, and kept my bed all day. I had the boys make my bed away from the noise of the donkeys and dogs, and retired at sunset for the night. My fever was still high, and my strength was fast passing away. I thought that my time had come, and calling the boys to my bedside, I gave them directions as to my burial. This is the second time since I have been in this country that I have given directions as to what I would like to have done after I was gone. I told the boys to dig a grave and sew me in my blankets and bury me. Then they were to return home at once, and take a message to my wife and child. As I finished, we committed ourselves to God, and I went to sleep, expecting never to see the light of the morning.

August 19: I slept fairly well during the night. My head was dull, and I could not think clearly. I still had a high fever. I learned from the natives that I was near the camp of Mr. Walker, the old hunter. I had often met him in Bulawayo, and he had invited me to call on him when I was north of the Zambesia. I was glad to accept his invitation.

"My God shall supply all your need according to his riches in glory by Christ Jesus." With the help of the boys I was soon in his tent, and he cared for me the next week, which I spent in bed. I slowly recovered my strength, and as soon as I was able, I started on again. As Mr. Walker had been hunting in this land for the past six years, he gave me much valuable information in regard to it. I found him the best informed in regard to the country of any man that I met. I told him what I wanted, and he directed me to several places that he thought would suit me.

307

Windows

He kindly loaned me his aneroid, so I might know my elevation at any time.

August 25: I left Mr. Walker's tent in the afternoon, and started for Monze's. As I was still weak, we could not travel very fast. We made our camp in a native field for the night. . . . It consisted of a high bush fence made circular, and about thirty feet in diameter. Inside of this all the loads were placed and the beds made. A quantity of wood was collected, and a good fire was made across the entrance. I had my bed just back of the fire. It was made by cutting two poles about seven feet long, and placing them side by side on the ground and about three feet apart. The space between them was filled with grass to the depth of about six inches. This made a comfortable mattress, on which the blankets were spread. A short log at my feet prevented the grass from working down into the fire. The carriers made their beds on either side. One of the boys was to keep up the fire all night.

August 26: We walked twelve miles for the day. We traveled up a river, so water was plentiful. The country was very rough, and covered with scrub brush. We saw a large herd of water antelope.

August 27: We had a long walk to the hot springs. We took the wrong path, and traveled eighteen miles to reach a point eight miles from our night camp. We remained at this place four days, looking over the country. There is some excellent land here, but the water is scarce. The government will not permit the ground to be pegged in the vicinity of the springs. The springs belong to a series extending from the Kafui to a point south of the Zambesia. I saw several of them. The water varies in temperature from the boiling point to simply warm. In some springs the water appears to be pure, while in others there are minerals. The natives have many traditions in regard to them, and they visit them regularly for worship.

August 30: We walked eight or ten miles in the

308

evening, and came into the wagon road eighty-five
miles from Kalomo and fifteen miles from Monze's.
There were hyenas about the camp all night, so I did
not sleep much. I can not say that I enjoy being
serenaded by three or four hyenas. The country is
very rough, almost mountainous.

August 31: We traveled the fifteen miles to
Monze's. He is the chief of the Batoka nation. The
first part of the journey was in the hills, and then we
came out in the open, elevated, rolling prairie. We
arrived at the kraal at sunset. It is a dirty Batoka
village, inhabited by people, cattle, sheep, goats, dogs,
fowls, and vermin. There is nothing except the large
herd of cattle to indicate the rank of the chief. He
received me very kindly, and after the usual exchange
of presents,—he gave me a goat, and I presented him
with a blanket,—I announced my mission. He said
that he wanted a school for his people, and asked
what he could do for me. I told him that a guide to
show me the country would be very acceptable. He
promised to send his son, and he was at my camp the
next morning at daybreak.

September 1: I looked carefully over the ground to
the south and west, but found nothing that suited me.
The combination that I desired was elevation, good
soil, and proximity to the natives.

September 2: I started very early to the north and
east. I took my guide and two of my carriers with me.
We traveled hard all day, but saw nothing that was
desirable until about dark, when I came to just what I
wanted.

September 3: I had a good look around the spring
and over the surrounding country in the forenoon, and
in the afternoon I pegged a farm of five thousand
acres on the Makei River directly east of Monze's
kraal. I pegged about three miles of the river front, so
as to include timber and the fountain. This farm has
six native kraals on it. It is the best farm that I saw in

309

all my travels in the country. There is sufficient in the fountain to irrigate a good garden, and plenty of water in the river for stock.

The soil is black along the river, and of a chocolate color on the high land. The elevation is four thousand eight hundred feet. The natives grow corn, Kaffir corn, sweet potatoes, peanuts, ground nuts, beans, pumpkins, and a kind of vegetable marrow. I returned to my camp on Friday, and started for Kalomo on Monday. On the return I visited two other places that were suggested to me, but I did not think them so good as the place that I selected.

On my arrival at Kalomo, I submitted my farm to the government for approval. They accepted it. . . .

I made a hasty trip home, visiting a mission on the Zambesia on the way. I arrived home, October 3, very tired, but otherwise in good health. My carriers could not keep up with me, so I left them behind, and they arrived nearly a week later. During my absence I had traveled three hundred miles by rail and about seven hundred miles on foot. [W. H. Anderson, "Notes From My Diary," *Review and Herald,* March 17, 1904, pp. 14, 15.]

Daniells had hoped to shepherd the church to the Second Coming without seeing death, but younger leaders realized by 1922 that he could not vigorously go on much longer. So being mindful of Mrs. White's admonitions against "kingly power" they decided not to renominate him for the presidency at the 1922 General Conference session at San Francisco.

The terse diary of Sherman E. Wight, a member of the nominating committee that year, bears on the change of administration:

310

Daniells Decades

May 21, 1922. Sun. We held a meeting of the nominating [committee] nearly all day. We decided to place our vote before the delegates. It was 29 for [William Ambrose] Spicer and twenty (20) for Daniells.

May 22, 1922. Mon. Today a meeting of the delegates was called in the Polk St Hall and they received the report of the committee which was 29 for Eld. Spicer and 20 for Eld. Daniells. They turned the report back after Eld. Daniells refused to accept of the vote.

May 23, 1922. Tu. Today the nominating committee reported Eld. Spicer for president and Eld. Daniells for secretary. They were elected. [Sherman E. Wight, MS Diary. Held by the compiler.]

Who could correctly measure Daniells' accomplishment? Only heaven can correctly evaluate a man, but his peers had their opinions:

(Carlyle B. Haynes): A very princely man . . . Arthur G. Daniells. It was during his administration that the great denominational activities were organized and greatly extended; that millions of dollars for a world program of missions were raised; that the mission enterprise of the denomination pushed into every continent and practically every country on earth; that the ministry was built up, strengthened, and revived, and that a greater evangelism was launched.

Raised up to save this denomination in its gravest crisis, he remained a tower of strength to the end.

(Taylor G. Bunch): Elder Daniells has without doubt been the greatest leader and organizer in the history of the Seventh-day Adventist denomination. Under his wise generalship the denomination became a world-wide evangelical movement. [*Review and Herald,* April 18, 1935, pp. 8, 9.]

311

for further reading:

Daniells, Arthur Grosvenor, *The Abiding Gift of Prophecy* (1936), chap. 32.

Kuhn, Mae Cole, *Leader of Men: The Life of Arthur G. Daniells* (1946), 130 pages.

Olsen, M. Ellsworth, *Origin and Progress of Seventh-day Adventists* (1926), chaps. 26-32, 35-41.

* Robertson, John R., "Arthur Grosvenor Daniells" (MT thesis, SDA Theological Seminary, 1966), 143 pages.

Spalding, Arthur W., *Origin and History of Seventh-day Adventists,* Vol. 3, chaps. 5, 9, 15.

Spicer, William Ambrose, *Our Story of Missions* (1921), 372 pages.

Weeks, Howard B., *Adventist Evangelism in the Twentieth Century* (1969), 320 pages.

Index

Index

315

Index

317

Index